Charles grew up in Paris and Tokyo. After graduating from business school, he undertook the cycle journey described in this book with old friend Gabriel de Lépinau. His entrepreneurial skills have seen him involved in several business start-ups and he is now in charge of the international expansion of a major e-travel company. He lives with his wife and two young daughters in Provence, in the south of France.

D1099091

# Cycling Out of the Comfort Zone

## Two boys, two bikes, one unforgettable mission

Charles Guilhamon

Translated by Juliet McArthur

Originally published in French in 2012
as *Sur les traces des chrétiens oubliés*
by Calmann-Lévy, Paris

First published in Great Britain in 2017

Society for Promoting Christian Knowledge
36 Causton Street
London SW1P 4ST
www.spck.org.uk

In addition to the images reproduced in this book, further photographs of Charles'
and Gabriel's journey can be found at:

http://spckpublishing.co.uk/product/cycling-comfort-zone-two-boys-two-bikes-one-
unforgettable-mission

*British Library Cataloguing-in-Publication Data*
A catalogue record for this book is available from the British Library

ISBN 978–0–281–07745–8
eBook ISBN 978–0–281–07746–5

Typeset in India by Lapiz Digital Services, Chennai
First printed in Great Britain by Ashford Colour Press
Subsequently digitally printed in Great Britain

eBook by Lapiz Digital Services, Chennai

*To Gabriel, whose friendship I value enormously*

*To all those who welcomed us,*
*our hosts for a few moments*
*or a few days,*
*each one providential*

*To Manki*

SERGE To be modern is to be of one's own time!
MARC As if we could belong to a time other than our own.

Yasmina Reza, Art

God didn't write that we were the honey of the earth, my boy, but the salt.

Georges Bernanos, Journal of a Country Priest

# Contents

# Foreword

*I want to see for myself and experience the reality of this world first hand
... I don't want an ordinary life. There's no such thing.*

So writes Charles in his mission statement for the epic journey
on which he is about to embark. Charles and his childhood friend
Gabriel, both in their mid-twenties, then set out to see the world
first hand on their recumbent bicycles. They do not choose to see the
popular cycling destinations or cross continents for the sake of it, but,
rather, ride through lands and cultures that we rarely hear about.

And their adventures are daring indeed: they brave a ride
through the deserts of northern Iraq; they dice with the aggres-
sive truck drivers of Kolkata; they visit refugee camps in India and
a church in Nepal that has recently been bombed; they scramble
over the high passes of Tibet; they survive a wild boat trip down the
Amazon; they risk kidnap in North Africa. Through testing themselves to their limits, they learn much, and grow greatly.

But more than wanting to simply grow as humans, they also want
to grow as Christians. By having a rule of only one euro a day for
most of the journey, and not staying in hotels, they depend on God's
Providence and the hospitality of his people.

Indeed, after stepping out with such faith, they find, time after time,
they are looked after and, again and again, the local churches give
them shelter, food and fellowship. They are fed and cared for not just
physically but also spiritually, as they witness the lives of the people in
these communities and hear their stories. At times Charles is inspired,
at times strengthened, at times bewildered, by the varying expressions
of faith he sees. The brave church of Kurdistan. The suffering church
of Orissa. The forgiving church of Nepal. The loud, dancing church of
the Amazon. The quiet monks and nuns of North Africa.

And what stories he records for us.

There is the priest in Iraq who has refused to flee despite the danger.
'This country has suffered much for the love of Christ. We've always
responded peacefully. I can't leave this land, this soil ... it's mixed with

the blood of martyrs. Our country is rich. We must give all we have, even our lives, to build, here in Iraq, a people united in peace.'

The man in Nepal who lost his wife and daughter in a bomb attack, but who had forgiven their attackers. 'When we search his face,' writes Charles, 'we find neither distress nor anger, neither fatalism nor rebellion. His eyes are full of tenderness. His face shines with that same light that I've seen before in monks and devout believers.'

The priest in China who spent decades in a concentration camp, but who says to Charles, 'I'm very optimistic about the future. This is the paradox at the heart of the Christian view of suffering: suffering doesn't have the last word, it can be a trampoline to joy.'

It is not just in their response to suffering that the Christians encourage Charles, it is also in the attitudes and devotional lives of those he meets. A materially poor parishioner explains to Charles how, for his wife's birthday, he gave her 'a magnificent view of a field of cornflowers that he had recently spotted when he was out walking.'

Regarding prayer, a nun in North Africa counsels Charles, 'The important thing is to take the time to meet God. That's why, when I ask the Lord something, it would be sad if I expected him to answer my prayer immediately. Because then it wouldn't be a person to person relationship; it would just be self-interest.'

Charles is honest in his self-reflection, such as his typically Western ailment of being in a rush: 'Always the need to get there and, once we're there, to leave again as quickly as possible and go flat out to reach the next place.' As the journey progresses, however, he is taught to slow down and be still. He is teased by a Senegalese monk, 'You French people, you're always in a hurry. You're always running after time. For us it's the other way round: time pushes us along!'

It should be noted that Charles and Gabriel are both Roman Catholics and the church communities they visited are all part of the Catholic Church. This is a book that will help Catholics to understand better their truly global family. It counters well the pessimistic future of the Church we so often hear about in the West. Charles writes, 'Personally, after all I've seen, I don't believe in the catastrophe scenario at all. The church that we've met is resourceful and full of life.'

But it is also a book that people of any faith tradition can enjoy. I am not a Catholic. I grew up in the Anglican Church and have regularly attended Anglican or independent Protestant-charismatic churches for most of my life. Sadly, some Protestant circles I have spent time with are suspicious of Catholics, but in recent years I've come to believe that, for all our tragic, historical conflicts, and even ongoing areas of theological disagreement, we are all part of the same Church and we are all called to talk, work and pray towards the healing of our divisions.

The breakthrough in understanding for me came on my own bicycle trip across the world, during which I was looked after by Orthodox believers in Russia, Pentecostals in South Korea, and Catholics in Papua New Guinea and Pakistan.

Two Catholic priests I remember particularly. In a haunted gulag town in north-east Siberia, I was hosted by Father Mike of Magadan. His deep spirituality, his total commitment to his people and his endearing sense of humour made a huge impression on me. Later in the journey, I stayed with Father Lawrence of Angoram in Papua New Guinea. He was a former accountant from South India, who now devoted his life to bringing peace and love to the violent community where he was stationed. Only the week before I rode up, unannounced, to his house, someone had tried to kill him with a machete. He showed me the nick in his porch where the knife had got stuck after he sidestepped the blow.

Charles sums up my own feeling well when he writes:

> *Visiting church after church over the last six months, we've dined and talked with hundreds of priests, monks and lay people. We've experienced several forms of worship, some of which didn't do much for us, prayed in dozens of languages, and encountered cultural differences that have demonstrated a huge gulf between us and our hosts . . . .and yet, every time we enter a church and every time we meet a priest or monk, the same minor miracle is repeated: we feel at home.*

On learning of this worldwide Church, suffering, persevering, witnessing, loving, I am challenged as to how I live my own life. A life in which I often bow more to the idols of comfort, safety and vain fulfilment, than Christian love and service. One of the saddest parts of the book is when Charles and Gabriel ride the home straight through France and find that the people of the local churches, when they knock on their doors, are too preoccupied to take an interest in them or even give them a bed for the night.

I hope that this book will help us, like Charles and Gabriel and the Christian communities they encountered, to live our lives more daringly, openly, generously and faithfully.           *Rob Lilwall*

Romania
Turkey
Syria ✗ Iraq
Paris
Morocco Algeria
Mauritania
Senegal ✗

Nepal
Tibet China
India
Thailand ✗

Brazil

Cycling, walking, sailing
Powered travel
✗ Village stopover

El Cheapo Airlines

N
W — E
S

© Gabriel de Lépinau

# 1

# Departure

## In which we work out the whys and the wherefores

'The Church? Nobody gives a damn. A round-the-world-tour? People go around the world all the time these days. As for going by bike – it's hardly original.'

That morning in early June we were ensconced on the leather sofa of a Parisian apartment overlooking the trendy Canal St Martin. In three short sentences, the man sitting opposite us has just demolished the reason for our visit. Fortyish, tousled light-brown hair, V-neck black T-shirt, Pierre B. is a television producer. We'd been told he's a risk-taker – the type who might be game for a project like ours that others would reject out of hand. So we came to him with our proposal for a documentary: around the world in one year, mostly cycling, but also some walking and canoeing, to meet Christian communities that are extremely isolated and, often, experiencing persecution.

Gabriel and I had known each other for 12 years. Sons of expats living in Tokyo, we met in Japan and had been good friends ever since. We'd travelled together many times and, over the last few years, there'd been this yearning, which never really left us, to go further afield, for longer. Gabriel had just finished his degree in agricultural engineering and was working for a company selling yogurt and biscuits. I was nearly through business school. If we didn't make up our minds now, it would probably never happen.

All right. Decided. But where would we go? And what did we want to achieve? We needed a clear objective that would keep us on track and be achievable in a year, after which I'd return to finish my studies.

'A beer tour of the world.' It seemed like a great idea at first. Going to meet the brewers of today. Understanding the problems of obtaining a

1

pure water supply and enjoying that delectable beverage wherever we went. No, we'd come back with beer bellies. Forget it! Perhaps a wine tour of the world? More refined. No, that wouldn't work either: if we were smashed half the time, how would we stay on our bikes? Something else then. A world tour of sustainable housing? A world tour of social enterprise? No, too clichéd, predictable. And, anyway, enough of sustainable development and the triple bottom line.

Since we were so difficult to please, our great travel plans were shelved. Nothing grabbed us enough to make us want to ride a bike for a whole year. I was within an inch of ditching the whole business when, one evening in Corsica during a weekend away, my mobile phone rang. I remember as if it was yesterday. There was a warm breeze. In the darkness I watched the distant luminous wake of a ferry on the horizon. A name came up on the screen: Gabriel.

'I've got it.'

'Uh? You've got what?'

'The reason for the trip. I want to go, provided the purpose is spiritual.'

(Eloquent silence)

'The trip . . . I'm keen as long as this year away enables us to get closer to God. What do you think?'

> *'The wind blows wherever it pleases. You hear its sound, but you cannot tell where it comes from or where it is going.'*  (John 3.8 NIV)

I was slow to catch on. Yet Gabriel had just put his finger on what should have been blindingly obvious to us both: all these years, the thing that had kept our friendship strong was, more than anything else, the faith we both shared. Our Catholic faith.

'The Church! The Church is interesting, isn't it? We'll go and meet Christians from all over the world; Christians who are persecuted, outnumbered, isolated, worlds away from the magnificent Church of Rome! We'll meet men and women of faith, simple people, forgotten by us in the West. Some of them we've never even heard of. We'll see how they pray, what keeps them going, what difficulties they face. Ever since I was little, I've been told I have Christian brothers. Do you know your Christian brothers? We have no idea what they're like.'

2

As usual Gabriel's voice was calm, measured. He never gets overexcited. He's as steady as I'm hot-headed, as easy-going as I'm enthusiastic, as blond as I'm dark: in short, as Scandinavian as I'm Mediterranean. That day, however, I could tell he felt passionate about the idea. This time we'd nailed it. We'd leave in exactly a year – enough time for me to finish my internship in Italy and for him to work for a few months. While I was studying and he was working, we'd get ourselves ready. It was an excellent plan.

'An excellent plan.' I'm repeating this little mantra to myself when our interviewer suddenly delivers us a whacking blow on the head: 'The Church? Nobody gives a damn. A round the world tour? People go off around the world all the time. As for cycling, it's hardly original.'

Yet the expression on his face belies the severity of his attack. Am I dreaming or could it be that he actually likes us? His cheeky grin can mean only one thing: he's sizing us up. I think people actually do give a damn about the Church, be they staunch believers or confirmed atheists, disillusioned doubters or faithful followers. If only through its history, and the heritage and values it has handed down to us, the Church affects far more people than we might care to admit. We try to stimulate his interest.

'Out of the 1.2 billion Catholics in the world, 200 million are unable to live out their faith freely and openly. We say the Church is one, and yet it is, by its very nature, diverse. Is it the same being a Christian in the desert, in Tibet and in the Amazon? How do Christians in the Middle East live out their faith? Where are the most recent converts? Is the Church in France representative of the Church worldwide? Is there a shortage of candidates for the priesthood in other countries? How do Catholics get on with other religious groups?'

The itinerary? It would be decided from day to day, but we envisaged stopping for three weeks at a time in seven isolated Catholic villages, in Syria, India, Tibet, Thailand, the Amazon, Senegal and Algeria. The choice was based on our research about the lives of Catholics in those areas and our own personal preferences, but also because, together, they form a great mosaic representing the Church in all its diversity. We also planned to travel through Turkey, Iraq, Nepal, Mauritania . . .

When Pierre calls us a few days later, he's keen. And he's already found a name. Our documentary will be called *Face to Faith*.[1]

One month later, in the church of St Cécile de Boulogne, we attend a special farewell Mass. At home the previous day, I made an exact inventory of what I will take in my panniers: Bible, journal, knife, two T-shirts, polar fleece, waterproof jacket, sleeping bag, three-quarter-size sleeping mat, silk sleeping-bag liner, mosquito net, pepper-spray canister, some medicines, two water bottles and our camera. Nothing superfluous because every gram counts.

Loads of friends come to see us off. My 88-year-old grandmother seizes the opportunity to clamber on to my bike, much to everyone's amazement. I feel a lump in my throat as I kiss her goodbye.

Others strum guitars and sing praise songs. Our mothers and sisters are crying bucketloads of tears. For me, the accumulated tension of the past few weeks was released last night; in my room, surrounded by stacks of cardboard boxes, all of a sudden tears streamed down my face on to the parquet floor.

Amid a round of applause and smart remarks about our incompetence, we set off. Our friend Alexandre[2] has come with his family and, of course, his bike – the one on which he completed his world tour in 1994. He accompanies us as far as the outskirts of Paris, thereby saving us the embarrassment of getting lost within the first few minutes of a journey that is to be thousands of kilometres long. He shares with us the wisdom of a seasoned traveller: 'You'll be drinking plenty of Coca-Cola! It's so refreshing . . . and it boosts your energy. You'll see how it gets you going!'

I am only half listening, the months of preparation passing through my mind. I think of all the providential events that have brought us to this point: Pierre, who agreed to produce a film about our expedition when we didn't even know how to hold a camera; the 20 young people, friends or friends of friends, who helped us because they were touched by our project; and the more or less kind and friendly

---

[1] French title: *Il était une foi.*

[2] Alexandre Poussin is a travel writer. He has written several books, including *Africa Trek*, co-authored with his wife Sonia.

reception of the Church of France clergy. I think of Frank, a sound engineer, who managed to find us top-quality microphones in the nick of time, and the priest from Rocamadour, the town in south-western France famous for its shrine of the Black Virgin. We met Frank by chance in Paris and promised we would visit the shrine in the rock on our way home to give thanks. And then there were the grants we were repeatedly refused, but also, and most amazing of all, the anonymous donors who sent us a combined cheque for €3,000 one week before our departure, when we still didn't have the funds to cover our costs. I think of all those in the schools with whom we will be in contact, the friends who have been unable to come to see us off and the superb Mass we've just attended.

Several months ago, we each wrote a 'personal statement' for this trip – a way of expressing what it meant to each of us and checking we were both on the same wavelength. Mine went:

*Milan, 15 September 2008*

*This project is a dream I have nourished for years. A dream of adventure, discovering the world, facing the unknown, the unexpected. I want to see for myself and experience the reality of this world first hand. I want to understand what makes the world go round.*

*I don't want an ordinary life. There's no such thing . . . I want to put God at the centre of my life and for him to be my guiding light always.*

*I love the idea of heading off into the unknown, with no idea of where we'll sleep or who we'll meet. I love the prospect of trusting myself totally to God and his Providence, no matter what happens. We'll rely on our own resources for transport, since we'll be cycling, but in other ways we'll be depending totally on the people we meet!*

*I choose to go with Gabriel. I couldn't imagine doing this expedition with anyone else; it's the result of many years' friendship, knowing each other, our strengths and also our weaknesses. We're very complementary and, under normal circumstances, we encourage each other's growth. Supporting each other for a whole year will be part of the challenge. We'll have to work at it but, united with a common purpose, I think we'll make it.*

*We're going to accomplish a very special project, not one that will necessarily look good on our CVs but one that has a greater significance. We want to be a reminder to people today that we all belong to one Body.*

Alexandre leaves us at Porte de Bagnolet after offering us a Coca-Cola – according to him, the first of many. We ride for another hour and, finally on our own, we pitch our tent in an empty field. We discover the comments that our friends and family wrote on our bikes earlier. F.-X., the youngest in Gabriel's family, hit the nail on the head: 'Don't push your luck too far!'

If only he knew . . .

# 2

## Europe

### In which we realize the virtues of a gammy knee

Only five days since we left and we've already been welcomed by
Marie-André, who opened his front door and fridge door to us, and
Georges and Davila, who put us up in their grown-up son's bedroom.
Who says the French only look after number one?

Joy of joys! We've finally been able to try out our bikes. And they
work! We took possession of them three days before D-day and only
just had time to assemble them before we left. Now, in the running-in
period, bolts are coming undone with monotonous regularity. The
novel feature of our trusty bikes is their recumbent design. You ride
with the handlebars beneath your backside and your legs parallel to
the ground, sitting back into a supportive, foam-padded seat. They're
the perfect cross between a deckchair and a bicycle, providing the
ultimate in comfort cycling, although they're not the ultimate in
cool. Recumbents were Gabriel's idea. Right from the start we discovered they're no magic cure for sore thighs – inevitable with any
kind of bike – but I had to admit, they provided a considerable degree
of comfort.

Anyway, everything seemed to be going well, incredibly well, but,
as of yesterday, it's all over.

We left in a headlong rush to get away, as you might race down
a staircase, missing most of the steps. Desperate to leave France as
quickly as possible, we needed to get cracking and cross the border,
which was, for us, synonymous with passing a point of no return. The
road was ours; we were unstoppable. But we had barely reached Strasbourg when I developed a painful tendonitis in my left knee, which

brought us to a grinding halt. I couldn't manage even one more turn of the pedal. I felt ridiculous, humiliated.

The bells of the Church of St Jean are ringing. I limp down the stairs, cross the courtyard and join Gabriel at the entrance. We push open the heavy, soundproof glass door and find a pew for Compline.[1] The monks and nuns of the Monastic Fraternity of Jerusalem take their places in the church, men on the right, women on the left, just like in the Eastern Catholic Church. Their chants, inspired by Byzantine liturgies, soothe my heart. The women's voices are exceptionally pure. The hymns, sung in a sublime four-part harmony, calm my mind.

Stuck here in Strasbourg because of my temperamental knee, we knocked on the door of this community. They welcomed us like royalty. Brother Ivan-Pierre, the Prior, took care of our every need. And so we found a haven of peace in the middle of the city; all we needed – gentleness, thoughtfulness, an encouraging smile. At St Jean's the brothers and sisters live separately and come together for Mass. They work for part of the day; some have paid jobs. The rest of their time is devoted to prayer, domestic chores, service.

The Mass ends. The brothers and sisters make the sign of the cross. In the gathering dusk of the concrete church, some remain prostrate, silently praying, while we steal away to bed.

This first stage of our journey is extraordinary, simply because it's not what we had chosen. It's the first demonstration of the divine Providence that we were so keen to experience and, over the course of the year, never let us down. When I was discouraged and disabled, my pride in my boots, we stumbled on a caring Church community. Only a few days ago, we were drowning in all the practical preparations for getting away. Now we're presented with this perfect opportunity to distance ourselves from all that in this unexpected retreat. In the monastery, with the monks and nuns, we put things back into perspective: we're not here just to clock up the kilometres or set a new record. As Pierre was quick to point out, a world tour is no big deal these days. Our purpose is different: we want to meet the Church, and our encounters with Christians will determine our route. In case we'd forgotten, this forced stop reminds us. As the Psalm says, 'The LORD is my shepherd; I shall

---

[1] Compline is the last service, or office, of the day in the Christian tradition of canonical hours.

not want'.[2] We're daring to trust as much as we can. Faith will keep us on the right track and, in order to put our faith really into action, we've made some very simple down-to-earth guidelines. Our own rule of thumb for the journey: never pay for accommodation; allow one euro per day for food in poor countries, three in rich countries. This will force us to take the opportunities that come our way.

As I slip between the sheets, I think back to the words Gabriel's little brother wrote on his seat. We're going away with one thing in mind – to let go the brakes, cruise a little. Take things as they come. Leave room for 'chance'. For the time being, my knee is out of action, but I know that we'll get back on the road again. We're confident. I realize more and more that 'the wind blows wherever it pleases'.

After a week with the monks, we start cycling again. Thanks to the EU, we cross from France to Germany as easily as crossing from Brittany to Normandy, but even in the first few kilometres, my knee starts causing trouble again. The pain is almost as strong as the previous week. We come to a stop, exasperated, on the side of the road. 'Want a lift?'

A van driver has just stopped by the roadside. In a flash we decide to hitchhike and load our bikes into the back. He drops us at a motorway rest area where two Germans of Turkish origin take over. They drop us in Baden-Baden.

Gabriel calls out to a raucous group of guys drinking outside a bar, asking where we can find a roof for the night. With a beer-sodden shout, one of them bursts out in English with a strong German accent, 'In Germany nothing's free. If you want a room, go find a girl and fuck her.' Charming.

We spend the night in a park under a weeping willow, 100 metres from a brothel and 300 metres from a casino. Ambience plus.

We reach Munich by hitching rides and taking the train. Louis, Gabriel's brother, meets us at the station. He's been there for several months on a university exchange. My knee's still problematic. There's no way we can continue our journey. We look for something

---

[2] Psalm 23.1 (KJV).

else to keep us busy. Nicolas, a friend of Louis', tells us about the von Poschinger family, who are building a chapel in their garden. Since we have no better idea, we turn up at their home, 40 kilometres outside Munich, in the heart of the Bavarian countryside. They're a traditional Catholic family who attend Mass every week, the men wearing their leather breeches, or, lederhosen.

One evening we go into the village for Bierfest. Hundreds of Bavarians are eating at tables set up in the streets. We're with the von Poschingers' daughters and their son, who is about our age, named, unsurprisingly, Ludwig. We munch on roasted peppers and sausages, then get acquainted with what is called, in Bavaria, a glass of beer: a one-litre mug. We hit it off straight away with the bar staff and waitresses, who ply us with drinks on the house. Soon we're drowning in double doses of the amber nectar. Loath to refuse a present, we feel duty bound to drink them all. (For us, respect for our host is sacrosanct.) Ludwig is delighted and, before we know it, we're sozzled . . . enough to be first on to the dance floor, which is in the barn, decorated for the occasion. On the bare earth floor, I'm spinning and twirling with a 50-year-old blonde wearing traditional costume, a blue dress with a black bodice over a billowing white blouse. Soon other couples form. The party is in full swing. Before long, we're up on the tables, singing with Ludwig and his crooners, backed by the village orchestra – a band of big, brawny blokes in short breeches and Austrian waistcoats, belting out tunes as they puff into their trumpets, pouring sweat, to the thumping of the drums.

A brief aside here. I hear some readers complaining: 'Hey, false advertising. Strasbourg? Munich? Is that the Church in the middle of nowhere? We've been conned. What about the persecuted Christians? What a rip-off! Scandal! Money back!' Please, just give us time. Every journey has to start somewhere and we can't jump straight to Iraq or Tibet or Mauritania without telling how the journey started . . .

We stay four days with the von Poschingers. The demon tendonitis continues to hound me. My knee is still no better. Back in Munich we decide to keep going, gammy knee or not. We buy a rail ticket to Istanbul and plan to spend a few days in Romania en route with a priest whose address friends have emailed us from Paris.

It's the longest day imaginable – a 24-hour marathon of jumping from train to train, struggling with our arms full of all our gear. The Hungarian railway conductors try to force us to buy extra seats for our bikes. We politely refuse. They back off, then come back in for the kill, one after the other. Something tells us that if we pay the money it won't end up in the coffers of the national treasury. In desperation, one of them, a fat guy with a moustache, calls out, 'All right, let's cut the red tape, just shout us a beer and we'll call it quits.'

Travelling by train puts you opposite a complete stranger, often for several hours at a time, and forces you to look at each other eyeball to eyeball. That's how we met Mika, a 35-year-old Hungarian with rodent-like front teeth and an impeccable Oxford accent, who has lived in England, Israel and Russia. He's well-travelled, pleasant. He gives us a running commentary on the Hungary that we're not cycling through: the dramatic corruption, the huge inequities, the fall of communism, which hasn't changed anything much, its lost territories and its stormy relations with its neighbours. At his request, we teach him a few words of French: *tu me manques* (I miss you) and *je t'aime* (I love you). He gets off the train just after the Romanian border to meet face to face with his fiancée, whom he found on the internet. Bog takes his place. This little dude suits his three-letter name – he's so cocksure and pushy. He's a Pentecostal and, after talking to us for about two minutes, he asks if we're Christians. When he was 18, he was a drug addict and an alcoholic. In a lucid moment, he prayed to Jesus to help him kick his addictions. He then became seriously ill, which forced him to cut his ties with his friends and come off drugs. Today, convinced that the illness was a divine blessing, he preaches all over Romania to any who will listen. Standing by the doors as he is about to get off the train, Bog announces, 'God has done great things for me. He can do the same for you!' And so we are blessed; blessed by Bog.

We finally reach Beclean station, in northern Romania. It's eight thirty in the morning. We have, scribbled on a scrap of paper, the address of a possible contact, Father Alin, who was recommended by a friend. We wander around the drab, characterless streets. The ugliness seems almost deliberate: no beauty anywhere. The footpaths are rutted and dirty. Weeds cover empty lots; street lights cast a macabre, dim light.

An old woman opens the door and smiles straight away. Alin is still asleep. He's her son. We must come in, sit down and have a good breakfast. She speaks only Romanian, but makes herself understood with much gesturing and miming. As she puts on the kettle, a little blond boy appears and clings to her skirt. Then a young woman of about 30 comes in, kisses the older woman and takes the child in her arms. This must be Alin's sister and his nephew. We're all seated around the table when a man with a neatly trimmed beard arrives.

'Hello, I'm Alin. Welcome to our home. I hope you enjoy your time here.'

He speaks perfect French, almost without an accent. Leaving us no time to reply, he pats the child on the head and kisses the woman – on the lips! Either relationships between siblings in Romania work a little differently from ours in France or he slipped or else she's not his sister. But he is a priest. Unless we have misunderstood? Perhaps he's a deacon, which would mean he'd be allowed to marry. But he's definitely wearing a dog collar. Seeing Gabriel's wide-eyed expression, I realize that he's as stunned as I am.

'This is my wife, Ana-Maria, and my son, Benedict.'

Alin is amused by our bewildered expressions. We hadn't realized that in the Eastern Church it's not uncommon for priests to be married. The Church here is part of the Greek Catholic Church, which has been connected to the Catholic Church since the seventeenth century, but has its roots in the Orthodox Church and uses the Byzantine liturgy. To us, Latin to the core, one of the most remarkable things about this Church is that deacons, before they are ordained, can choose to marry. In Romania, about 90 per cent of Greek Catholic deacons choose to marry.

I have always been struck by how journalists love to air their opinions on whether or not priests should be able to marry. Unfortunately, they are rarely sympathetic and often show a poor understanding of the issues involved. It has become a societal question. According to a TSN-Sofres poll carried out in 2009, which appeared in the daily newspaper *La Croix*, more than 80 per cent of French people support the marriage of priests. Also, 80 per cent of respondents identified the celibacy of priests as the main reason for the decrease in vocations to the priesthood. It's understandable now why Alin's situation hit me like an electric shock and why Gabriel couldn't help himself asking Alin, although we've only known him for five minutes, if he thinks that ordaining married men could be a remedy for the shortage of candidates for the priesthood in countries like France. Who better to enlighten us on the question? His reply is unequivocal.

'No, certainly not. I have heard it said that in France the celibacy of priests is at the heart of the reason for the shortage of priests. It's not true. Not at all – and I say this as a married priest. I think that if there are fewer priests today, it's because there are fewer and fewer young people who know how to love and serve others, who are willing to commit themselves, in whatever field it may be. Ten years ago, in Romania, out of 50 people who sat the preliminary exam for admission to seminaries, 25 were accepted. This year, only two people applied, despite the fact that deacons are allowed to marry. That hasn't changed! So the issue is not celibacy, but commitment. People are afraid to commit themselves for life.'

We spend several days in Beclean with Alin and his family. We sit through long services full of incense and a liturgy we don't understand. We accompany the young priest to visit an old woman who wants to make her confession, attend a youth meeting and share in family mealtimes. Between meetings and Masses, we piece together, little by little, the incredible story of his life. Alin was born into a Christian family during the brutal and repressive reign of the communist leader, Nicolae Ceauşescu. His grandparents, Orthodox Christians, were the only ones who were actually practising Christians. At the age of seven, without really knowing why, Alin knew for sure he would become a priest. He entered a small Orthodox seminary and then went on to the main one. But, disappointed with his spiritual directors, he left and found a job. A few years later, his world was turned upside down again.

'God came to find me, even before I had begun to search for him again. By chance I met a Greek Catholic priest who taught me how to listen to what Jesus taught us, to read the Bible and pray.

'In 1948 the Russian-influenced communist regime used the Orthodox Church as a vehicle of propaganda to spread its ideology to even the most isolated villages. The Orthodox Church used this situation to settle its accounts with the Greek Catholic Church, formerly the Transylvanian Orthodox Church, which seceded in 1700, when it recognized the authority of the pope. The Greek Catholic bishops were all imprisoned; some were beaten to death. Many priests died in prison. All the Greek Catholic churches were confiscated by the state and given to the Orthodox Church. Until the collapse of the communist regime in 1989, Catholics could not conduct public worship and used to meet secretly in private homes or under a tree to pray.

'I don't mean that everyone in the Romanian Orthodox Church collaborated with the Communist Party. We recognize the Orthodox Church as our sister; that's very important! But there were certainly some very delicate situations; and some serious wounds, which still remain open today. The Catholic Church was destroyed down to its very foundations and the Orthodox Church was destroyed from within. For me, an idealistic, naive young man simply wanting to live out the truth of the gospel, it was quite a shock.'

In 1989, Catholics regained the right to worship in public, but out of the 200 churches and monasteries confiscated by the state, only about 100 have been returned. There is a little church in Alin's home village. In 1998, with the help of his parents, who were converted by his contagious faith, he managed to get the church building back and brought in a Greek Catholic priest. The fledgling faith community suffered renewed persecution.

'The police, the mayor and some Orthodox priests joined forces to abuse and humiliate us. We were locked inside the church. We were even beaten.'

In the Bistrita region, in northern Romania, relations between the Orthodox and Catholic Churches remain very strained.

'We must keep praying for peace, that all those who claim to be part of the Christian Church, be they clergy or lay people, may live in harmony. Persecution of Christians by atheists or Muslims is common, sad though it may be. But when persecution comes from other Christians, our own brothers and sisters, it is even harder to accept. I often say that with all these conflicts, Christ's robe has been torn apart in Romania.'

Far from discouraging him, the persecution that the community experiences only strengthens the young man's faith. He has the passion of a new convert. He renewed his commitment to serve God as a priest, but this time within the Greek Catholic Church. He entered the seminary in Cluj and from there the bishop sent him to finish his theological studies in Paris.

Having settled in the little town of Beclean several years ago, Alin has one aim in mind: to give the youth back their dignity as Romanians and encourage the religious groups to live peacefully together. One evening he drives us a few streets from his presbytery to his youth centre, which is set up with a table, sofas and a football table. He holds youth meetings here for the group he started. He insists on having Catholics, Protestants and Orthodox mixing together among the 60-odd members of the group. He tries to instil into them an open-minded outlook on the world and takes them on trips to other European countries so that they learn about other cultures and ways of life. 'They learn to look together towards Christ, instead of remaining, like their parents, stuck in a past that divided them and tore the Church apart.'

# 3

## Turkey

## In which we learn the importance of a fair allocation of biscuits

6 AUGUST, 1 MONTH AND 1 DAY AFTER DEPARTURE
'Istanbul.' It's the only word we catch of the torrent spurting from the carriage loudspeaker. Never mind – it's the only word that matters. Our train journey is finally over. Last night, Alin, his family and friends, 12 in all, took us to the station. 'I'll say Mass for you every day until you get home', Alin murmured as he wrapped his arms around us.

Between Europe and Asia. West and East. The Black Sea and the Mediterranean. Istanbul, where two worlds meet, two civilizations merge. Istanbul, gateway to the East. Veils, turbans, moustaches, muezzins calling from lofty minarets; a thousand and one enchanted mysteries; its famous, unconditional welcome. As I step on to the platform, I really do believe it's going to work out; our journey's going to take off from here.

I love those first, precious moments of arriving somewhere new. I'm suddenly struck by the new sounds and smells and, subconsciously, I start tying them to what I already know. The aroma of cinnamon wafting from a spice stall takes me back to mugs of hot mulled wine in the mountains; the scent of vanilla brings to mind an old friend's perfume. A man sitting cross-legged outside a tea salon reminds me of a wonderful afternoon I once spent strolling around the souks of Tangiers.

The most incredible sense of freedom floods through us. No friends, no family, no contacts, not even a hotel reservation or plane ticket. We've arrived and not a soul knows we're here. It's intoxicating. If no one is expecting you, there's no timetable to keep to. You have the luxury of just standing around on the platform, gawking wide-eyed, chatting with a passer-by or soaking up the sun and watching the swarming hoards go by. You're more relaxed than the tourist who sees his six days' holiday rapidly coming to an end and hasn't a minute to waste. Your first few steps are slow, hesitant, a little awkward, for fear of intruding into this new world opening around you.

We push our bikes along the banks of the Bosporus and take a random left into a crowded street. Istanbul is a vibrant city, full of contradictions: it's difficult just making sense of what's happening around us. We roam the town, between minarets and baroque churches, strolling along broad avenues with enticing shop window displays, swarming with couples in European-style clothing, then plunge into dark, deserted alleyways. The centre is modern and touristy. Turkish people queue at cash machines before spending heavily in Western-style department stores, boosting their profits, but just a few hundred metres away, we're surrounded by hens, dogs and children begging.

Curious, we take a look inside an old, abandoned building. At the foot of the steps, unshaven men are playing cards on cardboard boxes, sipping tea from tiny glasses. We try the stairs. On the third floor, we're drawn by the sound of voices and come across two workers in singlets, sweating over a machine from some bygone era. In a huge, dilapidated room, lit only by light falling through the broken windows, among piles of rubble, they're drilling holes in plastic washers and sticking them together. They look up, surprised to see our bewildered faces, then resume their work, taking no further notice of us.

We know that the Church has a real presence in Istanbul, so we're not worried about tonight – it won't be difficult to find a place to sleep, a community to take us in. We try a church and then a monastery. We're stunned by their outstanding inhospitality. Apparently we're not as charming as we thought. Sometimes they are 'terribly sorry', sometimes not. Finally, as night falls and daylight gives way to irritating yellow lamplight, a community of Salesian priests invites us in, calling '*Ma, non c'è problema!*'

Old Father Felice, who greeted us at the door, sits us at the table with his colleagues. The large refectory hall is under renovation while the children are away for the summer holidays, so we'll be able to have an uninterrupted conversation. Giving Gabriel a reassuring wink, I bravely strike up a conversation, armed with my few flamboyant words of Italian learned during my internship in Milan. I swallow my second-declension verbs, along with my pride, when they reply after a moment's hesitation in the most impeccable French: 'We're Salesian priests!'

We talk over slices of goats' cheese and honeydew melon. Jokes fly between the four priests, who seem to be permanently smiling.

'The Order was founded in 1859 by an Italian. By our own St Jean Bosco, Don Bosco, as he is known. Now we have centres all over the world. We specialize particularly in education.'

'This is a school, here?'

'Yes, and recently we've been taking in a lot of young Iraqis.'

I can hardly believe my ears. It's one thing to read the news in the comfort of your own home, but quite another to be exposed to the reality. In a few short years, Turkey has become the preferred buffer zone for Iraqi refugees trying to get into Europe, Australia or the United States. Their transit can take several months, sometimes over a year. With his mouth full of food, one of the other brothers chips in: 'They're arriving in their hundreds, forced out of their own country. They often have the same story to tell: a hurried departure after receiving death threats. They leave with a few pieces of family jewellery or some silver, sometimes even a little cash, but mostly they haven't had time to sell their houses and their resources are very limited.'

'The heartbreaking thing is that the persecution doesn't stop at the border. Refugees are vulnerable. Slumlords take advantage of them: they put up the rent every month until the families can no longer pay. Everyone knows it's happening, but people just turn a blind eye.'

The youngest priest, a Syrian, who hasn't spoken yet, explains: 'We try to help them, as our resources and vocation allow. The children come to school during the term and we take them on holiday during the summer.'

The European Union's borders are certainly watertight and we know that this exodus of refugees, ready to overflow into the West, is controlled by Western powers, who keep the floodgates closed. Over the next few weeks, we plan to follow the route of this tide of fleeing Christians, but in the opposite direction – back to its source in Iraq. We fear what we'll find there.

Charles' knee is still weak. Luckily a tractor was passing . . .

Lost in thought, we each lay three cushions on the floor in the little room our hosts have given us for the night. The concrete floor is covered in dust and the ceiling bears the scars of old water damage, but, luxury of luxuries, there's a bathroom. We take a cold shower, then lie down, enjoying the relative coolness of the evening and sleep like babies.

The Church in Istanbul seems to be upside down, having more clergy than members of the congregation. The city is riddled with churches. Together they make up a curious jigsaw: Dominicans, Jesuits, Franciscans, Salesians, Little Sisters of the Poor, Syrians, Chaldeans,[1] Greek Catholics. Most churches have been renovated, ready for visitors. Many are quite ornate, but they seem rather empty. Who does this great army of clerics serve? Where are the believers?

We tour the city, cycling at low speed. I want to put my knee back to work gently, on the city streets, before we head out on to the highway. Our bikes, so underused until now, attract attention. Heads turn as

---

[1] Eastern Rite Catholic Church, in full communion with the Catholic Church.

we pass; faces light up with a smile. I get my first puncture on Independence Avenue, the Champs-Élysées of Istanbul. It's my *rite de passage*. Sitting on the footpath, my every action under the scrutiny of the crowd, I'm all fingers and thumbs as I remove the wheel and try my best to repair the tyre. A street seller, feeling sorry for us, gives us a kebab dripping with oil and a pot of yogurt.

We buy a map of Turkey. No need for a detailed one; we'll take the main roads. Our departure is set for the following morning after Mass.

In the sultry morning heat, we pass the Galata Tower and cruise along to Independence Avenue. It's impossible to miss the Catholic church, built in classic Venetian style: red bricks and white stone railings. We stop in front of the heavy metal grille, pass through the colonnaded porch, take several steps down and enter the crypt of the church of St Anthony of Padua. At the entrance, two men fix their eyes on us and ask what we're doing there. Timidly we murmur, 'We have come for Mass. Monsignor Yakan suggested we come.'

Open Sesame! They push the door open and signal for us to enter. The service has already started and the crypt is full to bursting. Standing room only. The women sit on one side, their heads covered with white lace veils, and the men on the other. In front of the altar, a dozen young girls form a little choir. The priest officiating wears a white robe and red cape with gold trim. It's Monsignor Yakan, Patriarchal Vicar of the Chaldeans of Turkey.

Only metres away from the busiest street in Istanbul, for the duration of Mass in this dimly lit crypt, time stands still. At first we're surprised by the rough, strident nature of the chants, but soon we're transfixed by their beauty. They're praying in Soureth, a language descended directly from Aramaic – the language of Christ and the first Christians. It's still spoken today by the Chaldeans of Iraq and elsewhere. We're touched by the poignancy of the moment and the fervour of this strange assembly.

Their faces are inscrutable, drawn; all eyes are fixed on the priest. They're all Iraqi refugees. Some arrived yesterday, others months ago. They've left behind family members, friends, lovers and, in many cases, their dead.

The service ends. We join the people as they climb the steps quietly towards the exit. Outside, the prelate greets the congregation, encouraging, listening to news, asking after family members.

A young mother glows with happiness: 'At last! We have our visas!' This family is leaving for the USA, for Chicago. The promise of a new life, with no hope of returning.

When the crowd disperses, we're finally able to talk to the prelate. Behind the beaming face and welcoming smile, we sense the man is busy, with numerous important matters urgently clamouring for his attention, but he kindly takes a few minutes to talk with us.

'These believers come from many church backgrounds. Today there were Protestants, Catholics and Orthodox believers. They all come from Iraq and the countries bordering Turkey. Most are Iraqi refugees. There are five thousand two hundred here in Istanbul and every day new families are arriving, while others leave for the USA, Canada, Australia. Europe as well, but not many. Europe is quite stingy with visas.'

We sense some bitterness in the voice of this man who has been struggling day and night to accommodate the influx of refugees.

'The problem with us Christians in the East is that we're not united. I often wonder to myself how we Christians, Eastern or Western, can share the Lord's Supper while ignoring a member of the same body who is suffering somewhere else in the world. Just now, we were singing and praying in Aramaic . . . the language of Jesus, the very person who said there is but one Church, and that oneness is of the utmost importance! Here in Istanbul, there are 12 Churches. Each claims allegiance to a different apostle, saint or founder. They all have their own particular strengths, but they are all parts of the one Church. The Church is the sun that lights up the world, and there's only one sun!'

A woman comes to greet him and kisses his hand reverently.

'Turkey is a second Holy Land. It really is! Saint Paul travelled extensively in Turkey and the amazing events in the Acts of the Apostles happened here. It was in Turkey that the first Christian community was born. You are very lucky to be here with us!'

★

We're pedalling side by side and chatting, with the sun blazing down on us more harshly every minute. It's good to feel my muscles being stretched, my shirt dripping with sweat and my heart thumping. I've got a new lease of life. Monsignor sees Turkey as a second Holy Land and so do I! For me, it'll always be the land of my resurrection as a cyclist. Each turn of the pedal is a gift.

We meet a fruit seller on the roadside. Richard Gere in the flesh – almost. The salt-and-pepper hair, the twinkle in his eye. Moments later, we find ourselves inside his house. Barefoot, sitting on the carpet, we're surrounded by plates of bread and butter piled with tomatoes and onions, bowls of fruit and drinking chai – traditional Turkish tea.

If Turkish tea tasted good, it would be well known. Diluted in water, it's highly sweetened to hide its bitter taste. Natural, apple-flavoured, strong or downright insipid – there's one for every type of bad taste. They drink tea in Turkey for the same reason we have a drink or a coffee together in France: for the sake of a good conversation. With our weird bikes and white faces, when we enter a village we're always surrounded by a crowd of children and old folk who stare at us and flood us with questions. The most daring among them will proudly shout out an invitation for chai. Despite not understanding a word of Turkish, we know by some sort of unwritten code that we're duty bound to stop. Our hosts bring out chairs and tables and sometimes sweet treats and we sit on their front porch or in a café and drink tea together. Great discussions follow, in which everyone waves their arms around, pointing, miming, mixing up English with Turkish and drawing pictures to get their message across. Finally, hands on our hearts to show our gratitude, we thank them profusely and leave. Ten tea stops a day, though, is for grannies, not cyclists. We have to keep up our pace. We left Istanbul a week ago and our current rate of progress is about right. We're covering about 100 kilometres per day.

This evening, the countryside is fabulous. We're on a road that stretches between rounded hills bathed in a golden light. The sun reddens as it sets, slowly giving way to darkness. An evening breeze rustles the dry grasses, bleached by drought. Young boys herd goats with jangling bells. A dog barks in the distance. We pitch our tent among the rocks and bushes in a spot that overlooks the whole valley. As darkness falls, Gabriel jots down the events of the day while I mix up a big bowlful of our usual pasta with vegetables. About 500 grams of pasta and over a kilo of seasonal vegetables – that's what it takes to get us up and going the next day.

'Hey, do you enjoy riding roughshod over the weak and powerless?'

Suddenly, dessert tastes more sour than sweet. We're sitting round the fire eating 'Made in Turkey' Bisquy biscuits. Between crunches, Gabriel has just knocked me for six. As is his habit when something is irritating him, he didn't say anything at first. He's been rather silent and morose for several days now. He must be brooding on something. The time has come to get it out in the open.

'Pardon? Ride roughshod over who?'

'Well, it's like, er, in the time it takes me to eat one little biscuit, you've already downed four. What am I meant to do? Stock up so I don't miss out? Put an option on half the packet or do nothing while you scoff the lot, since it doesn't seem to bother you?'

He stuffs in a whole mouthful and puts on a rather constipated smile. I can't believe my ears. It's late in the day; I'm completely thrown. He's accused me of treachery.

'Oh, go on. Eat your stupid biscuits.'

Flashback to the school playground. We're four and a half. He's calling me names. I'm calling him names back. I admit the case in my defence isn't brilliant, but then maybe that's because I've got nothing to say. He's right. I've been caught red-handed.

Thanks to the wretched Bisquy, we decide on some very simple rules. It's not easy to live 24/7 with someone, even if it is your best friend. If we simplify things that are within our control, we can save our energy for more demanding matters. We adopt a routine, like an old married couple: I sleep on the left of the tent, Gabriel on the right; we do the filming and take photos on alternate weeks. The one not filming does the interviewing and doesn't interfere at all with the other's job. We write up the day's entry in our common journal every other day and we also take turns leading daily prayers. Above all, no matter what, our allocation of food is always strictly equal.

I realize that for the next few months everything depends on how we keep these little everyday routines. There is a certain inconsistency in wanting to go and meet the Church, the members of this great body of believers we claim is One, while we can't even 'be the Church' at our own basic level. We're going to have to change, be a little less selfish, but it will be for the better. We'll be stronger. Our little mini-Church of two will be founded on our daily prayer together – the best time to forgive each other and move on. From now on, more than ever before, our friendship will be a threesome: Gabriel, Charles and our Father God.

Because of the August heat, we get up at an unearthly hour to try and get a head start on the sun. A quick breakfast, tidy up the tent, do our stretches, prepare the bikes and *avanti!* The hope of a Sunday Mass spurs us on. Since we left Istanbul, we haven't come across one church or met a single Christian, but now, 130 kilometres away, there's a large dot on the map – Konya. It's a city, the biggest we've seen for a long time. Perhaps we'll find a church there. We reach our highest pass so far, at an altitude of 1,400 metres. The perfect opportunity to reflect on why recumbent bikes are popular in Holland: they're great for the flat, but, on steeper slopes, they become instruments of torture. The whole load – 15 kilos of bike, 20 kilos of equipment and 80 kilos of muscle and bone – is taken on our thighs and knees (you can't stand up on the pedals).

'That's it! I'm on a diet, starting tonight!'

'I'm offloading half my stuff at the next town!'

'Those guys in the Tour de France are absolute heroes!'

'No way! They're psychopaths!'

The first stop of the day is at a service station, where we know we'll find a tap with drinking water and decent toilets where we can wash. We've noticed that the Turks are as great at showcasing their spotless petrol stations as they are at polluting their roads and coastline. Cans of oil and other dangerous concoctions are stacked neatly in pyramids. The shop sign is gleaming. The service is impeccable. As we sit on the steps of the washrooms savouring the most delicious mandarins, it dawns on us that there's a fundamental difference between our two countries. While the French attendant takes no notice at all of oil stains on the forecourt, the Turkish pump operator uses every ounce of his energy to remove them. We watch in amazement as one diligent attendant generously tips at least 200 litres of water on to the forecourt and conscientiously scours the stains with a long-handled scrubbing brush. A few hundred kilometres to the south, Syria is close to dying of thirst while upstream in Turkey they're busy building dams. A delightful irony in the sharing of water resources.

We cover the last few kilometres. The gradient steepens, we pass one last saddle, and suddenly the horizon opens out before us. The town of Konya stretches along the foot of the cliffs. During the descent, Gabriel shows off his knowledge of the area.

'According to legend, Konya was the first town to be built after the flood, but it's known today primarily for its "whirling dervishes" – an order of Sufism founded here by the poet and mystic Rûmî in the thirteenth century. It has now spread all around Anatolia.'

There are two groups of dervishes still active in Konya today. The Mevlevi Order have fallen out of favour with Muslim traditionalists. Their dances enable them to enter into communion with the 'Perfect' in a sort of mystical journey.

Today, Konya is Turkey's seventh-largest city, with a population of two million. The centre is swarming with people. Within the space of a few kilometres, we pass from the countryside to the big city, where Western mores flirt with Islamic traditionalism. We pass seductive glamour girls and women veiled from head to toe on the same footpath. Night is falling. We stop some passers-by.

'*Kilesi? Katolik?*'

'Yes, it's that way.'

So there is a church here. Tomorrow we'll be able to go to Mass. After going round and round in circles and getting completely lost, we finally lean our bikes against the wrought-iron gate of the only church in town – a modest building of pink stone, with two slate-roofed towers, in a little park enclosed by cast-iron railings, right in the middle of the city centre. We ring. No response. We ring again. A thin woman slowly walks across the garden and stops behind the gate. A second soon follows – she looks exactly like the first. Italian, sixtyish, rather thin. They're nuns. I dig out some of my rusty Italian.

'Good evening! I am sorry to disturb you . . . We're doing a long journey by bicycle to meet the Church in the world. We've come from Paris. Can we put up our tent in your garden?' The response is immediate.

'I'm afraid that will not be possible.'

'Yes, it is impossible,' adds the other. Just like Thomson and Thompson in Tintin.

'Er, we could sleep out in the open?'

'No, I am afraid not.'

'Can we come to Mass here tomorrow?'

'Yes, there will be three sessions of Mass.'

'Good. Do you know where we could sleep in Konya?'

'Yes, there are cheap hotels.'

'The problem is that we never pay. It's our rule. I know it doesn't seem very smart but . . .'

'Oh! Well, in that case, you won't find anything. You'll have to pay here. Really! Everything costs money, you know!'

I'm getting fed up. I sense that Gabriel is, too. The little ladies simply won't listen. Maybe they're terrified of us – our beards, our dishevelled appearance, our size.

'Sisters, could we at least leave a few of our things with you? We'll pick them up after Mass.'

After some hesitation, they agree to keep our bikes in the shed at the back of the garden. We leave with the bare minimum for camping out – a sleeping bag, a sleeping mat and, as always, just in case, a pepper spray canister. A restaurateur who sees us pass spontaneously invites us in for dinner and some young men in Western clothes on the terrace of a nearby café invite us to share a hookah. They speak English, which makes them exceedingly rare specimens in this region.

Then, with no better option in sight, we make our way to Aladdin Park, right in the middle of the city centre. We hope to bed down on one of the many lawns, amid the families and groups enjoying the evening there, but the raucous music blaring from the fairground bombards our eardrums and, anyway, the park is teeming with people. We walk around a little more and eventually find a quiet corner outside a nearby mosque.

As I slide into my sleeping bag the smell of cat pee assaults my nostrils. I can't stop ranting.

'Famous Catholic hospitality? Well, you could've fooled me. So much for welcoming the needy. We go off visiting the Church and end up sleeping by a mosque. Unbelievable!'

Gabriel is only half listening. 'Yeah, yeah, yeah. Poor us.'

Sleep comes intermittently. We're woken by a curious passer-by who pokes his nose into our faces to inspect us, then by some cats, then by some kids. When the sun finally shows up, we wriggle out of our feather coffins and walk a woozy walk back to the church.

This time the gate is wide open. In the garden we'd crossed yesterday to drop off our bikes, we come across an Iraqi family who are also going to Mass. They're refugees. More refugees. The father, Youssef, a great big chap with a moustache, quickly fills us in on their situation.

'I'm from the village of Bartela, in the north of Iraq, but I work for a newspaper in Mosul. I received death threats in my office. I had to leave the country virtually overnight, taking my wife, my two sons and my two daughters with me. I don't have any work here and neither do my sons. I have sold my wife's and daughters' jewellery in order to rent an apartment, but we are nearing the end of our reserves. We've been here for nearly a year. We would like to go to Australia, the USA or Europe as soon as possible.' His story is like that of so many others.

The sisters preparing for the service look embarrassed to see us, but they greet us kindly.

'Here, this is the French translation of the readings. Is there anything else we can help you with?' The nun walks away, but then turns back. 'And please, we absolutely must talk after Mass.'

We worship and pray with Youssef's Iraqi family and a group of Spanish pilgrim-tourists. They will soon return to their air-conditioned coach, but, meanwhile, here we all are, from such diverse backgrounds, sharing the Eucharist with two Italian nuns. I forget my bitterness of the previous night; I'm deeply moved.

After Mass, the sisters invite us to sit in their little flower garden, where a delicious draught of cool air plays around us. One of them soon returns with some slices of bread and a jar of NUTELLA! They've suddenly risen in my estimation. These lovely nuns are offering us the very thing they themselves miss, the thing that reminds them of their home country. As we enjoy the bread and Nutella, they ply us with questions and confess how guilty they feel.

'We were scared last night. We had no idea who you were.'

Their sincerity is touching. We don't know how to stop their stream of excuses.

'Have you been here for long?'

'For 15 years. We belong to the Brotherhood of the Risen Christ of Tavodo.[2] Our mission is to ensure the Church has a presence here.'

'We're the only ones; there's no priest in Konya.'

The solitude seems to weigh heavily on them. Without any clergy attached to the church, it's only when a priest accompanies a group of pilgrims that they can attend Mass, the essential nourishment for any Catholic, let alone a life consecrated to God.

'This year is the year of Saint Paul. That's why so many pilgrims have come to Turkey and to Konya. But today seems to be an exception; there weren't many people at Mass.'

The other nun explains. 'This little church is called Saint Paul's. We try to keep the memory of St Paul alive here in Konya. As you know, Paul was a great traveller. On his first trip into Asia Minor he was chased out of Antioch [called Antakya today] and went to Iconium [called Konya today]. There he preached the gospel and founded a Christian community but was forced to leave because of the opposition of the Jews. It's all written in the Acts of the Apostles. This little church was built by the Assumptionist Fathers in 1910. It's the only one of their churches still standing; all the others were destroyed or turned into mosques as the Christian community slowly died out.'

Konya. Two million inhabitants. Five Christians, two of whom are nuns. Discretion and the ability to engage in dialogue – these are the qualities they need for their mission, because proselytizing is strictly prohibited in Turkey, and especially in Konya, where fundamentalist Muslims make sure that the activities of the Church remain behind the walls of the compound.

'Once a week we leave the church doors open to encourage interaction with locals. Sometimes young people come in, just out of curiosity, as do tourists as well. And we often have great discussions with them.'

In 15 years the nuns have witnessed only one conversion to Catholicism in the city, an old lady on the point of death. It's tempting to question their presence here when they're not really 'achieving' anything much.

---

[2] Based in Trento, Italy.

'But we are simply a presence! Free, with no hidden agenda.'

It's a far cry from the power struggle of times past when it was a matter of not capitulating and keeping the church going at all costs so as not to lose the city to the Muslims. But I think the two Italian nuns are there simply 'to be'. They are monuments to selfless love. Having been uprooted from their home country for the sake of Christ, they lead a very simple life: they pray for the world around them and devote their time to various charitable works. It's for God, with God, to God. In God they find their purpose. The words of Jacques Maritain could well be said of them: 'Success is not the important thing. Success doesn't last. The ineffaceable fact of having been there, that is what matters.'[3]

In the late afternoon as we're leaving, one of them slips a little plastic bag into Gabriel's pannier. Some sweets and biscuits for us.

It's weird, but every time a dog sees us on our bikes it inevitably decides to come and annoy us. *In doggie memory, people have never before cycled with their feet in the air, and they're certainly not going to start now.*

As we pass through a village looking for somewhere to spend the night, a great brute of a dog charges at us. There's no doubt in my mind: it's a Kangal, one of the notorious breed kept by the original shepherds of Anatolia. We've been advised that the best strategy in these situations is to stop and face the dog, which then quickly stops thinking of you as its next meal. But with this mountain of muscle bearing down on us, devouring metres with every bound, we decide not to test the theory. It's every man for himself! Like cowards, we run for our lives but can't manage to shake him. Oh no! The road peters out and suddenly there we are in the middle of a field of carrots. The wheels dig in, the bikes lurch from side to side. We're bound to hit the dirt any minute. My heart's pounding wildly; my arms feel like jelly and sweat is pouring down my face. A few metres in front of us looms a solid row of trees on the edge of a forest. I'm going to die in Turkey. My life passes before my eyes.

[3] From the Preface of Cardinal Jouret's book, *Exigences chrétiennes en politique*, Paris: Egloff, 1945.

'I think he's gone,' whispers Gabriel.

We get back on the road, taking care to avoid the farm from whence sprang the wild beast. We're not far from Tarsus. As the sun begins to sink into the clouds on the horizon, once again we find ourselves being chased. As we leave a service station, two young men follow us, one on a scooter, the other on a motorbike. This has happened nearly every day since we've been in Turkey, and often we're escorted by a group of nosy, loud-mouthed young Turkish motorcyclists. So this time we're not worried, and we respond to their questions and jokes. They finally leave us. At sunset we arrive in Tarsus, where we'll spend the night. It's here that St Paul was born – Paul of Tarsus, the one the Italian nuns at Konya talked about. Having zealously persecuted the new Christians, with the approval of the Jewish religious leaders in Jerusalem he headed off to Damascus to arrest the disciples of Jesus there. This was in AD 36, a few years after Jesus' death. As he's approaching the city walls he's struck by a great light from the sky. 'Saul, Saul, why are you persecuting me?' Within a few moments he does an about-turn and becomes the most passionate of all the believers. He preaches in Damascus and then returns to Jerusalem. But no one trusts this former persecutor. Threatened with death, he flees to Tarsus, his native city, where he studies the Hebrew Scriptures. He realizes that salvation is not to be found by observing religious traditions but simply through God's grace. He then preaches this grace to the new believers.

We're pondering these weighty matters as we enter the city of Tarsus. Not having done our homework, we've no idea what to expect. We find the church easily. Surprise: it's been converted into a museum. No Christians left here. Opposite the church, the members of a large family are dining outside in their garden in the cool of the evening. A little girl smiles at us and comes over to the fence, but her father, a hairy man wearing a singlet, barks ferociously at us. Obviously we don't understand a word, but he makes his wishes quite clear. I think he's asking us if we would kindly get the hell out of there. To top off this pleasant little interlude, I suddenly realize that the two young guys who rode along with us earlier have emptied the pockets of my rear pannier.

We have three bags on each of our bikes, one on each side of the seat and one on the luggage rack behind the seat. This rear bag is impossible to keep an eye on without dislocating a cervical vertebrae.

It would have been no trouble for them to empty it. They've relieved me of my magnificent Swiss Army knife. I'm annoyed, but quickly consoled when I realize they're obviously not the brightest bulbs in the box: the video equipment is all still there inside the bag.

'Really, it's like stealing a Renault 5 surrounded by Lamborghinis on the Champs-Élysées.'

But the situation is critical; there's no time for philosophizing. The hairy hulk on the lawn next door is baring his teeth. We need to make tracks, fast.

We're stopped by another family who are dining on their terrace, a few streets away; they invite us to stay and eat with them. They're as welcoming as the other family was hostile.

Another evening, after clocking up 120 kilometres, we stop in the little village of Ceyan to buy supplies for dinner. While Gabriel is selecting the cheapest products with which to knock up a princely feast for €2 maximum, I guard the bikes outside. Gabriel finally emerges from the shop.

'Fine dining for us tonight,' he trumpets.

We head off, in a hurry to set up camp before dark. I'm in the lead and Gabriel's behind me. Suddenly, in front of us, weaving in and out of the oncoming traffic, between cars and trucks, a kid of about 12 riding a bike comes hurtling out of nowhere, shrieking at the top of his voice. In a flash the whole street freezes and every eye is riveted on him. When he reaches us he lets out a barbaric scream that sends chills down my spine. Everything happens very fast. He circles us, his bloodshot eyes bulging, narrowly missing cars and pedestrians on all sides.

I turn around. Too late. Gabriel's on the ground. The little devil has pushed him violently into a car parked on the roadside. He then aims for me and slams into me at full force. I fly through the air and end up stretched out on the road. My bike's knocked over; my saddle bag is torn open.

'Hey, you little wretch! You're going to pay for this!'

Gabriel's already after him, but he's impossible to catch – he's riding so dangerously, chopping from lane to lane, almost crashing into trucks and mowing down pedestrians. He taunts us gloatingly and onlookers have a good laugh at our expense.

We turn off the main road and stop on the first corner. Our mini-thug is crafty but not very clever. As he tries to catch us up, he falls straight into our ambush. I grab hold of him. He's thrashing about and screaming like a wild animal. I let him go. Now he's on foot, running towards a group of shopkeepers who've gathered on the other side of the road. I catch up with him, determined to give him a good thumping – a fatherly one, of course. But as I approach, 10 or 12 men come forward and grab me by the arms.

One of them wags a finger in my face. The message is clear: 'Hands off the kid, or else!'

The child crows with delight. I should have realized it before. This is a concrete example of how, in a Muslim society, the strong protect the weak. In desperation, reluctant to pass up this occasion for justice to triumph, I let rip:

'Hey you, I'd give you a good hiding, you little . . .'

'*Deli, Deli,*' they shout in unison, scowling.

'Crazy, crazy!' Ah, so that's it. He's the village idiot. He hasn't been right in the head since he suffered an electric shock as a little boy. The men laugh at my astonishment. They ease my increasing embarrassment, taking me by the hand and clapping me heartily on the back. Having narrowly avoided a punch-up, we finally part on good terms.

I rejoin Gabriel and we ride off under a blazing sunset sky. Our little idiot keeps on following us until darkness falls. He keeps his distance but we spot his red jacket when we turn round to see if he's still there. Later, as we snuggle into our sleeping bags in a roadside field, a chilling shriek splits the silence of the night.

We hit the mountains 15 kilometres further on. Then we endure a long and painful climb. Sweat pours off us in rivers. After 70 kilometres, at one in the afternoon, when the sun is at its most vicious, we cross a white line on the ground below a blue sign that says ANTAKYA. Antakya – that means the end of Turkey, the beginning of Syria, and the satisfaction of knowing we're making good progress.

At the time of the Acts of the Apostles, in the first century AD, Antioch, as it was called then, was the third-largest city in the Roman Empire after Rome and Alexandria. It was also the ancient capital of the Seleucid Empire, which succeeded Alexander the Great. It was the jewel of the Orient – a paradise of laurel trees, lush gardens, waterfalls and fountains.

As usual we criss-cross the town, looking for a church. A succession of locals point out the way.

'Go that way.'

'A bit further on, over there.'

'On the right. See the green light? Well, keep going from there, and take the first on the right. Understand?'

Not really knowing where we're going, we end up outside the town. At the foot of a rocky hill there's a sign pointing to the entrance of St Peter's Church. This is where the first Christians gathered. Peter and Paul would have preached here. The former enjoyed enormous prestige among the Christians as the apostle of Christ, while the latter, the one-time persecutor, had only his faith and his fervour for the gospel going for him. Paul was called to Antioch by Barnabas, to preach with him there. Together they were a tour de force; new converts flocked here from all over Antioch. It was a multicultural city and a melting pot of religions: there were Jews and Greeks, philosophers and worshippers of Apollo, Christians and colonists from all over the known world with their own religions and beliefs. In this pluralist environment, Paul preached to the Jews for a whole year. Then, throughout his life, he kept on returning to encourage the fledgling Christian community here.

Paul's refusal to impose the rite of circumcision on the numerous pagans who converted to Christianity was effectively a breach of Jewish Law. Those of Jesus' disciples who were still in Jerusalem were at first horrified by this violation of the Law, and summoned Paul and Barnabas to meet them there. The apostles decided that Paul was right, so from then on baptism was the only requirement for new converts. Those who believed in Jesus were no longer called 'Galileans' or 'Nazarenes' but were seen as a separate group. It was here that they were first called Christians.

We stand before the rock church. A beautiful, ornate façade scales the wall of porous rock above us. Below it yawns an enormous cavern carved out of the rock. Inside, a throne hewn from ancient rock stands behind a stone altar. The first Christians would have met together here, risking persecution. I imagine them praying, their senses on high alert, ready to flee at the least sign of danger.

We leave to look for a church that's less like a museum and where the Christians are still alive. We ask the way, taking care this time to explain that it's not St Peter's Church we're looking for. The streets are bordered by high walls. We imagine they conceal stately houses surrounded by shady courtyards. With 200,000 inhabitants, Antakya is as big as Tarsus. Among the minarets we finally spot the distant spire of a Catholic church.

*Katolik kilesi.* A yellow sign posted at the entrance to a tiny passageway points out the last few metres. In the narrow corridor we come across some Italian tourists of generous proportions. With difficulty we inch our way past and come out into a vast courtyard, brimming with life.

'Look! An orange tree!'

Gabriel, the friend of animals, insects and plants. This is a guy who once, on a year-long trip, recorded the equivalent of 90 minutes of film for the French animal protection group, 30 Millions d'Amis. The house is built in the Moorish style, as are all the noble, old residences of Antioch. Orange trees, grapefruit trees, Virginia creeper – everything is green. It feels like a cool, fresh oasis of life. A stairway with a wrought-iron railing leads to the first floor.

In the middle of the courtyard a thin man with silvery grey hair and large square glasses is talking with a group of tourists and pilgrims. The flurry of activity going on all around doesn't seem to trouble him. He talks calmly, giving his listeners all his attention.

'Welcome. I'm Father Domenico. How can I help you?'

When our turn comes, we don't have to try to explain. In less than no time we're settled in a room upstairs, overlooking Antakya. A real bathroom. In warm water we rinse off the accumulated dust and dirt of the last few days, emerging refreshed and lighter.

In the late afternoon Father Domenico's rush hour is over and he's finally free to talk with us. We find him on the terrace in the shade of a Virginia creeper. Although there are five Patriarchs who bear the title of Bishop of Antioch today (three Eastern Catholics, one Orthodox and one Jacobite Syrian), surprisingly not one of them lives in

Antioch and so Father Domenico is the real successor to Saint Peter! He, a Capuchin[4] friar and Catholic parish priest, and Father Boulos, priest of the Orthodox parish.

His face bears the weary look of one who never rests. But his voice is full of passion.

'This area was the Jewish quarter: the houses of the first Christians were probably around here! Now there are only very poor people living here, and us.

'I came to Turkey in 1966. I lived in Izmir first, for 20 years, and then I came here, to Antioch, in 1987. There was nothing here then, only derelict houses. We began celebrating Mass in the home of one of our parishioners. This house was given to me by a Christian family in exile. It was almost in ruins. We worked on it for two years! It was the first of these traditional old houses to be restored. The Catholic Church no longer existed in Antioch, and then, all of a sudden, it came back to life. Now it's even on the tourist route. The mayor brings her VIPs here if she wants to impress them. We've had local government officials, government ministers and army generals coming through. We've even had Jewish and Muslim families holding their festivities in the courtyard after their circumcision ceremonies.'

He chuckles as he talks about how incredibly successful it has been. Above the entrance, he's placed a marble plaque inscribed with the words 'Turkish Catholic Church', so that everyone knows this is not a foreigners' church. We are very taken with the straightforward way he relates to his Muslim neighbours and the nearby mosques, as well as the local authorities. Turkey is full of paradoxes; it's Western and Eastern at the same time, secular and religious, and its Islam vacillates between liberal and fundamentalist. Catholics are sometimes caught between social pressure from Muslims and secular regulations that give the Church quite an ambiguous legal status. However, Father Domenico shows no sign of wanting to claim that Christians have suffered any discrimination.

'In Turkey, the Church does not exist, from a legal point of view. But in reality, it does exist! Here, we are a small reality, but an important reality, nevertheless. We engage in dialogue with non-Christians,

---

[4] A branch of the Franciscans.

particularly with Muslims. It happens very naturally; they come to visit the church and to talk. John Paul II used to say that we must create a "dialogue in an atmosphere of mutual respect" so that it becomes a source of peace. That is what we are endeavouring to do.'

The nuns in Konya were less optimistic. But the situation here seems different.

'You know, Turkey is an immense country, and incredibly diverse. We don't have any problems here at all. One proof is that we celebrate numerous baptisms, often for people who have had no religion, because yes, there are Turks who don't have a religion. They're not all Muslims. But before being baptized, the candidate has to undertake four years of training. Baptism must be held in the church, in public, with the agreement of the family.'

The church bells cut our discussion short.

'It's time for Mass. Are you coming?'

We enter a large rectangular room that's been made into a chapel with pews and an altar. Twenty centuries after St Peter and St Paul, this is where the little Christian community of Antioch meets. The chapel is full. Mass is celebrated in Turkish by Father Domenico. A man about 30 years old strums the guitar, his eyes closed. He plays with great feeling. The ceremony is fervent and full of joy. After the service, Father Domenico greets everyone at the door. We then return with him to the same seat we'd left an hour earlier. He's radiant, jubilant.

'So did you see? Do you understand? At Mass there weren't only Catholics. There are 70 Catholics in our community but also many Orthodox Christians and Protestants. The young man playing the guitar, he's the son of the Orthodox priest!'

A little girl hangs on to his arm. He gives her a fatherly look and says, 'That's enough.' She runs off to play with her friends.

'A few years ago the Orthodox Patriarch of Antioch, Ignatius, came from Damascus to visit the city. I was able to speak to him about the Orthodox young people to whom I give Communion during Mass. Me, a Catholic priest! Do you know what he said? "God will reward you for your good work!"'

I think nostalgically of Alin in Romania. If only he could see this. If only those young people he ministers to could see it.

Father Domenico continues: 'Catholic and Orthodox aren't so very different. Christians must walk hand in hand. We've had enough of labels: Protestant, Orthodox, Catholic . . . we're all Jesus' disciples. Of course there have been divisions in the past . . . But the important thing is to live the Christian life together now.'

He's brimming with zeal; his eyes sparkle.

'Here we've decided to celebrate Easter[5] at the same time as the Orthodox Church. This year there's only one week's difference but last year there was five weeks' variance between the two dates. If we don't show ourselves to be united, how does it look to outsiders? We aren't perfect, and we certainly have our weaknesses, but Jesus calls each of us to be a witness of love and unity.'

He explains that all year long he collaborates with his Orthodox colleagues as if they were priests of neighbouring parishes. They lead the liturgy and prayer meetings together, organize discussions with the local authorities and run combined charity programmes. On 29 June every year the two communities climb Mount Silpius to pray together in Peter's cave.

'Living out the Christian life.' He keeps on repeating the expression; it's his catchphrase, the fruit of many years of living for God.

'It seems to me that the large churches in the West, with thousands of members, don't allow the Christian message to be "fleshed out" in real life. To live out the Christian life is to live side by side with one's brother, knowing how to love and forgive him, and this is not easy. Loving one's neighbour. It's a wonderful idea, but when you get close to others, with all their faults, well, that's a very different thing.'

I can't help thinking of the incident with the packet of Bisquy a few days earlier, which led us to take stock. Unimportant little actions. Very important little actions.

'In the church today we need to form small communities, to bear witness to the Christian life. The time for large communities is over; those were the days of the triumphal Church, the Church of the past!

---

[5] Since 1988, with an authorization conceded *ad experimentum* by the Holy See, Antioch Catholics celebrate Easter on the date set by the Orthodox calendar. So, at least in Antioch, the celebration of Easter in the two churches is at the same time. This has removed an argument commonly used in the Middle East to criticize the division in the Church.

Jesus gave us two signs that would mark us as his disciples: unity and love. And these aren't just empty words! Living out the Christian life means applying what the gospel says and seeing that it actually works: loving our enemies, turning the other cheek; if someone asks for your shirt, give him your coat as well. We must try. If we don't, these are no more than fine-sounding words.'

Daylight has given way to electric light and the mosquitoes are starting to bug us. Father Domenico stifles an enormous yawn. The crickets sing us their lullaby.

Tomorrow we have our own 'little and important' thing to do: we cross the border.

# 4

## Syria

### In which we find ourselves back in the times of the first Christians

24 AUGUST, 1 MONTH AND 19 DAYS AFTER DEPARTURE

We left while it was still dark, heading due east for about 50 kilometres towards the Syrian border. Now the sun is high in the cloudless blue sky. As we approach the border the vegetation looks progressively more stunted and hostile. Apart from the tarmac on the road there's nothing but dust, sand, dead wood and scrubby bushes. We ride along beside a tall wire-mesh fence. The carcass of what must have been a horse, left half eaten by scavengers and the wind, hangs on the barbed wire. Yet in this hostile environment stands a very large fig tree drooping with the weight of its fruit. We pick some, filling a plastic bag. From the top of a watchtower a soldier gives us a military salute. We cover the final metres to the border post, passing a queue of hundreds of stationary trucks roasting in the sun. The drivers are filling in time: some are asleep; others are drinking tea and chatting in the shade of their vehicles. We pass a first barrier, leaving the Turkish flag behind us, and cross the no-man's land that separates the two nations. We repeat the operation with the Syrian officials, who stamp the visas we obtained in France. The customs officers seem surprisingly lethargic considering the long line of goods trucks waiting at their door. But they're charming. In less than an hour we're in Syria.

All we've done is cross a border, but suddenly everything changes. The climate, the terrain, the geology, the architecture, the language, the faces, the culture, the agriculture, the clothing, the humour – it's a completely different place. This is all the more surprising since, historically, the Hatay region, which we have just left, was partly

Syrian. It was handed over to Turkey by France in 1939 to ensure its neutrality in the war, which was then in its early stages. The Syrians have never forgiven the French for this, and many official maps of Syria still put Antioch and the area around it inside Syrian national territory. That's why we thought that the southern tip of Turkey would resemble Syria. And yet they seem worlds apart. They share only one common feature: the numerous mosques that stand along the roadside.

After about 50 kilometres we reach Aleppo, the 'capital' of northern Syria. We've been given the name of the bishop of the Chaldean Syrian Church, Monsignor Audo. He's also a Jesuit. We hope he'll be able to point us towards a Christian village where we can stay for several weeks. Meanwhile we cycle all over Aleppo looking for a place to spend the night. We ask passers-by where we might find a church but no one can help us. Finally, we stop at a cyber-café where, for a few coins, we google Aleppo + church + Catholic and note down the telephone number of the first entry.

A man's voice answers the phone, assuring us that it's fine – we can come. 'Ask for Terra Santa. It's near the university. Everyone knows it.' He hangs up.

It's on the other side of town. When we finally arrive we find a school, a Christian school judging by the mosaics on the white walls surrounding the grounds. A custodian lets us into the compound. The pathways are potholed and half covered with weeds; paint is peeling off the walls. But most striking of all, it's intensely empty – a phantom school. There's no one here.

'Was that you on the phone?'

We jump. Behind us stands a thin, smiling European monk who holds out his hand, which we eagerly shake. While we're still looking confused, he pre-empts our questions.

'This used to be a school! But that was quite some time ago – I'm in charge of the place now. It's a Franciscan retreat centre for the Christians of Aleppo. They can come here and use the school facilities. Every evening hundreds of Christians come for picnics here! You'll see tonight.

'You've just arrived, haven't you? I don't suppose you know the history of our country. This school was closed in 1967, like many other

He turns and walks away.

faith-based schools in Syria, after a government directive was issued stipulating that they must accept the state's nomination of a director who would not necessarily be a Christian. We had the policy of secularism to thank for that. But it only worked in one direction: Qur'anic schools would never have been entrusted to a non-Muslim. Schools also had to adopt the public-school teaching manuals and teach in Arabic, even though teaching in English or French is precisely what gives a Christian school education its value and richness.

'Since the nationalizations of 1967, much water has flowed under the bridge. President Bashar al-Assad himself went to a school run by nuns, and he's been relatively tolerant towards the opening of new private Christian institutions, like Monsignor Audo's, for instance.'

'Monsignor Audo! We've heard so much about him. We'd love to meet him!'

'I'm sure he'll show you his school. He's doing a great job there.'

He stops outside a little room in which two camp beds have been set up.

'Here we are! This is your room. I wish you an excellent stay in Aleppo.'

He turns and walks away. It might be the last time we see him because finding him again in this labyrinth will be not be easy.

Nicknamed La Blanche for the marble and pale coloured soil in the area, Aleppo is a hive whose worker bees are yellow taxis and their buzzing is the blaring of horns. Local Syrians give us directions but they're not much help. The atmosphere is generally rather strained because we've arrived in the middle of Ramadan. Hunger and thirst puts everyone on edge, which is quite understandable. Drivers don't give us enough room; they charge straight for us and then pull out suddenly to overtake, constantly honking their horns.

I haven't yet replaced the knife I lost in Tarsus, and I want to take advantage of this larger town to buy one. It's amazing what you can do with a knife: slice bread, spike vegetables, whittle wood, cut string, cut up an inner tube, open a can, spread jam . . . In short, I'm lost without one. Off to the souk to remedy the situation. Aleppo's souks are considered among the richest in the Middle East; they're even listed as a UNESCO World Heritage site. We go from stall to stall: gold, wool, cotton, ceramics, spices, jewellery and, of course, soap.[1] It's a labyrinth of lanes, caravanserais, centuries-old vaulted stone arcades, tiny squares linking yet more alleys, shops large and small, and everywhere traders hawking their wares. Behind us a young voice calls for us to step aside: it's a child perched on top of a donkey. Enormous fabric pouches swing wildly as it walks, battering its flanks. Within quite a small perimeter the souks form more than ten kilometres of tangled alleyways where the housewives of Aleppo rub shoulders with European tourists looking for souvenirs. In the arcades, where no sunlight penetrates, we lose all sense of time and direction. We wander around for hours, at first just feasting our eyes on it all, and then on the lookout for a knife.

Gabriel shows his Swiss Army knife to a vendor and gives him a friendly, encouraging smile.

'One the same, please,' he says in English.

The guy panics, glances furtively around him, takes Gabriel's hand with the knife in it, and pushes it back towards his pocket. He gives an embarrassed laugh, retreats into his little shop and closes the curtain. Great sales pitch. Beside us, a man wearing a traditional *djellaba*[2] bends down to drink from a tap fixed to the wall. He rinses his mouth and spits out, without swallowing; it's Ramadan. The next few shops we visit, it's the same; the vendor gets scared, avoids looking closely at the knife and sends us packing. Finally one deigns to enlighten us.

'Put that away. It's prohibited. Weapons are forbidden in Syria.'

'But it's not a weapon, it's a knife. Like a kitchen knife or a pair of scissors.'

'Put it away, I said. It's forbidden.'

We can't get any more out of them. We stop in front of a little bakery to buy a loaf of bread. Pushing on the door, I notice a group of men seated in the back of the shop. One of them calls out to me at once. 'Peace be with you. Have you eaten? No? Come and join us!'

---

[1] Soap from Aleppo, a clever blend of olive and laurel oils, is known worldwide for its dermatological qualities.

[2] Traditional long, loose-fitting outer robe.

Gabriel and I sit down at the table in this kitchen-cum-storeroom, lit by one naked light bulb, with six older gentlemen who are smiling at the idea of breaking the fast with a couple of white guys. It's a veritable feast. Dishes appear one after another and disappear as quickly as they arrive. The eight of us clean up the lot: a dish of *mahchis*,[3] turnovers, pistachio macaroons and all sorts of pastries. We came for a snack and we're treated to a full meal.

We're always surprised by this magical welcome, which is offered again and again everywhere we go. It's really quite extraordinary. In the East, hospitality is unconditional and the stranger is welcomed everywhere, no matter who he is. In France, so often we don't welcome people as we should. And yet our Catholic faith teaches us to open our door to the stranger, to show real love, to make ourselves available. But we're afraid; we're too complicated. We don't know how to seize an opportunity to meet people. We tend to make it conditional, to question others' motives. What if he takes me for a ride? And what if someone else is needier than them? We're just great big cowards, really, and we're handicapped when it comes to reaching out spontaneously to others. But there's nothing new under the sun. Jean-Jacques Rousseau described it when he wrote *Reveries of the Solitary Walker* in 1783!

> *I have remarked that Europe alone sells hospitality. All over Asia you are lodged gratis. I comprehend that conveniences are not so easily to be had there. But is it nothing to say, I am a man and am received by humanity? 'Tis pure humanity which gives me a covering. Little privations are easily endured, when the heart is better treated than the body.*[4]

'So, do you like Halab[5] cuisine?'

'You bet!'

It's exquisite. A treat for the taste buds. I imagine generations of tourists and travellers, caravans stopping here en route for Mesopotamia, discerning gourmets who must have licked their lips at the thought of stopping to eat in Aleppo. They say that Aleppo's cuisine is

---

[3] Stuffed courgettes.

[4] Jean-Jacques Rousseau, *The Confessions of J. J. Rousseau with Reveries of the Solitary Walker*, vol. 2, London: J. Bew, 1783, p. 293.

[5] Aleppo in Arabic.

one of the most delicious in the world. We finally struggle out of our chairs and ride uncomfortably back to Terra Santa.

In the park-like school grounds that we left strangely empty earlier, we now find dozens, maybe hundreds of people of all ages, eating and making quite a racket: children running around, young people standing in groups chatting. Tables are set and then cleared as more people arrive. Each group brings a complete meal to share. But the feasting here has nothing to do with breaking the fast. These people are all Christians and don't celebrate Ramadan. These must be the people our Franciscan host was talking about a few hours earlier. They meet here in the evening to spend time together as a community.

It seems to me that in France, church groups and church meetings are usually organized for a specific purpose or for particular causes. For example, you might go to a 'dinner for street people' or be part of a group that visits the elderly, prisoners, the sick and so on. But when the priest suggests a church social event, drinks or dinner, he's not exactly overwhelmed with responses. Personally I've never been very enthusiastic about those kinds of get-togethers. But this evening, mixing with the crowd and noticing the great atmosphere, I see how stand-offish I've been. They've understood for a long time something I'm only just now putting my finger on. It's exactly what Father Domenico in Antioch was talking about: he called it 'living out the Christian life'. When I came to faith I also came into a community. Believing in Jesus means also believing that others are placed in my way, as I am placed in theirs – people I don't know and don't choose. You cannot believe in your own Jesus and just come to Mass on Sundays, staying in your own little corner. There's a dimension that goes beyond ourselves in the sense that we believe together. It's one thing to know it, but quite another feeling it this evening.

As we retire to our luxury suite, we notice a light at the end of the corridor. Peering inside a small room we see a man with a moustache, sitting on a camp bed identical to ours. Another man, younger than the first, is smoking by the window. The room is a mess; suitcases and their contents are strewn across the floor. The man in the singlet smiles warmly at us. We feel a connection straight away. They're from the north of Iraq. Refugees. The younger man is his second son. He's a surgeon. His sister and his mother are outside with the Syrian Christians. The whole family is in transit, on their way to Turkey. They're hoping to join their elder son in Europe. They're taking the same route as us but in the opposite direction. In a few days, no doubt, they'll be worshipping in the crypt of Saint Anthony of Padua in Istanbul. After Mass they'll ask Monsignor Yakan for help with obtaining visas.

How painful it must be to leave everything behind and commit to an unknown future, with no going back.

We stay in Aleppo for a few days to try to get information about crossing the Iraqi border. According to our somewhat fluid plans, we need to be in Iraq in one month's time. But a series of unfortunate events prevents us finding the officials from the Iraqi consulate: first we get the wrong address, then it's shut for some unknown reason, and then we arrive too late in the day.

On the other hand, we manage to meet Monsignor Audo in the diocesan centre, opposite the largest mosque in the city. Late one morning, without any prior notice apart from an exchange of emails a few weeks earlier, we ring the doorbell. The man who opens the door is all smiles. He has white hair brushed neatly to the side and eyes so blue they're nearly translucent. Monsignor Audo.

'You're the cyclists! You're not too tired? I'm in a meeting right now, but would you like to stay for lunch?'

A few minutes later we're on the second floor, in the dining room. A tiny slip of a lady with silvery hair, who barely comes up to my elbow, is busy at the stove: Jeannine is the bishop's cook. She cooks for him and a young seminary student, Jamil, who takes private Bible classes with Monsignor Audo. The interior is elegant in the Middle Eastern style. In this ostentatiously rich interior, we realize how surprisingly down to earth he must be to invite two young bearded guys wearing shorts to lunch. During the meal the image we had of Eastern bishops – high and mighty dictators, far removed from the common – goes up in smoke.

The Chaldean diocesan house in Aleppo, with Jeannine, Monsignor Audo's cook. The quality of her cuisine is inversely proportional to her size

'"IBM"! "I" for *Inshallah* (if God wills it), "B" for *boukra* (tomorrow) and "M" for *maalesh* (no problem). You can go anywhere with that! "IBM"! Understand?'

The man exudes intelligence and sensitivity. After plying us with questions and listening attentively to our answers, Monsignor Audo tells us that he is of Iraqi origin but has Syrian nationality; a Jesuit since 1969, Bishop of the Syrian Chaldeans for over 20 years and also a Bible scholar, he's involved in translating the Bible into Arabic. Since he's been bishop he's seen two waves of Chaldean Christian refugees from Iraq: the first in 1991, after the Gulf war, the second from 2006 until today.

'Since 2003 our community has continued to grow because of the influx of Iraqi refugees. At present about half have been able to get a visa and leave, and now in 2009 there are between 15,000 and 20,000 Iraqi Chaldeans in Aleppo, out of the 200,000 or 300,000 Iraqis in Syria. We've had to mobilize all our resources. We've organized sanitary programmes, language training, IT training, bought fuel for winter, paid rent for some, run catechism classes for thousands of children . . . We can't solve every problem, but we do as much as we can. Here Christian love is definitely in action.'

At first the Iraqi priests who arrived with their compatriots were called upon by the diocese to help. Now there's a Syrian priest specifically appointed by Monsignor Audo to look after the refugees and ensure that ongoing care is provided. All the Chaldean parishes in the country are called upon to help. Each has a welfare committee dedicated to helping refugees. These committees organize social aid (food and medicines), cultural aid (schooling and organization of training sessions) and religious aid (catechism, sacraments, youth meetings and liturgical celebrations). Monsignor Audo also explains that Syria is very welcoming towards refugees, offering access to free education and health care.

The meal ends. We move to the sofa for coffee.

'Last year we opened a school here, in the grounds of the diocesan house. In Syria, on the one hand you have some very good schools that are expensive, and on the other you have public schools where the standard of teaching is low. We wanted to open a Catholic school that would provide a good education, accessible to families of modest means. It's open to all the Catholic communities of Aleppo, to the Orthodox and also to a few Muslims, so that all parts of Syrian society are represented.'

Muslims in a Catholic school! The Jesuit understands our surprise.

'Christians really do have a place in Syria. I don't say it's always easy or that it's a straightforward position to be in, but we really do have a part to play. The foundation of the regime is not Islam, it's "Arabness." And we are Arabic in culture, as well as being Christians. We're Arab Christians! That's one of the reasons why I'm so committed to translating the Bible into Arabic. I sincerely believe that our culture can provide a platform for dialogue with Muslims.'

Monsignor Audo keeps talking as he takes us to visit the new church.

'You know, we often see the fanatical side, but Islam is very varied. It's also complex. It has its hopes, its questions about faith and modern society. I believe our mission as Christians is to be well grounded in our faith, confident. To be always open to dialogue. We mustn't be afraid, especially not of fundamentalists.'

When you realize the number of refugees the diocese welcomes, his words make sense.

He continues: 'In Syria, proselytizing is forbidden, but we can discuss, ask questions, bear witness to what's in our hearts and how we pray. Muslims respect the faith of authentic believers, even if it's different from theirs. Christians must be both discreet and courageous at the same time.'

We walk down the steps and across the courtyard. Monsignor Audo turns a key in the lock of a little wooden door. We go through the vestry into the Chaldean Cathedral of Aleppo. It's just been renovated.

Monsignor Audo himself supervised the work. The result is superb, luminous. Before doing a tour of the property, he kneels before the Holy Sacrament. We pray in silence. My thoughts turn to the Iraqi refugees we've met.

He walks with us to the gate. We exchange looks.

'Monsignor, in France, we don't talk much about Christians in the East. We know very little about you. But you Christians here, how do you see us?'

'I studied in France and I appreciate all that I learnt from the French: precision, honesty, a sense of rigour, rationality. There's a great depth that's largely unseen. These days we hear a lot about the problems of the Church in Europe, particularly in France. The lack of candidates for the priesthood, for example. In spite of everything, I believe that in your country there is great faith, good, honest people. That's why we mustn't be afraid – a light is going to shine. It's already there, but at the moment it's subdued. But there's still a ray of hope. In the East we have a very rich history and we hold on to our heritage. Here we don't easily renounce our faith, whereas in the West I would often hear people say, 'I've lost my faith.' To us that sounds absurd; it's almost laughable. Faith isn't something you can lose, just like that! It's part of our life, our personality, our history. My parents and my ancestors, they defended it with their blood! It's our identity.'

He pauses. He knits his eyebrows.

'On the other hand, we have our own problems. Our faith could easily become a social thing, a community faith. Here in the East we lack the personal aspect of faith that you have more in the West – the dimension of free choice of faith and Church. I believe we could complement each other better. Didn't Pope John Paul II say that the Church has one heart and two lungs, breathing in concert and in their own authentic way? The two lungs are the Eastern and Western Churches.'

As we leave Monsignor Audo we feel we've been in the presence of a great man. We spend the afternoon with the staff of Caritas. Thérèse must be about our age. She studied French at university and now works here with the Iraqi refugees. She takes us to visit an Iraqi family.

We climb the stairs of a building just like all the others. The hallway is bare, with concrete stairs. A woman opens the door and smiles when she sees Thérèse. One brief glance takes in the whole apartment: a bedroom, a closet, a living room and a bathroom. On the balcony a woman wearing a black headscarf stands contemplating the street below. I imagine her posted there all day, surveying an area she's never lived in, watching people she doesn't know, in these streets that hold no memories for her and shops where no one knows her name.

The master of the house, a man with crooked teeth, a shaved head and a gentle expression comes over and shakes our hands warmly. A little boy of about four hides in the folds of his mother's skirt. They invite us to sit down on the sofa and bring us tea and pastries. Even among refugees, and the poorest of the poor, a warm welcome is the rule.

'We've been here in Aleppo for three years now. After the war, the situation in Iraq became very difficult. All around us people were being abducted. Our parish priest was held for 20 days. When they released him, he was covered in bruises. They smashed his face with blows from a hammer. I was working in the church as an assistant to the priest. Sometimes, when my wife was alone at home with our son, armed groups would come to the door and demand money. In the street, terrorists would ask for your identity card, which showed your religion. If they saw that you were a Christian, you'd be put to death. I couldn't take it any more. I ended up leaving with my whole family. We didn't have time to sell the house. At the moment, terrorists are squatting in it. We shared this apartment with my sister and her family for a few months, and took it over when they left. I can't work here in Syria; refugees are not allowed to work. Our family in Europe and America are helping us.'

He tells us he's willing to go anywhere. He just wants to be able to earn a living. His whole family has emigrated, except his sister-in-law. His son will no doubt never return to Iraq. Everyone dreams of leaving the country but most don't have the means. According to him, there's no future for Christians in Iraq. Not any more.

'There's no one there now. Iraq . . . it's over for us now. Why go back? Here, we've forged a very strong link with the Chaldean Church. I pray for all the people in the world who are suffering, in Iraq and elsewhere. I know that God is always close to me, and with him there's always a solution. My faith is still very strong.'

We finally leave Aleppo. We're heading for Tal Arboush, a village of about 40 families near the Iraqi border. The bishop recommended we stay there and he let the two nuns who are posted there know we are coming. They're expecting us. We've got 300 kilometres to cover. By way of a map, we have Monsignor Audo's directions, which he gave us last night.

'Tal Arboush is a village of Chaldean peasants of Iraqi origin, built on the banks of the Khabour River. Head due east until you reach the village of Hassake. For 250 kilometres there's nothing, just desert, the beautiful Syrian Desert! Once you reach Hassake, ask the way from there. There's only about 20 kilometres to go after that.'

The terrain is quite different from what we saw before Aleppo. In the desert the road is dead straight and absolutely flat. Dust infiltrates everywhere. The heat is suffocating. But the prospect of a prolonged break ahead does wonders for us. We pedal like crazy. There's no shelter for miles around. We adopt the old Bedouin custom of wearing multiple layers of clothing. Sweat soaks the layer next to the skin, and as evaporation is blocked by the other layers, the least breath of air that reaches that layer produces a refreshing tingle on our skin. Under our cycle helmets we wrap our *chèches*[6] around our heads like a turban, bringing them down around our necks and across our mouths to shield us from the dust.

We've left the town of Manbij behind us. Already we've put 100 kilometres on the clock since we left this morning, and it's not yet

[6] Arab headscarf and turban.

Overnight stop with some Bedouins in the desert. No mobile phone coverage, but the men all have mobiles

midday. The road winds between pink rock cliffs. Then all of a sudden the horizon stretches out before us. Desert as far as the eye can see. But a few hundred metres ahead flows a great river with patches of green along its banks, and little houses here and there. The Euphrates! Its source is in Turkey, to the north, in what used to be Armenia. It crosses Syria and continues into Iraq, where it joins the Tigris before flowing out into the Persian Gulf. Once we've crossed this river there'll be no more sand or wind until Hassake.

The closer we come to the river, the more enticing it is. Our dust-covered bodies cry out for it, with a thrill of anticipation. As we cross the bridge to the far bank, a group of children wave us over. The youngest is barely old enough to walk; the older ones are teenagers. They whip off their T-shirts and dive in head first. We immediately follow. We're like two huge tea-bags: the water around us slowly becomes discoloured from the grime coming off our bodies. We swim with the children, relishing the coolness of the water, diving again and again, until a man with a smiling face and curly hair appears on the bridge; he's the father of some of the children. He's come to call them home for lunch and he invites us too.

51

Still dripping wet, we enter the little concrete blockhouse. There are no windows, which keeps the house cool. We sit down on the carpet. Our host's name is Hassan. He sits down beside us, with his youngest son on his lap. His wife and two daughters appear in the doorway, with tanned skin, nut-brown eyes and colourful scarves on their heads. They place silver trays down in front of us: fresh tomatoes, ewes' cheese, olives, flatbreads. Hassan and his family spoil us. Just because we're passing by.

After a short siesta, Hassan introduces us to his brothers and their wives, who live in neighbouring houses. Together they work the land and go fishing. This place is paradise. They live a few metres away from the Euphrates and never lack for water.

We hit the road again. The worst part lies ahead. We'll need to ration our water and save our energy. After 80 kilometres, as the sun starts to sink over the horizon, we're still in the middle of nowhere. It's flat as far as the eye can see, apart from the pylons beside the road, spaced at perfectly regular intervals. We plan to sleep under the stars. As a cool evening breeze caresses our necks, we can make out some hazy shapes in the distance that look like houses. We decide to push on, in the hope of finding a welcome there for the night.

When we finally reach this minute hamlet, we meet a Kurdish family who've just finished fasting for Ramadan. They invite us in at once to eat with them. Again the welcome is simple and genuine. The women drink tea and eat with us. We communicate with our hands, and soon everyone is laughing. They laugh when we ask if we can sleep near their house under the stars. Leaving us no choice, they make a place for us on the floor between the grandfather and the second son.

We pull out our sleeping bags, which intrigue them enormously. As the family members lie down to sleep and Aziz, the father, stands in the doorway smoking, we go out on to the terrace. Sitting with our backs against the wall, we whisper Vespers, or Evening Prayer, just as thousands of monks and nuns around the world do at the close of day. Not too loud, so as not to spoil the majestic silence. Aziz watches us. He understands that we're praying.

We leave early the next morning, stepping over our neighbours' beds without making a sound. It's still dark but we have almost

200 kilometres to go before we reach Tal Arboush. Dead straight. Kilometre after kilometre. Each exactly like the last. There are no sand dunes in the Syrian Desert, none of the smooth, sculpted forms of the Sahara. Just stones and fine dust.

At a service station in the middle of nowhere we refill our water bottles and drench our clothes. It's now one in the afternoon and the sun is vicious.

'We should stop. Make a sunshade with our *chèches* or even put up the tent. We'll get going again at about five o'clock.'

Gabriel is right. But I want to reach our destination as quickly as possible.

'Let's keep going for a bit.'

But my head starts feeling heavy and waves of nausea sweep over me. We need to find some shade urgently. Beside the road a shelter emerges out of the haze: an earthen hut, no windows, abandoned. We dive inside. It's almost pleasant compared with the furnace outside. Gabriel sets up our camping stove and cooks some rice from a packet that's been in his pack for weeks.

'It won't be the Ritz – it might be rather disgusting – but we need to keep up our strength.'

Now I can't even stand up and I fall into a deep sleep on the ground. I'm suffering from sunstroke. I'm woken with a start. I've just heard a muffled bang outside. And then another. I'm not imagining it . . . They're explosions. When I open my eyes Gabriel is already outside.

'What the hell's going on?'

'They'd better not fire at us, the damned idiots!'

He's waving and shouting. I join him. I must be hallucinating. About 50 metres away, a guy in Western-style clothing with sunglasses and the red and white chequered Arab *keffieh* on his head is holding a magnificent Kalashnikov! With the butt against his shoulder, concentrating intensely, he aims into the distance and fires. An expert marksman, I'm sure. Never mind that weapons are forbidden in Syria, and despite its being impossible to find even a Swiss Army knife, this damned lunatic is firing a machine gun less than 200 metres from our shelter. He finally sees us and panics. Dropping his weapon into the open boot, he leaps into the car and races off.

'Hey!'

Towards six o'clock we get going again to devour the last few kilometres. I concentrate on the regular movement of the pedals. Every turn of the wheel brings us closer to a glass of cold water.

We pass Hassake and arrive, exhausted, at a service station, on the way out of the village of Tal Tamir. Only 20 kilometres from Tal Arboush. It's getting dark.

My head is spinning. My vision is blurred. My muscles no longer respond. I lose my balance and fall to the ground. Inside the service station, four men are drinking tea. One of them takes pity on me and offers us a ride to Tal Arboush in his pickup. We accept, promising ourselves we'll return later to cover the last 20 kilometres by bike.

I faint almost as soon as I hit the car seat. I remember seeing headlights, a doorway and a kindly little nun. Then walking like a robot to a bed. Taking sips of water. For two whole days I lose all sense of time. I'm feverish, nauseous and have persistent diarrhoea. A spectacular start to our stay with our first Christian community!

## First isolated community: Tal Arboush

'Here we are in Tal Arboush!'

'Tal Arboush is a little Christian village. There are only Christians here.'

'Forty Christian families, Chaldeans!'

'So what is a Chaldean?'

'A Chaldean is . . .'

Today we start filming material for a 15-minute spot that we have to send to Pierre, our producer, by the end of the following week. We stand in front of the camera, which rests on its unipod stand, and look into the lens as we talk.

We arrived in Tal Arboush two weeks ago. Having settled in at the Convent of the Daughters of Charity,[7] we spend our days out walking, stopping to visit each house. The village is tiny: two streets, laid out in a cross shape, lined with about 40 little houses made of concrete and sheet metal.

---

[7] St Vincent de Paul.

The bells start ringing and we have to stop filming. It's Sunday, and they're calling us to Mass. The children who were crowding around the camera take us by the hand and drag us to the little church.

Newly renovated, it stands right in the middle of the grounds of the convent, next to the library. When we enter we're confronted with a sea of lace headscarves; the women wouldn't dream of attending Mass without them. The villagers file in. Men sit on one side, women on the other. They use the same liturgical rite and the same language, Soureth, that was used at the Mass for refugees we attended in Istanbul. Except that here people are relaxed, their faces peaceful and the children smiling. This is their home. We sit next to Charbel, the young village heart-throb. He has a James Dean look about him, except for one detail that wouldn't look right on the American star: a huge, colourful tattoo of the Virgin Mary that takes up his whole forearm and echoes the tattooed image of the cross on his biceps. It doesn't seem out of place here. Religious symbols are ubiquitous in Tal Arboush: in houses, streets, doorways, gardens, on jewellery and even on the biceps!

Today a priest from a neighbouring town has come to celebrate the Eucharist. He looks majestic in his rich green and gold robe. Compared to the Roman rite we're used to in France, the Eastern rite used for Mass here is far more centred on the consecration of the bread and wine: the whole Mass rises towards this summit. God made humbly present as food. At the end of the liturgy some old women remain on their knees, arms folded across the chest. Others pray in front of each of the statues in the church. Near the door there's a crucifix hanging from a gilded bust of the Holy Family. One of the women kisses the figure right on the lips.

Once we get over our initial feeling of dislocation in these foreign surroundings, our life here doesn't seem out of the ordinary, at least on the surface. We adopt the rhythm of the villagers' lives. We've met Jimmy the hairdresser, Hady the chauffeur, Charbel the handsome young farm worker, Roman and Yvan, the twins of the village who are our age. They try by all means possible to learn English, and no doubt hope we'll prove expert language teachers. Finally there's Sister Shamiran and Sister Marguerite, who welcome us into their home. We do the rounds of all the families. We spend time praying. We give them a hand with their chores and take walks in the surrounding area. Because of the heat, the pace is slow. Everything takes time; nothing works efficiently.

I'm convinced that in this year of travel in which every day is precious, we're wasting valuable time here. But we've chosen to waste it. Lose it. Rather than being on the move all the time, we want to stay and spend time in seven villages, starting with Tal Arboush. Three weeks. It's not much but better than nothing, to get a real taste of life here, a better understanding. So we can learn to love better.

Each fleeting encounter we have along the way is magical because it's unexpected, spontaneous, freely given; because anything can be disclosed since we'll never meet again. But some conversations take time; both parties need to listen, observe, wait patiently when difficult personal experiences are shared. A precious understanding is built up through what is spoken and, very importantly, what is unspoken. In this our first stop we give up being masters of our own time in order to try to embrace the rhythm of those we're with. It's a good way of letting go.

For the first few days, once I had recovered from sunstroke, I found time hung heavy on my hands. I didn't want to adopt this rhythm, so unnatural for me. I didn't have enough faith; I didn't really believe it could achieve anything. After five days I feel I've seen what there is to see and suggest we leave straight away. Gabriel refuses.

'We said we'd stay two to three weeks. We're staying. We'll take the time.'

Two months since we left, and still I'm in a rush. Incapable of accepting the time it takes travelling from A to B. Always the need to get there, and once we're there, leave again as quickly as possible and go flat out to reach the next place. All the symptoms of a life that's perpetually on fast forward. I finally resolve to see this time in Tal Arboush as a special invitation from Providence to reverse the trend. I remind myself that being patient doesn't mean putting my life on hold; that I need to learn to live at a different pace, not keeping my eyes riveted on my watch or my speedometer. To live more calmly, to open my eyes, my ears. Put simply, to live better and, therefore, live more.

Great intentions but, on my own, I feel inadequate. I ask God to teach me to be gentler and calmer.

Since our departure we've been praying Lauds, or Morning Prayer, in the morning, and Vespers in the evening, in communion with the Church around the world, especially monks and nuns living the monastic life. I really liked this idea of Gabriel's – praying in unison with the worldwide Church at the same time as we were going to meet the members of this Church. I thought it was great. Beautiful. But I wasn't very used to this type of prayer, having only practised it when I'd been on short retreats. To say the least, reciting a whole series of psalms, hymns and prayers, leftovers from a more formal era, written in outdated language that, frankly, seemed rigid and incomprehensible, had never done much for me. What I was offering God in prayer was essentially my commitment: in spite of our tiredness, we pray; we set apart time for God. A Trappist monk from the Abbey of Sept-Fons said 'Prayer is an offering of your presence to God.' That's what I was trying to do. So outwardly I was praying but inwardly finding it hard going. Again, I was in too much of a hurry – even while I was trying my best to meditate on a verse, I was already scanning the next.

But in Tal Arboush – after persevering relentlessly for two months to pray better, using all my willpower – I no longer have to force myself. Without really knowing why, I've started looking forward to these times of prayer, even feeling a certain need for them. I just have to let myself go and relax. And that's when grace enables me to begin to really enjoy praying the prayers set for each time of day that have been used by Christians down the ages – the Liturgy of the Hours.[8] Certain verses continue to resonate throughout the day. I begin to realize how beautifully poetic the readings are, and the slow, regular rhythm of the chants finally begins to strike a chord in my heart. Prayer permeates my being, overwhelms me, warms me. It soothes my anxieties, brings me peace as it wraps itself tenderly around my heart. And now I know by heart the Benedictus, the Magnificat and the Nunc Dimittis.

I feel I have made a little step forward.

This morning we're going to dust off our bikes and put them back to work. We want to nail the last 20 kilometres that we missed because of my sunstroke. The journey to Tal Tamir passes without mishap.

[8] Often referred to as the Breviary, the terms refer to the official set of daily prayers and readings prescribed by the Catholic Church.

But when we try to find the service station we come across a police roadblock.

In Syria the army and secret service are everywhere, controlling everything. Syrians feel they're constantly being watched, and need to be always on their guard. For the entire month that we're in Syria – except for our desert crossing – we're under constant surveillance by plain-clothes policemen on motorbikes who tail us everywhere, changing the guard every 20 kilometres. They're so obvious: if they get ahead of us, they use cunning tricks such as pretending to check the oil level or do up their shoelaces on the side of the road, to let us pass before they start tailing us again. It's annoying but we get used to it.

This time the soldiers are very surprised: no one has told them we're here. Suddenly they spring into action. A soldier with an AK-47 slung across his bare chest signals for us to sit down. He's a downmarket version of Rambo: he and his brothers-in-arms are half-shaven, and they shuffle along in their big, baggy outfits, unbuttoned down the front, revealing their hairy torsos. Some wear no shirt, others aren't in uniform at all. They swagger about, making a show of their machine guns and giving us the evil eye. Overall they look like a bunch of clowns who've been given more authority than they know what to do with.

They scrutinize our passports, inspecting under all the seams. Unable to make head or tail of them, they tell us to write down our surnames, first names and the names of our parents. But we have too many names for their liking; why the heck have we got three names each? They make us start all over again. Then they copy them on to a scrap of paper, scowling at us, and ask us again about our names, in case we've slipped a few more on to the list. Then they telephone their superiors. On the road below there's a group of men wearing the *keffieh*, standing around a flock of sheep. Their trucks are parked in a circle, and a man in the middle is shouting out prices: it's a livestock auction.

Our guards start their questioning again.

'Where do you live?'

'Tal Arboush.'

'But aren't you French?'

'Yes, we are.'

'So what are you doing there?'

'We're staying with friends. We're on holiday.'

'Your friends, men or women?'

'Women.'

'Women. You're staying with women?'

'Yes.'

'Are there several of them?'

'Yes, two.'

'What age?'

'You don't ask a woman her age, but I'd say over 65.'

'They live together, these women?'

'Yes.'

'Two women live together without a man? And you, you are staying with them?'

'Yes. Yes, they're sisters. Catholic nuns.'

The poor chap is horrified and visibly disgusted by the whole thing. He has no idea what we're talking about. He ends up returning our passports and serving us tea. Then he lets us get back on the road, assuring us that everything is in order. We return to Tal Arboush under police escort: two soldiers, one in civvies and the other in uniform, follow us at a distance to the sisters' home. They fire questions at them about who we are. Sister Marguerite is not at all surprised.

The next day, while we're out walking beside the River Khabour with some of the villagers, Gabriel gets ready to do some filming. One of the villagers looks worried.

'No, you mustn't take photos. Or at least not of the river because the water level is low this year. It's a very delicate subject. The police wouldn't like you filming it.'

Same scenario when we want to visit a high school that some of the local children attend. We wait patiently in the principal's office for an hour, while he completely ignores us. The English teacher who invited us looks embarrassed. Smiling nervously, he serves us tea.

'The children asked us if we would come. Do you think we could drop into the classroom to see them?'

'I don't know.'

He translates our question into Arabic for the principal, who doesn't reply but instead gets up from his desk and leaves the room. Our English teacher follows closely on his heels. We sit there waiting for a good five minutes before he returns alone.

'I'm sorry, my friends. It's not going to be possible. You need authorization. You cannot visit the school.'

'Not even just to pop into the classroom briefly?'

'No, it's not possible. I'm sorry.'

We leave. It all seems quite absurd.

However, others explain later that there are reasons for such authoritarianism and the omnipresence of the state.

In Syria the regime is run by a minority group, the Alawites, which is a dissident sect of Islam that has taken great liberties with Muslim teachings. The Sunni regard them as a marginal group within Shi'ism and harshly condemn them. Alawites represent about 10 per cent of the population, hardly any more than the number of Christians of all the various Churches combined. Nevertheless they assumed power, taking over the Syrian army at a time when both Sunni and Christians considered military duty beneath them. It's understandable that the government, which has to deal with a Sunni majority, tries to protect its rear.

There's no doubt that Christians have a place in Syria. When the country gained its independence in 1946, the secular state, which was inherited from the French, was not contested. The foundation of the regime is really an Arab identity rather than Islam. Syrian identity papers don't show one's religion. There are no questions about religious affiliation in the Syrian census. Christians are just like other citizens, even if their situation hasn't always been the most straightforward. Indeed, when the first Syrian constitution was written in 1950, the Muslim Brotherhood wanted to impose an Islamic state. A compromise was adopted: Islam would not be the state religion but the President's religion. Political and religious equilibrium hangs by a thread in Syria, particularly for Christians. A political victory for the Sunni majority could endanger freedom of worship, but if support for the Ba'ath Party[9] – under the guidance of the Alawites – were too overt, relations with the Sunni community would deteriorate. That's why the 2001 uprising could have had tragic results for the Christian minority. Its place has always been secure because the government has

[9] The original Ba'ath Party was founded in 1947 in Damascus. Its objective was the unification of the Arab states into one nation. It came to power in Syria (1963–6, then since 1970) and in Iraq (1963, then 1968–2003). The Ba'ath party supports secularism, Arab socialism and Pan Arab nationalism.

always been run by another minority, but what would happen if the Sunni fundamentalists succeeded in overthrowing the government? Despite all this, Syria is actually the Arab country in which Christians can most overtly express their faith.

Several days later we gather for the feast of the Holy Cross, an occasion totally forgotten in the West but celebrated royally here and throughout the Middle East. It originates from the fourth-century tradition of the veneration of the Holy Cross, remnants of which were said to have been discovered by Saint Helen.

The celebration starts with a procession of women and children, led by the two nuns, to the cemetery, which overlooks the village from the top of a nearby hill. The graves are rough and many of the crosses have been knocked over by the wind which, at this very moment, pulls at the women's headscarves, blowing their hair in all directions. The priest blesses the tombs and the people recite the usual prayers. Each family has come to pray for their dead and also, in a way, to put themselves right with God in readiness for when their own turn comes.

Their faces look serious, meditative; heads are bowed, eyes closed. But as soon as the priest has given the final blessing, the mood of the congregation changes completely. We don't know whether to laugh or cry. The women dig deep into their bags and bring out a mass of sweets, cheap lollies, pastries and all sorts of treats, which the children hand around, delighted. They blissfully disregard the fact that they're in a cemetery and that the very practical, flat stone serving as a table is the corner of Grandma's tomb!

'We celebrate among the dead! In faith, death is a joyful thing!' Sister Marguerite explains.

When evening comes, a delegation from Tal Arboush accompanies the sisters to Hassake, the nearest town. Gabriel and I are invited as the French representatives, much to our delight! The Hassake Cathedral is packed. After Mass the priests lead the procession out of the church. Some of the congregation carry an immense wooden cross, so large that the horizontal section gets stuck in the frame of the church door.

With the time taken to dislodge it, and the sudden halt at the head of the cortege, there's a terrible bottleneck and tremendous pushing and shoving in the central aisle of the cathedral.

**Bonfire for the feast of the Holy Cross**

The procession continues through the streets of the town to the sound of the brass band, with people waving flashlights and singing Christian chants. They're celebrating the cross and they're not doing it quietly! How different from Turkey, where all religious expression is prohibited! In a little square between the houses, we form a circle around the cross. A man lights a bundle of boxwood twigs placed at the foot of the cross. Children let off fireworks to accompany the bonfire. Faces glow in the orange light of the dancing flames.

If we needed further proof, this evening's celebration confirms Monsignor Audo's words: Christians certainly do have a place in Syria. The way most of the media report the massive emigration of Christians from the East doesn't give a clear view of the reasons that force Iraqis and Syrians, for example, to leave their country and try their chances in the West. Nor do they distinguish between the two. Many Iraqis experience terrible persecution, which is not the case for Syrian Christians.

'I had stone brought in specially from Spain,' Jimmy calls to us one day with a triumphant smile, showing off the house he's having built at the entrance to the village. With his wife and two children, he left Syria five years ago to work in a hairdressing salon in

Sweden – a hairdresser with a mop of jet-black hair in the land of blondes. And his wife has had her hair dyed to Swedish blonde to show off to everyone her expatriate status. In summer they return to Syria, and their family and friends drool at the sight of his very smart phone and fancy car.

For us Tal Arboush is a haven of peace. However, life is hard for farmers here, who have no work in winter and sell their harvest in summer to the state at pre-set quota prices. Many of the young people dream about the promise of life in the USA and Europe. Charbel, the James Dean of the village, confesses he's just waiting to be able to leave the country for good. He prefers to forgo marriage here in the hope of building a new life in another country. His sister Ritta, who is an English teacher in a Muslim school, travels 100 kilometres to and from work each day in a minibus, which costs her a quarter of her salary. She'd also like to leave. Their older brother is engaged to a young Assyrian woman who was born in Germany: they met on the internet and, thanks to her, he'll be able to obtain a European visa. They're not leaving because it's difficult for Christians here but because of the attraction of Europe and the USA.

As the sun goes down, blushing delicately in the evening sky, the young people get together on the sports ground for their daily match of footie. The players are comical to watch, a mixture of all sizes, shapes and ages. In the streets, chairs have been placed outside on the steps so the old folk can enjoy the evening breeze; the grandmothers survey the scene with toothless smiles, while the men talk and clap each other on the shoulders with intermittent bursts of laughter. You'd think you were in a Pagnol[10] novel. You don't need an invitation to dine with your neighbours.

'They seem so happy. I'm really impressed with them,' Gabriel keeps on saying.

We're struck by the living, breathing spirit of brotherhood that reigns in Tal Arboush. The villagers weave strong links of friendship and learn to live out the message of the gospel. It's impossible not to be moved by the profoundly peaceful atmosphere in this Christian

[10] Marcel Pagnol, much-loved early twentieth-century French novelist, playwright and filmmaker – the well-known 1980s films *Jean de Florette* and *Manon des Sources* both directed by Claude Berri, were based on his work.

enclave. When the Daughters of Charity[11] took over the mission in Tal Arboush in 2003, there had been no nuns living here for ten years. The villagers had no one to shepherd them. Over the last ten years the sisters have re-established the mission and the pastoral care. The results are impressive.

By their daily life as much as by their traditions, the villagers seem to be close to what the first Christians must have been like. Fleeing Iraq in the 1930s, Assyrian families settled along the border, forming 30 or so villages along the banks of the river Khabour. Tal Arboush is the only one made up of Chaldean Christians; that is to say, Assyrian Catholics, the others being Orthodox. In Tal Arboush they speak the language of Christ.

We remember the words of Father Domenico when we were in Antioch: 'It isn't enough to see your neighbour at Mass on Sunday. The real challenge is living in harmony with your brother.' In Tal Arboush this brotherhood is also seen in their relationship with the Orthodox Christians in the surrounding villages, who are also both Christians and Assyrians. Marriages between the different churches are commonplace.

'Orthodox, Catholic, it's the same thing!'

The old woman says this with a mixture of goodwill and authority as she downs a glass of peach cordial. We've been in Tal Arboush for three weeks now. We've ended up feeling at home here, putting down roots, gaining a better understanding of the people. But tomorrow we're back on the road. We've taken up residence in the sisters' garden, among the trees, flowers and swings, with Sister Marguerite, an adorable little slip of a woman about 60 years old, with a gentle face and deep, dark eyes, who speaks French with a lilting voice. During our stay she's been our guide, our mother. Always giving out to others unconditionally, she seems to us to be the epitome of a saint in action.

A group of young girls interrupts our discussion. They've come to say hello to the nuns, play in the garden and beg a ride on our bikes.

[11] Having become famous because of the film of Gérard Oury, *La Grande Vadrouille*, the Daughters of Charity, or Sisters of Charity of St Vincent de Paul, changed their habit and no longer wear the headdress that made them readily identifiable. The order, founded by St Vincent de Paul in 1633, works with the poorest of the poor.

Since we're leaving tomorrow, they summon the courage to ask for one last turn. With our funky bikes, and our goatee beards, we're the number-one attraction, particularly for the school-aged kids. Especially Gabriel, who is apparently the spitting image of the Turkish actor Kıvanç Tatlıtuğ, whose films flood the screens all over the Arab world. At home there's Brad Pitt, George Clooney, Ben Affleck and the rest. But here, well, there's Kıvanç Tatlıtuğ. And Kıvanç Tatlıtuğ reigns supreme in the heart of every member of the fairer sex. Apparently he's caused numerous divorces in the Middle East: the woman swoons at the exploits of the superstar, under the jealous eye of her husband, who promptly demands a separation. It's understandable that Gabriel is rather pleased with this similarity. He's come to within an inch of signing his autograph, but the people are content with a selfie with him. Having had a go on his bike, the groupies shout out in unison, 'Photo, photo!' Ever the professional, the star obliges.

We buy some eggs and invade Helene's kitchen. She's one of the young women of the village. We want to make some *clafoutis*[12] and fruit cakes for our leaving party. It takes us a good three hours and Helene remains sceptical as she surveys the results.

We drop in to see Jimmy the hairdresser, who jumps at the opportunity to cut our hair; it's Gabriel's third haircut in 24 hours. Usually he has his hair cut at home – he can't believe his luck. Jimmy is a true artist. He pulls out all the stops for us: clippers, razor, scissors, clippers, scissors, clippers again. We come out an hour and a half later, as clean as two new pennies, each of us sporting a beard that's nothing short of a masterpiece.

As night falls the women and children arrive at the convent. We've invited all the villagers to come and share the cakes as a way of saying thank you and goodbye. Strangely, not one man comes. There must be about 40 people in all. Our friends sit down in a circle and try the cake without ever really saying whether they like it or not.

We speak in French; Sister Marguerite translates into Arabic. We thank them, apologize for our camera, which has certainly been too intrusive at times, explain what the rest of our trip and the project involves, and hand over the first 'object'. Gabriel brings a wooden

---

[12] A French dessert consisting of fruit baked in batter.

cross out of his bag: about 20 centimetres long, it's engraved with a dove carrying a sprig of boxwood in its beak. It was made for us by a French friend of Gabriel's. We wanted it to be a present to our first Christian community, a symbol of giving and unity.

'We left France with this little cross, made especially by our French friend for your village. We give it to you and we would like you to give something else, a gift for the village that will be the second stop of our journey.'

Silence. Puzzled expressions. This idea, which seemed absolutely fantastic when we were leaving France, is about to undergo its baptism of fire. If it doesn't seem meaningful to them we can kiss the whole idea goodbye – this 'relay of faith', which we want to be a sign of the universality of the Church. Just at this moment two young girls come forward. They hold out a string of rosary beads that they've made themselves. Sister Marguerite has had it all in hand. Rescued!

'We'll present it to a village in India in several weeks' time, as a gift from you. Pray for them if you would, and they will pray for you as well.'

The first link in the chain . . .

**To Syria from France – a cross for the Christians of Tal Arboush**

# 5

## Iraqi Kurdistan

### In which we suffer with the Christians

21 SEPTEMBER, 2 MONTHS AND 16 DAYS AFTER DEPARTURE
The customs officer stamps our passports with a friendly smile:
Republic of Iraq – Kurdistan Region.

'Welcome to Kurdistan. Enjoy your stay.'

We daren't look him in the eye or show any emotion for fear he'll
change his mind. Hurriedly pocketing our passports, we leave the building. We've just made the border crossing that, recently, everyone has
made into such a big deal; and with no difficulty at all, apart from one
soldier who needed convincing that bikes never have registration plates.

Two flags fly side by side. On the left, the Kurdish flag has a yellow
sun in the middle of three horizontal bands, red, white and green; on
the right, the new Iraqi flag bears the Arabic words *Allah Akbar*, God
is great.

Gabriel takes a deep breath. 'Phew! We're through.'

It's not really particularly difficult. All you have to do is show your
passport when you're asked, and smile at regular intervals. But we
can't help feeling paranoid that they won't let us go through. We have
been dreading the border because it's like a cinema trailer, giving us a
foretaste of what it will be like inside the country. But the film itself,
for us, will be several weeks long. If the border official is friendly, does
it mean that all the other Iraqis we meet will be welcoming too?

And now . . . *Inshallah!*

In spite of our straightforward crossing we still feel decidedly
uneasy. The sun is already low in the sky, and soon darkness will fall.
So far we have no contacts and therefore nowhere to spend the night.
And to reduce our options even further, we haven't a cent between us
– the only cash machine in Kurdistan is in Erbil, the regional capital

– and no map to show us where we are. But Providence will take care of everything. It has up until now; there's no reason it should stop.

I can't help feeling surprised to see people driving on the road, stopping at red lights, pedestrians chatting on the footpaths and children walking home from school wearing their school rucksacks. I don't know what I was expecting, but it wasn't this. Really, we know nothing about this country. I was imagining a scene from a film – explosions, machine-gun fire, bombed-out cars. Especially as people have been warning us about Iraq for weeks.

Feeling nervous, we decide to ride close together. As we have no idea where to go, we take the only option available: get back on the road and follow the signs: Zakho 2 km.

The road is straight, bordered by large stretches of sand and wasteland. Brand new 4x4s with tinted windows, battered pickups and cheap Japanese cars overtake us honking their horns. Wind laden with dust prickles our nostrils. Zakho comes into view.

'What'll we do?'

'Try to find a church.'

Apart from the customs officer, we haven't spoken to anyone in person yet. At the top of the list of my worst nightmares about Iraq is the idea that all Iraqis detest Americans, and therefore Westerners in general. How are they going to react to us? I wanted to keep a low profile but it's a lost cause: Gabriel has just stopped in the middle of a roundabout in front of an army post. He calls out in English to one of the officers, who doesn't understand and calls his colleagues.

'We would like to know if there are any Christians in this town. Do you know if there are any Christians? Or a church?'

Their eyes grow as wide as saucers. They obviously don't see many tourists.

'There's a church very near here, at the bottom of this street. Hey, your bikes are weird! Are they designed like that so you can have a siesta while you ride?'

They return to their post, laughing their heads off, forgetting about the traffic while we do a lap around the roundabout. We freewheel down the hill to the church. Ahead of us, kids are running around in the street playing with plastic machine guns – like kids the world over, except that here there's a sad irony in it. Passers-by stare at us as if we're from another planet. We hear singing coming from the doorway of the church; Evening Prayer has started. We catch the last few minutes and as we're leaving we see the bishop in the porch. Our first Iraqi Christian. We call out to him. The man, an imposing individual, stops, looks at us and says nothing for a few, long seconds before grudgingly pronouncing the word 'Silence!'

Charming. Really. With his walking stick he points at the logo printed on Gabriel's T-shirt: 'Silence'.[1] Oh yes!

He smiles roguishly, obviously pleased with his opening line. 'Come. Let's go and have a cup of tea.'

We follow him to the diocesan house, 100 metres away. The bishop is fat – he seems to be choking in his priest's collar – and chain-smokes Dunhills; when one goes out, another replaces it as if by magic. Monsignor Patros Harboli, Bishop of Zakho, seems absorbed in his thoughts. He throws out comments at regular intervals; up to us to catch them as they fly by.

'The general situation is quite grim. Kurdistan is safe. Don't go to Mosul. Relations between Christians and Muslims are good. What are your names? Do you have a visitor's visa? A lot of Europeans come here. I can't have you for dinner tonight. Iraqi Christians are heading for extinction. What will happen to the Church if our young people leave? It would be better if you French people did something constructive rather than coming here to cry with us. Saddam razed numerous Christian and Muslim villages in Kurdistan.'

And then nothing. Monsignor has seen enough of us. It's time to go.

It's pitch dark. We're looking for a place to sleep. We knock on the door of a Syrian priest who calls from the balcony of a two-storey house; he's sorry but he hasn't any room. Our experience with the nuns in Konya has cured us of persisting when we're obviously getting nowhere. We go on our way. We just have to get used to it. People are wary; suspicion is everywhere. We return to the bishop's house. He's ordered a hearty meal for us! When we've eaten he sends us to his warden's quarters. He offers us two mattresses in his own room. The fan on the ceiling above our heads gently cools us; our aching muscles relax. Before drifting off to sleep, I have one last flash of coherent thought:

---

[1] 'Silence' is one of the sponsors of the Tour de France, seen on the cycling jerseys of the contestants. Gabriel wears this jersey, which was given to him for cycling.

'That's all very well. We're off the hook for tonight. But what are we going to do tomorrow? We don't even know where the Christian villages are.'

'Yeah. Well, we'll see tomorrow. What worries me more is not getting any breakfast. And as far as I'm concerned, that sucks.'

At this point in the conversation there's a knock on the door. A cheerful face appears. A cheerful face that speaks English. The face of an angel.

'Good evening. My name is Abouna[2] Mouffid. I passed by the diocesan house and Monsignor said you were a bit lost. Would you like to come to my place for breakfast tomorrow?'

We can't believe our ears. Out of the blue.

'Excellent. Of course, yes. We'd love to.'

'Great. Then I could give you a few ideas of where to go. There are quite a number of Christian villages in the mountains, especially with the influx of refugees. But you have to know where to find them! I'll show you! So I'll see you tomorrow.'

The door closes. Our host rolls over in his sleep. Gabriel heaves a contented sigh. In the darkness I'm smiling from ear to ear. Our guiding star, always. Time after time, Providence brings people across our path just when we need.

We're meeting at seven thirty on the other side of town, in the second Chaldean parish of Zakho, where Abouna Mouffid is the priest. He tells us that the compound is guarded day and night. But at eight o'clock in the morning we find everyone is fast asleep. We take it on ourselves to rouse the guards and wake up the whole household by hammering on the iron gate. Abouna finally appears on the balcony, looking perky, clad in shorts and singlet. He gives orders to the guards, who let us in and sit us down for breakfast. Abouna soon arrives, dressed and clean-shaven, followed by Daniel, a man of about 50 with grey hair and a moustache. He wears round, silver-rimmed glasses. Between two slices of bread with fig jam, Daniel explains that he's in charge of diocesan development projects for the Iraqi refugee villages. Through his work he knows the mountains well. The reason he's here so early in the morning is because Abouna asked him to point us in the right direction.

[2] Abouna means 'Our Father' in Arabic, and is the title given to priests by Christians in the East.

During the course of the conversation we discover that over the last few years Kurdistan, the northern part of Iraq, has become the only part of the country where Christians can still feel at home and live in peace. Those who don't have the means to emigrate to Europe or the USA settle in the north. And so the Kurdish villages, where Christians were hunted down by Saddam's troops, have been repopulated with Christians exiled from the south – one of the ironies of Iraq's history.

'Many families flee Baghdad and Mosul because they're victims of persecution. In the mountains where you're going, you'll see a great many refugees. Our role is to try to find them work, help them start new businesses, and provide education for the children. We help them build a new life; everything from arranging microcredit to finance the opening of a new shop in a remote village, to hiring a teacher for children who've had to leave their school in the city.'

Daniel rips a sheet of A4 in two. On one half he draws a map of the Christian villages spread through the mountains, among the Muslim and Yezidi villages. This half sheet of paper, with misspelt names and approximate distances, is to be our compass for our entire stay in Iraq; it will prove to be more precious to us than gold. And while we wolf down one last piece of bread before leaving, Abouna Mouffid tries to sound reassuring: 'You'll be okay as long as you don't ride at night, and don't take the road to Mosul. You'll be passing very near it. So don't take the wrong direction after the checkpoint. Mosul is to the right. To the left, it's fine. If you go left, there's no danger, but to the right, there are murders every day. Last week, a man had his throat slit and he was left lying on the roadside, with the threat of death to whoever tried to move him. Don't get mixed up, that's all.'

★

Since Strasbourg, everything has gone smoothly. Whenever we come across an obstacle, Providence puts a guide on our path. And now, once again, the way is charted before us even before we've bought a map of the country. The landscape is magnificent. Grass-covered mountains of pale ochre dotted all over with little shrubs; rivers bordered with patches of lush green; steep roads that zigzag upwards like a bootlace, rising to the heavens. We pray as we ride. The beauty that surrounds us is disconcerting. Almost overwhelming. The effort of scaling one hill after another frees our minds, and God fills our hearts.

We stop for lunch on a mountain slope, between two big rocks; a huge plateful of pasta uses up the last of our food supplies. We've no money to buy any more; tonight we'll need to find a place to stay. At five thirty it's already starting to get dark. I think back to Abouna Mouffid's warning: 'Don't ride at night.' According to Daniel's map, we shouldn't be far from the first Christian village. In a little hamlet where we stop to fill our drink bottles, some people tell us it's five kilometres away. We ride for an hour – still nothing. We climb hill after hill, straining our thighs. Darkness shrouds the mountains in deep silence. Sometimes a pickup or a 4x4 lights us up in its headlights and slows down to overtake. At these moments our hearts race and blood pulses through our temples. We're reluctant to use our bicycle lights. As we come round a bend, we see lights ahead – music and snatches of conversation coming from a row of houses. I leave Gabriel with the bikes and go in for a closer look. It's a family gathering; the music is coming from the stereo of a car with all its doors open. They're having dinner around a barbecue. The sight of some delicious-looking brochettes on the grill makes my mouth water. Acting as though it's completely normal to feed any old tramp who interrupts their party, they wrap up some meat in newspaper for me. But they can't have us to stay. The village we're looking for isn't far away, they tell us. After less than a kilometre we reach another house, with an enormous wooden cross standing on the terrace. We knock on the door; a man appears. He's a Chaldean.

A few moments later we're drinking *café au lait* with him, except it's more like a *lait au café*. Our man speaks very bad English and calls his cousin, Benham, to help him. Benham speaks perfect French, like many older Iraqis. He explains that he went through a seminary taught by French nuns, before deciding in the end to get married.

Benham wears a tweed jacket and horn-rimmed glasses. His words are precise, his gestures measured. He takes us to the house where Thomas, the head of the village, lives. Inside there's a large room with sofas all around the walls. From what we understand, Thomas's house is the equivalent of a presbytery, the place where the clergy live. Everyone congregates here to eat and talk. Tonight, even though it's late, there are about 15 people. They inspect us with great curiosity and bring a pile of enormous pastries, leftovers from a first-Communion celebration. And then, when we've just finished gorging ourselves, a mountain of platters arrives at the table, with enough food to feed an army: meat, stuffed vegetables, rice with vermicelli . . . We hardly feel equal to the task. What we found in Syria holds true here as well: in the East, the passing stranger is received like a king.

Benham and his family used to live in Mosul until six months ago. He tells us that he received death threats, but out of caution he can't tell us much.

'It became unliveable. Hellish.'

We think back to the testimonies of the refugees we met in Istanbul, Konya and Aleppo – leaving in a terrible rush, fearing for their lives. We don't force him to go on. And anyway, it's party day today, a celebration for the village children's first Communion. Communion with the body of a certain Jesus of Nazareth, put to death for what he declared, not so far from here, 2,000 years ago.

The sun is already high when we leave Thomas and his family. We realize we've sentenced ourselves to sweating bucketloads all day. We find it hard going; the heat is debilitating and our muscles are still recovering from all the kilometres we put in yesterday. Suddenly a big, white, late model Toyota 4x4 speeds past us, its horn blaring.

'Hey, Granddad, run us over, why don't you?'

The 'Granddad' parks on the side of the road up ahead. As we slowly catch him up, the door opens and a man in black jumps out: a beanpole of a man, sixtyish, closely cut hair, neatly trimmed moustache, piercing blue eyes behind square, metal-rimmed glasses. He's wearing a clerical collar.

'You're the cyclists! I'm Monsignor Rabban, Bishop of Amadiya! So pleased I saw you!'

Amadiya. We've heard that name somewhere before . . . It's the name of a well-known village perched on a rocky plateau, which is home to a famous fur market. There are still some trappers and their families living there. It turns out that Benham called the bishop to warn him we would be passing close to his village.

**An enthusiastic welcome to Komane village**

'We're a bit lost . . . The hills are so steep. Is Amadiya far from here?'

'No, you're nearly there. But why don't you come to the village where I grew up, Komane? It's quite close, and the diocesan house is there. You could stay for a few days and have a break. I'll call my nephew. He's the priest. You're most welcome!'

The 4x4 zooms off in a cloud of dust, leaving us speechless.

When we get to Komane I'm no longer Charles Guilhamon but Ben Affleck. Or more precisely, Ben Affleck the hero, emerging from his space rocket, having saved the world from Armageddon.[3] Children crowd around as we ride down into the village, which lies in a little hollow. Soon we're surrounded by 30 or more kids, all shouting and jostling to hold on to our panniers. We come to a halt in front of the church, where a priest is waiting for us. He's a short man and his face is beaming.

Green hills rise in the distance – an awe-inspiring view. In front of the diocesan house, old women with headscarves are making flat-breads. They knead balls of dough in their strong hands and cook them in a frying pan on a bed of red-hot embers. The little priest offers us a room. His name is Imad but we soon start calling him 'Abouna

---

[3] The final scene of Michael Bray's film *Armageddon*, with Ben Affleck and Bruce Willis.

Maalesh', which as Monsignor Audo explained to us in Aleppo means 'it's not serious' or 'no problem' in Arabic. Abouna Maalesh, or Father Happiness.

'It's easy,' he repeats endlessly, to justify his good mood. 'Life,' he explains, 'is easy when you trust in God. You can't help but be joyful.' He's always laughing.

Monsignor Rabban arrives late in the afternoon, with a plump little lady named Laura. A Lebanese journalist, she's here to write an article about Iraqi Christians. She's coming with us to visit a Kurdish family. On the way the bishop wants to make a point: 'Here in Komane there are both Christian and Muslim families, and everything is fine.'

He takes us to meet a Muslim family. Our host wears traditional Kurdish costume: baggy trousers, a waistcoat, and a turban on his head. Monsignor feels very at home here. Between gulps of tea he leads the discussion, juggling the two languages. He tries his best to explain the history of their land. The main thing we retain is that Kurdish history is a long succession of events in which the Kurds have suffered the loss of their dignity as a people, tragic criminal acts and double dealing by the world powers.

The origins of Kurdistan – literally 'land of the Kurds' – go back to ancient times. Today the Kurdish people are divided between Syria, Turkey, Iran and Iraq. After the First World War and the decline of the Ottoman Empire, the Treaty of Sèvres in 1920 provided for the creation of a Kurdish state. Three years later the Treaty of Lausanne redrew the boundaries in the Middle East, and the Kurds were deprived of the right to their own land; the European powers preferred to exploit the wealth of physical resources for themselves, particularly the rich supply of both oil and water. The Kurds, a proud people, revolted and were severely reprimanded: the British, as the occupying power in Iraq, bombed numerous villages, and were said to have used mustard gas on the town of Sulaymaniyah in the north-east of what is today Iraqi Kurdistan. During the 1970s, Saddam Hussein granted Kurdistan a certain amount of autonomy, but it was only a façade – the majority of the members of the Kurdistan legislative council were nominated by Baghdad. Ten years later, in 1980, the Kurds were still demanding self-determination when Saddam ordered a chemical weapons raid on the Balisan Valley. The result was a veritable genocide: 182,000 people died in these attacks. Whole villages were wiped out; only about a hundred out of every thousand escaped death.

'If you have no desire to know someone, you will remain forever strangers. And to know him, you must share his values. As a Christian, it's my duty to pass on this message. Kurdish history is very sad, full of misunderstandings with Arabs. I'm a Catholic bishop, but I respect all men, be they Christians, Muslims, Kurds or Arabs.'

After the first Gulf War in 1991, in which Saddam Hussein was weakened, Kurdistan became an autonomous region under American protection. The new Kurdish Assembly would henceforth include five Christian representatives (out of 100). The proportion of Christians has risen sharply since 2003 with the influx of refugees from the centre and south of Iraq.

'At the end of the 1990s, this was the only Christian village for miles around. There were only about 60 inhabitants. The situation is quite different today, with massive numbers of refugees coming from Mosul and Baghdad. Now there are Christians living all over the mountains.'

Monsignor takes us to have dinner with his brother. No sooner has he pushed the door open than his nephew jumps up and flings his arms around his neck. From then on he becomes a *papa gâteau* – a real softie – for the evening. The whole family clamour round the clergyman, and treat Gabriel and me with the greatest honour. During the meal Laura, the journalist, outlines the crimes perpetrated against Christians during the last few years.

She tells us of death threats, intimidation, letters containing bullets, kidnappings and exorbitant ransoms that had to be found within 24 hours, apartments requisitioned, murders committed in the middle of the street, car bombs exploded in front of churches, beauty salons blown up for harbouring vice, priests tortured, children crucified on doors, neighbourhoods filled with suspicion, decapitations filmed and posted on the internet, loaves of bread filled with explosives, wrapped as presents and sent to priests for the feast of Epiphany. There isn't a family in Mosul without a story to tell. Nobody escaped tragedy.

Back at the diocesan house we sit down with Monsignor in his office. Gabriel goes on the offensive. With all these stories of the persecution of Christians in Iraq, we can't understand why the bishop insists that Muslims and Christians generally live in peaceful coexistence.

'If relations are as good as you say, why is it that Christians are fleeing in droves to Europe or the USA?'

Monsignor's face darkens. He must be tired of having to repeat the same old story. He launches fervently into his explanation.

'You see, here in Komane, in Amadiya and the surrounding villages, some are leaving even though we're living in peace: they're taking advantage of their refugee status to emigrate, hoping to find an easier life in the West.'

'So the situation is the same as in Syria, where people are leaving not because their lives are in danger but because the West seems to promise so much more?'

'Not for everyone, as there are obviously some tragic situations. But it's certainly the case for some people, which grieves me. Generally speaking, I think Christians have lost their identity. Their faith needs to be restored.'

Identity. This famous 'identity' that Monsignor Audo was talking about a few weeks ago in Aleppo. The word was tossed around in Tal Arboush, and everyone's talking about it here as well. Christianity is in these people's DNA. They receive it at birth. I have trouble really understanding what that means, all the implications. For me, even if practising my faith means being involved in a community, like going to Mass for example, it is for me, first and foremost, a personal thing. But for them being a Christian is a way of life – it involves all their traditions, their history, their land, their blood. I certainly can't share this identity, but I can understand that the families who leave without hope of returning cut themselves off definitively from everything that has made them who they are.

Monsignor's voice trembles, a mixture of enthusiasm and disappointment.

'They really are a part of the Kurdish people! This is their home. It's our duty to help rebuild our country. Every Sunday I have to drive an hour to celebrate Mass in a village where the priest and his family have left for Turkey. Is that faith? We've lost the fire of our new-found faith. We've lost our courage.'

In some circles, Christian families migrating to the West are regarded favourably, but not by Monsignor Rabban. To him, as well as many of his colleagues, it's not the solution.

'If we all leave, it would be the first time in 2,000 years there hadn't been a Christian presence here. We need help to live peacefully in our own country, with our safety ensured and our rights protected! Europe and the USA are a false promise for Iraqi Christians. Those who emigrate lose everything that gives them their identity. Sometimes life can be even worse than here. A few years ago, when I was in Rome, I stopped at a church to pray. A man in tattered clothing was begging at the entrance. When he saw me he grabbed my arm and began to cry. He was from my village. He'd left several years earlier to try to find a better life.'

The comments are bitter but the man is a fighter. In Dohuk – a town further south in Kurdistan, the scene of bloody confrontations between the Iraqi army and Kurdish Peshmerga in 1991, as well as between Kurds themselves – he used to run a co-educational, secular school where Christians and Muslims received the same education. It's a centre where the different communities can come together and students' eyes are opened to the wider world; every student learns Arabic, Aramaic and Kurdish. That's where his daily battle is: showing that living together is possible.

The next morning, before leaving Komane, we attend Mass celebrated by Monsignor Rabban, with his nephew assisting. It's touching to see them officiating together, the patriarch and his disciple, uncle and nephew, the old man and the novice – one charismatic and self-confident, the other quietly cheerful. They both speak straight to the people's hearts and gently lead them back to God. Monsignor Rabban translates several passages of the Mass from Kurdish into French for us. With a long embrace, we leave the bishop and Abouna Maalesh. Behind them there's a building site; construction has been interrupted through lack of funds. However, we're sure that a new cathedral will soon stand here in the middle of the Kurdish mountains. There's already a large cross on the top of the roof – a daring gesture in a Muslim country.

Following Abouna Mouffid's recommendation to the letter, we take a left at the checkpoint, turning off the road to Mosul, and head for

Erbil. In the distance we can see the town of Alqosh, built at the foot of a mountain. There's another checkpoint on the road into the town. The soldiers let us pass when they understand that we've come from Paris by bike.

On the rocky slopes above us we can just distinguish the façade of a large building. That's the monastery we're looking for.

A blind monk, with a cigarette hanging from his lips, opens the door and takes us through to an outer courtyard.

'Welcome. You can spend the night here.'

Alqosh is in the Bible. It's the birthplace of the prophet Nahum, who lived from 650 to 612 BC. In 1948, most of the members of the Jewish community were expelled from the city, leaving the synagogue abandoned. The synagogue, which houses the prophet's tomb, is in ruins today. Since the Jews left, Alqosh has become a Christian stronghold. To live there, you must be from a Christian family going back several generations. There are *only* Christians living here! Thinking back to the imposing checkpoint barring the road, we realize why the protection is warranted.

The monk continues: 'We're Chaldean monks. There are 12 of us. When it was no longer safe for some of the brothers living in Baghdad, they left and came to join us here.'

Our monk isn't wearing a habit; he gets around in a tracksuit and flip-flops. He takes us to a large square courtyard, where we meet the other brothers. They're sitting on plastic chairs around a little fountain. Strong and thickset, they look like a bunch of Mafia hitmen. A man of about 40 with a crew cut and deeply lined face approaches me. His name is Gibrail, the Father Superior.

Speaking in Italian he says: 'I read an article recently that predicts that in 40 years' time, 50 to 60 per cent of the population of France will be Muslim. Are you crazy, you French? Why are you letting that happen? Are you a Christian country or not?'

'A Christian country.' How many times have we heard people tell us that we come from a Christian country? Often, when we say we're French, people seem to take it for granted that we must be Christians.

'Well you see, in our country it's quite different. Faith isn't really tied to your identity, as it is in your country.'

'So what? When Islam comes in everything is swept away, destroyed.'

The monk's words are violent and seem incredibly radical to us. But with my scant knowledge of Islam, I'm no match for this Arab Christian who has suffered from the oppression of the Muslim majority since the day he was born. People here make a distinction between Muslims and Islamists. Perhaps he's talking about fanatics. Perhaps he means that extremists are terribly dangerous. Maybe, but I get the impression that as far as Father Gibrail is concerned, the Qur'an carries within it the seeds of the sufferings of Christians in the Middle East and that the very essence of Islam is committed to fighting Christianity.

The exodus of Christians is seen as both a current suffering and a historical injustice. Although Iraq is 97 per cent Muslim today, the country has a long Christian tradition, from ancient times, when Christianity was planted here well before the birth of Islam in the seventh century. It's quite valid to say that the Christian community has a kind of territorial right to Iraq since the two main Christian Churches – Chaldean and Eastern Assyrian – are directly descended from the peoples who lived in Mesopotamia before the Christian era. Those who suggest that the Eastern Christians should 'go home' are completely wrong: Eastern Christians are already home.

The bells are ringing. The monks all stand up.

'Look! The children are going in for dinner. Let's join them!'

A bevy of boys of all ages and sizes crosses the courtyard two by two, stopping in front of the entrance to the dining room. There must be about 60 of them – the orphans of Alqosh. 'We opened this orphanage only a few years ago, to take in the child victims of war and terrorism. In the East, in principle, the family looks after its orphans. But these children were in extreme situations; some of their parents couldn't look after them.'

After dinner we offer them all a ride on our recumbent bikes, inside the courtyard; within minutes the peace of the monastery is shattered. Shouts of delight ring out into the night. Some of them tug at my heartstrings. They line up politely waiting for their turn, for fear they might miss out. Under the tender eye of the monks, they take turns riding round and round the courtyard.

The next morning we climb with one of the monks, Abouna Abraham, up to an ancient cave monastery where the hermit Rabban Hormez once lived. Our guide sets off at a good pace in spite of his 63 years.

'Would you prefer the road or the goat track?'

'Since we're not on our bikes for once, let's take the goat track.'

The area is a geologist's paradise. The folds in the rock are by turns pink, beige, grey, maroon, ochre. A flock of goats pass close by on their way down the valley. Abouna is puffing and panting. When we take our first break his eyes are red and bloodshot and he's short of breath. We assure him that we can carry on without him. But he won't listen; it's a question of honour. Abouna must go with us.

'*Andiamo!*'[4]

As he walks he teaches us all kinds of things about the mountain and its flora. When we arrive, he rewards us with a guided visit. What from a distance looked like black patches on the light-coloured rock face turn out to be a series of caves that the hermit and his disciples dug out by hand in the seventh century – the first cells of the monastery. There are beds, seats, tables dug out of the rock. It's an amazing sight. The cells open directly on to the cliff face overlooking the valley.

When we were in Komane we came across a group of students from Alqosh who were on retreat. We call one of them now on his mobile phone. He wants to pick us up from the monastery and take us to meet his family. Eder is 26 years old. He's the third son of a family of four children, two of whom have emigrated to the USA. He's short and stocky, and wears a tight, black T-shirt. He looks at us with piercing green eyes. It's a dark, moonless night. In the confined space of the car, Eder explains what his decision to stay in Iraq means to him. He's only slightly older than us – a student, just like me . . . Every morning he takes a bus with other young Christians to go to university in Mosul. Mosul! Everyone advised us not to go there, even by car. He goes there every day.

'I never know, when I leave in the morning, if I'll come home that evening. Yes, it scares me. It really does. But I have faith. You can't let fear rule your life. If you do, you're already dead. I'm no hero. I don't particularly want to die a martyr's death.'

His best friend was killed just because he was a Christian. The reality that Eder talks about is completely different from what Monsignor Rabban described. We go down several stairs, cross through a kitchen and sit down in a long, narrow room with no windows and cold white lighting. Eder's parents greet us; his little sister serves us coffee with milk.

[4] 'Let's go' in Italian.

He continues: 'My father was kidnapped. They demanded $20,000 ransom. His so-called crime was having converted people. But he never converted anyone. It was just an excuse to extract some money from us. Of course we paid, with the help of all the families in the neighbourhood. And he was freed.'

'Don't you sometimes want to take revenge? After all the bombings, do people ever retaliate?'

'No. You see, we're a peaceful people. I've got five guns, but I don't think I could ever use them against a human being.'

As the discussion progresses we gain a better understanding of the dilemma Eder lives with. On the one hand he'd like to leave, as his two brothers have done, but on the other he wants to be 'a Christian who is making a difference for Iraq'.

'We'd love to help rebuild our country, but it's impossible!'

'Why is it impossible?'

'Because the government is corrupt, and it's incapable of guaranteeing Christians their rights. Take my case, for example. I'd like to be an English and Information Technology teacher. But as a Christian, I can only work in a Church school and only in Kurdistan.'

Eder is touchingly sincere. He learnt English all by himself by watching American films, and he's now as fluent as a native speaker, with a strong Texan accent. He seems so brave and determined.

'Every day I pray to God, telling him that if I die today, I will at least have tried to be his child. We need faith, and we need to trust God, but sometimes it's hard.'

Eder takes us up to his room; he built it himself on the roof of the family home. It's like a million other kids' rooms. He puts on a CD of Céline Dion and we smoke *shisha* listening to '*Pour que tu m'aimes encore*'. An enormous dagger sitting on his desk attracts my attention.

'An American soldier gave me that. When the Americans arrived, we were all there in the streets to welcome them. They came to save us from Saddam. But since then, violence against Christians has only got worse and people say if that's freedom, they don't want it. It's worse than under Saddam.'

The more people we meet, the more we realize how complex the situation is: that the Christians aren't all in the same boat; that fundamentalists and Muslims are two different terms that mustn't be confused; that people of different faiths can still be friends; and that although persecution can have religious overtones, it's also the result of a climate of latent insecurity due to an unstable government.

We leave the monastery at dawn. The air is refreshing. Cool, even. For the first time since we left home we wrap up warmly. With an escort of barking dogs we pass the checkpoint on our way out, and we're back on the Erbil road. We ride on, knowing it's going to be a long day. I've learnt to deal with the strain by dividing the distances into little doses that I only need to swallow one at a time. Each ten kilometres that comes up on my odometer represents one step in this game of mental gymnastics. My legs simply obey. I know that all I need to do to keep going is look at my front wheel turning, and let myself be gradually hypnotized, turn after turn.

And yet it's impossible to maintain our momentum today. We thought the road would be flat but it's just one hill after another. It makes me mad; I want to stomp with both feet on my bike to teach it a lesson. Anger, pain, wounded pride assail me with a chorus of dark thoughts that stop me from pedalling consistently. I'm continually amazed at how obsessed I am by the pain in my legs when the countryside around us each day is witness to a much greater evil.

After 120 kilometres we stop for lunch in a tiny village. We're surrounded by a circle of kids, but their parents, who are putting grain out to dry on their roofs, continue their work and throw furtive glances in our direction. Sitting on a stack of concrete blocks, we unwrap our cooker and pots and start preparing our meal. But when our rice with raisins is nearly cooked, an army vehicle pulls up beside us. The villagers act all innocent. They say they called the police 'for *our* safety'! In fact they were just scared of us. The soldiers order us to follow them. What a pain!

'We've just done 120 kilometres and we need to eat. If we don't, we'll … And the rice is hot. It'll get cold. Can't you wait a bit?'

They roll their eyes around like marbles but much to our surprise agree to wait, and watch us downing mouthfuls of our peculiar stew. But one of the soldiers rapidly loses his temper. This time our stomachs must wait. Surrounded by policemen on motorbikes, we grudgingly follow their jeep for a few kilometres to the police station. The floor and walls are concrete, filthy and bare. Minimal furniture. Our officer's desk is framed by two deputies standing one on either side. The patrol leader who harassed us earlier hands him our passports. He opens them, then closes them almost immediately. Then he directs his powerful gaze at us and throws a laconic, 'OK, it's all right. Move.'

I'm furious. As a consolation for having lost time and missed our precious lunch, we plant ourselves on a little patch of grass facing the station and finish our cold stew. The soldier who stopped us is very embarrassed. He brings us a soda, some rice and then asks us straight out if we'd like to rest inside the station with the other soldiers. So we find ourselves in a bunkroom, sitting on a mattress in front of the television with six guys, their uniforms unbuttoned to the waist. They show us how to dismantle a gun. Evidently our education is sadly lacking. The most 'extroverted' among them is a brainless idiot, who is too fat for his uniform. With a cocky grin, he asks us about French women. Are they beautiful? Are they as liberated as they say? Is it true that none of them are still virgins when they get married? The others intimate that he's a Muslim in name only, because he drinks, smokes and has numerous mistresses behind his wife's back. His friends point the finger at him and burst out laughing, as if his wrongdoings were just childish behaviour. They're quick to point out, very seriously of course, that he's the only one.

The road to Erbil is tough going. A cloud of dust surrounds the town and its environs. We can barely see 30 metres ahead. Dust infiltrates us, stinging our eyes, prickling our nostrils and making us gag. We pass long traffic jams of 4x4s and pickups, their windows yellow with sand, and are forced to stop again at the checkpoint just outside Erbil, where we're interrogated by the 'Colonel' himself. He swaggers around showing off how big and tough he is, while his henchmen follow him drinking tea and smiling as if it's all a big joke. We stand facing him, awaiting the supreme verdict. He eventually decides our passports are in order and deigns to let us pass.

We reach Erbil, capital of Iraqi Kurdistan, and hence Ankawa as well, which is our real goal. Situated in the suburbs of Erbil, Ankawa was still a little village only 20 years ago. Today it's a decent-sized town within Erbil and it's continually growing as it provides asylum to thousands of Christian refugees, notably from Mosul and Baghdad.

Like many new towns, it's been built hurriedly and, in parts, poorly. Monsignor Rabban, as well as acting as bishop in the mountains, is Vicar General of Ankawa. He's not here at the moment, but again he's made his house available to us. The warden is expecting us and shows us to our rooms. We relish the luxury of a long bath.

The bishop's house is in a residential quarter. In this area women can go out without wearing the veil, dress as they want and take a taxi without their husband or their brother.

As we're getting ready to go out, a man calls out to us from the entrance of his office in the courtyard. With his shaved head, gangster hat, and too-big beige suit, he looks priceless. His name is Abouna Sabri, the curate.

'They told me you were looking for me. Can I help you?'

'We're a bit lost. We've come to find out about the church in your country.'

'Awesome, man!'

Abouna Sabri talks like a real Yankee. He spent many years in the USA.

'Come on, fellas, I'm taking you out for lunch.'

Like all the churches in the city, and most of the churches in the country, the Chaldean Cathedral is guarded by armed men. On our way out, Abouna introduces us to the guards who are sitting on plastic chairs in front of the entrance, their AK-47s between their legs. One of them, with a jovial smile and very round cheeks, claims he's never fired a shot in his life. The second, a little younger, is a former soldier. He assures us that personally he wouldn't hesitate to shoot if the situation was dangerous. But apart from this militia, employed by the Church to protect itself and deter terrorists, Ankawa seems incredibly peaceful.

He takes us out to an upmarket restaurant beside one of the main arterial roads in Erbil. Abouna Sabri used to be a weightlifting champion. After he'd had his moment of glory, he entered seminary and went to study in the USA. But he's been back for several years now.

'Because I like this place too much.'

'Really?'

'Yes, I like it here. And you, how are things in your country? I've heard that the churches are all empty and the young people never go to Mass.'

Some American and Korean soldiers are sitting beside us, their weapons gleaming. Nothing like the Iraqis' battered old Kalashnikovs. They're laughing and talking loudly.

'I know nearly all of those guys. I celebrate Mass at their barracks,' comments Abouna.

'Oh, and do many of them come?'

'Yes, quite a few.'

We stay with Abouna Sabri for several days, getting to know Ankawa and its inhabitants. He introduces us to one of his parishioners, a political science and international relations student, who is also a journalist, with a wife and little girl. Ano, 24 years old, is a busy man. A few years ago he created a one-hour programme for Christian viewers shown weekly on Kurdish television.

'The Kurdish government came to see me because they wanted Kurdish television to be for everyone and there still wasn't anything for Christians. I offered them this programme. I was very young when it started and not very experienced, but people liked the idea. It's been showing for nearly eight years.'

Ano takes us for a walk in the streets of Ankawa. He talks diplomacy, politics, territorial conflicts. He's a mine of information and full of good stories. One day we joined some of his friends at a café. One of them was Saddam Hussein's chef for 20 years. He's a Christian, as were all the other domestic staff of the late dictator, because 'Saddam knew that Christians are men of peace and they would be incapable of betraying or poisoning him.' We walk past the Chaldean cultural centre, a grandiose edifice built and financed by the Kurdish government, and visit a 1,000-year-old church that was rebuilt ten years ago in a style that's not at all in keeping with its age; inside it looks like some cheap hotel's function room.

Ano is our new guardian angel. He commandeers his friend Tony to take us to the airport to pick up Pierre, our producer, who is planning to join us three times over the course of our trip. When Pierre appears at the arrivals gate, he's lost ten kilos and we hardly recognize him.

'I've taken up running! Not bad, eh?'

It's great to see him again. He asks lots of questions, jokes around, brings us news from France. He's brought us a parcel from friends and family. We unwrap it, with a lump in our throats. I find a new Swiss Army knife, to replace the one stolen in Tarsus, and a pile of other presents: a bottle of pastis, luxury shower gel, chocolate, vacuum-packed cheese, books. Old school friends have even put pen to paper with words of encouragement. Nourishment for our bodies. And balm for our hearts.

Thanks to Ano, who has found us a fast car complete with a driver, we leave with Pierre for Qaraqosh – impossible to get there by bike because Qaraqosh is at the heart of the conflict between the rebels and the Kurdish government. Besides, it's a sort of Christian stronghold surrounded by Muslim villages. It's been subject to regular suicide car-bomb attacks. Before he starts the car, our driver, with shaved head, black shades and a rosary hanging from the rear-view mirror, sticks a gun into the back pocket of his trousers. Just like in a mobster Mafia film. We pile into the back. He takes a route that avoids the worst hot-spots. We pass several checkpoints without any problems. The American soldiers wear futuristic-looking, hi-tech outfits, whereas the Iraqi soldiers have faded uniforms, with oversized flak jackets and battered old helmets. When we're almost there, we run into trouble . . .

We'd been working on them for a long time, trimming, shaping . . . They were getting quite bushy . . . we could almost comb them. In short, we were quite proud of our beards. A beard is great: it protects you from the sun, gives you the cool adventurer look and considerably increases your virility! But above all, in Arab countries a beard allows you to fade into the background. For weeks, we've been fussing over them, putting up with the inevitable itchiness, persuaded that they'll be a great advantage for us in Iraq. It's not until we get to the checkpoint at Qaraqosh that we realize we've got it wrong. The guards make us get out of the car and escort us into the security post. I ask why. The clean-shaven soldier points to my hairy cheeks. The fact is the Kurds tend to be clean-shaven, and instead of a beard they wear a thick moustache. The officers mistook us for Arabs. We're the only bearded men for 20 kilometres around. The captain obviously understands nothing of our confused explanations. Fortunately Pierre has a contact in Qaraqosh. He calls him on his mobile and passes it to the captain, who rapidly resolves the situation. We feel very foolish.

Qaraqosh – 45,000 people. Christians make up 99 per cent of the population. Eight bell towers that point towards the heavens. Surrounding the town, a succession of brown hills. In the distance they look like sand dunes. And on the ground, fine dust, burning by day, icy by night. Water trickles along a muddy little canal, lined with all kinds of rubbish. In front of each church, and at every street corner, stand armed men – rough, unshaven civilians with battered Kalashnikovs slung over their shoulders. Qaraqosh is a huge safe haven for a wave of refugees fleeing Baghdad and Mosul. New organizations have been hurriedly launched to help the most disadvantaged. The Christians of Qaraqosh are proud of their land, proud of their culture and proud of their faith.

'We're going to die here.'

With a bantering tone, the man emphasizes the *here*, as if the thought gives him great joy. At the Qaraqosh press agency we video our interview with the only journalist who speaks French.

'We're going to die here, because our Christian faith is here! Since 1980 there have been three million martyrs in Qaraqosh. Do you understand?'

He makes some witty asides in Arabic; his colleagues split their sides laughing.

The atmosphere is incredibly light-hearted, given the setting.

'Look! That guy's the director of a women's magazine!'

'Ah, so he's the great specialist on women, is he?' A burst of laughter highlights my bad joke. With the physique of a weightlifter, he seemed anything but the sensitive and caring type.

'You know, we're in seventh heaven today!'

'Oh really? Why is that?'

'Very few French delegations come to Qaraqosh. And here you are, journalists, cameras, video. It's a great honour!'

Journalists? That was a quick promotion! We don't contradict him. We just keep listening.

'Some people emigrate because they want to live in peace. But here we give our life for our faith, to bear witness to others, especially those who aren't Christians. Perhaps you think our faith is naive, a bit simple. But that's not true. I tell you, our faith is strong. We see the Marie Virgin (sic) at Qaraqosh, you know. It's because we have a lot of problems that our faith is strong!'

As if to celebrate these great words, tea arrives on a silver platter. In the room next door there are dozens of machine guns stacked on racks, ready to be drawn in case of emergency. Above them hangs a portrait of

Monsignor Raho, the Chaldean Bishop of Mosul assassinated in March 2008. He received numerous death threats but didn't want to leave the city, even joking about it from the pulpit. However, one day after Mass some cars blocked the street and several men got out. They fired on the bishop's car with machine guns, killing the chauffeur and some deacons, and took the prelate away. He died three days later, probably from a heart attack. The captors demanded $1 million in ransom. Iraqi Christians regard him as a true martyr, one who died for his faith.

Later, in another part of town, we make our way carefully among piles of rubble and twisted metal rods. Bishop Monsignor Petros-Mouche is showing us around the building site for the new seminary of Qaraqosh, which he will run when it is built.

'More than just a seminary, this will be a humanist university, open to everyone. We'll teach the arts, philosophy and theology. This enterprise might seem completely foolish to you. How can we imagine getting enough students to fill a seminary when the Church in Iraq is disintegrating? How can we think of training priests to plant new communities of believers, while according to the media the Church is rapidly exsanguinating, dying? But a Church that's preparing for the future is a Church whose faith is not shaken; it's a Church which, quite rightly, continues to hope.'

'Our country is fragile, but we have the power of God,' the old man says simply. 'This country has suffered much for the love of Christ. We've always responded peacefully. I can't leave this land, this soil . . . it's mixed with the blood of martyrs. Our country is rich. We must give all we have, even our lives, to build, here in Iraq, a people united in peace.'

'Iraqi Christians have always been people of peace and patriotism, working to build a country that has been theirs for several millennia. Personally, I wouldn't leave. But I know that in staying, some are risking their lives, and I cannot guarantee their safety.'

Building a country that is united in accepting its own diversity; a mission that can only be realized through a hope in God.

Today Christians make up 1.8 per cent of Iraq's population.[5] Between 2009 and 2010 the number of Christians in Baghdad went from 450,000 to 150,000.

[5] Observatoire de l'Église en détresse.

## Iraqi Kurdistan

*For your sake we face death all day long; we are considered as sheep to be slaughtered. No, in all these things we are more than conquerors through him who loved us. For I am convinced that neither death nor life, neither angels nor demons, neither the present nor the future, nor any powers, neither height nor depth, nor anything else in all creation, will be able to separate us from the love of God that is in Christ Jesus our Lord.*

*(Romans 8.36—39 NIV)*

# 6

## India: Chennai to Kolkata

### In which churches appear out of the blue . . . every 100 kilometres.

7 OCTOBER, 3 MONTHS AND 24 DAYS AFTER DEPARTURE
A short flight from Iraq to India and we're back on our bikes. The transition is brutal: we're flattened by the heat and humidity. It's a drastic change from the parched atmosphere of the Middle East. Feeling woozy and woolly-headed, we drag ourselves through Chennai airport like slugs in an uncomfortable post-landing torpor.

Before we left Paris we met an expatriate Indian priest named Father Andrew, who immediately recommended us to his nephew, Edwin. Gabriel telephones him from an airport call box; Edwin arrives 30 minutes later. He has enormous black eyes and brilliant white teeth. We see his teeth because he's smiling . . . He's continually smiling. We pack the boxes containing our bikes into the boot (he's smiling), as well as the boxes containing our panniers (he's still smiling), and get into the car (he's still smiling). We drive across the sprawling city. The traffic is both shambolic and harmonious at the same time: everyone does whatever they like, without bumping into each other. It's coordinated chaos – and it works. Those who say Indians are crazy drivers are wrong; they're artists, more like it! We soon leave the main roads and plunge into a mass of alleyways barely wider than the car. Edwin drops us at his place, where we find his mother and brother. Like him, they never stop smiling. It starts to become embarrassing. We feel like grumpy old grouches beside them.

So far our interaction, though warm and friendly, has been rather silent because Edwin doesn't speak much English, his family speak none at all. But while we're reassembling our bikes in their little garden, under the gaze of interested onlookers, young Father Victor Rakesh turns up. He arrives with – surprise! – a big smile. He's accompanied by Sophie, a very beautiful young woman. They met at university when they were both studying for a Masters in social services. She speaks good English and acts as our tourist guide for the day. She has fine features; her voice is gentle but firm. She wears a perfectly fitted red sari.

'We'll be your hosts while you're here. Would you like us show you around the city?' asks Father Victor.

'Thank you, Father, but you must have better things to do.'

'No, no, we're very pleased to have you.'

Victor has taken it upon himself to look after us. He's a parish priest, but at the request of his friend, Father Andrew, Edwin's uncle, he has made room in his schedule to entertain us. We start with a visit to a restaurant with a self-service buffet.

'There is a fire in your mouth, no?'

As the chillies violate our virgin palates, Edwin, Sophie and Victor smile and nod their heads like bobble-head dolls.

'You'll be sleeping at my place tonight.'

'Father lives in a slum among the poor!' explains Sophie enthusiastically.

Father Victor vacates his bedroom for us, despite our protests, and goes off to sleep in the room next door.

At nine o'clock the next morning we arrive at Father Victor's chapel for Mass. Although it's still early, the heat and the humidity are already oppressive. The congregation, mostly women, sit on the carpeted floor. We've been told they're all beggars. But to us the young girls seem like princesses. A few pictures of saints decorate the white walls of the plain, rectangular church. When Mass has finished, Father Victor calls us up to the microphone. We make our way clumsily down the centre aisle, to the beat of the synthesizer, part of the little band on the right of the church. Little tots with beaming smiles place flower necklaces and scarves around our necks as a sign of welcome and respect, while a toothless old woman dabs orange-coloured cream on our foreheads. Everyone applauds.

'*Wanacome! Wanacome!*'[1]

We spend a marvellous few days with Edwin and Father Victor in Chennai; they wait on us hand and foot. Father Victor mobilizes one

[1] 'Welcome' in Tamil.

of his parishioners to repair the large chainring of my bike, which was damaged on the plane, while he takes us for a walk into town and introduces us to his bishop and fellow priests. Father Victor organizes everything as if his reputation depends on our being able to tell people all over the world that the hospitality in India is the best anywhere.

We go with him to Mass in the sanctuary of the Church of St Thomas. It's a large church built of dazzling white stone, so white that you'd think it was plaster. According to various apocryphal writings, Saint Thomas was the first to bring the gospel to India, around AD 50, and established the first Christian community on the Indian subcontinent. They have always been known as the 'Saint Thomas Christians'.

To top off his string of good deeds, the night before our departure Father Victor writes a letter of recommendation, full of Indian ceremonial expressions, addressed 'To whomever it may concern'. According to him the letter should open church doors for us all along our route through India. When we're about to leave, we find our bikes draped with myriad strings of orange and red peas. Then it's our turn to be decorated: once again, they swathe us with necklaces and dab oil on our foreheads. An old lady approaches holding a basin of strange-looking liquid with a candle floating on it; she waves her arms in circles around our faces, murmuring obscure incantations. Father Rakesh blesses us with great solemnity and wraps his arms around us. From the moment we arrived in India we have noticed something we will witness throughout our journey: Indians love pomp and ceremony, incense and oil, customs and rituals . . . They like religious celebrations to be thoroughly imbued with a sense of the divine, in sharp contrast with the humdrum of everyday life. After the magic spells and the Christian blessing, we're henceforth equipped to face the road hogs and honking horns.

Our goal: to escape from the stifling southern air and revitalize ourselves in the mountains, travelling right up the coast of India to the mythical Darjeeling plateau at the foot of the Himalayas. We realize we'll never be able to get a perspective on India as a whole or understand it all. It's an entire continent in itself, home to a great mosaic of cultures and peoples: 225 languages, spoken in 28 states. How can we hope to do more than seize a few passing impressions? So, as always, we plan to let go, to trust, and make the most of our encounters with people we come across by chance.

Bikes, motorbikes, rickshaws, buses, trucks, sacred cows pass perilously close to us, one after another. Some drivers wield their mobile phones, swerving wildly to get a shot of us. Since leaving Chennai we're almost always accompanied by at least one inquisitive onlooker, who asks all the same questions as the one before.

'How are you? Do you have tubeless tires? What are you doing this for? It's for charity, isn't it? Are those your oxygen tanks (pointing at our water bottles)? Have a good day!'

But today one of them, more curious than the rest, brushes so close to me with his sidecar that I swerve and land upside down in a ditch. My knees are covered in blood. I hurl every insult I can think of at him. And he doesn't even stop. He smiles, amused or embarrassed, I'm not sure which, and off he goes. Not a care in the world.

As the sun gradually sinks to the horizon, in an atmosphere heavy with gas fumes and smoke, we catch sight of a strange circular building on the other side of the road, bordered with multicoloured fluorescent tubes and topped with a red cross blinking on and off.

'Hey, what on earth is that?'

A Red Cross centre? A casino? Maybe a sound and light show?

As soon as we set foot on the bridge that leads to this extraordinary edifice, fountains start playing and jets of water shoot above our heads. Inside, a young girl of about 15 is busy decorating a statue that's already decked out with many strings of sparkling beads. Perched on a stepladder, an older man wearing a singlet is fixing some light fittings to the ceiling. From his neck hangs a rosary. When he notices us, his face lights up.

'Hello! I'm Father Paul, the priest of this church. What can I do for you?'

The priest! So this is a church and he's responsible for the aesthetic carnage we're looking at. You'd think you were on the set of *Saturday Night Fever*. We ask if we can stay the night.

'Of course you can sleep here. Welcome to our parish!'

The priest has a maid. And having only one servant, he's obviously not as well off as some of his colleagues. In India, a priest enjoys a social status similar to that of a French abbot in previous centuries. His standard of living is often well above the average for the population.

After scrubbing ourselves under a cold shower, we join Father Paul on the terrace of the presbytery for a cup of tea. The drone of the motorway traffic mixes with the cicadas' song and, close by, the church rainbow winks in the night sky.

'Your church is very special . . .'

'How's that? What do you mean?'

Oh dear, he's rather touchy. Better make sure I don't put my foot in it.

'It's the first time we've seen a church that's so . . .'

'Original?'

Yes, that's it. Original.'

'Ah!'

Our priest can hardly contain his pride.

'Do you know, here in India, we love colour! Colours! So we made the church colourful. Besides . . . I'm actually an artist myself. I've just finished some frescoes that are several metres long, based on the Ten Commandments. Would you like to see them?'

'Er . . .'

Everything becomes clear when we see his art work. It's like with Salvador Dalí – you either love him or you don't; it's the same kind of thing with this church. But Father Paul: you can't help but like him. He is kindness and thoughtfulness personified. He has olive skin and little, dark spots dotted all over his face. His hair is combed neatly to one side and he wears rectangular metal-rimmed glasses.

'The advantage is that you can't possibly miss a church like this.'

I'm grovelling now. But I still think Dalí is a much better painter!

'No, indeed, and that's exactly why you're here with us tonight! It's also our way of reaching out as missionaries. And, you know, many drivers stop in front of the statue of the Virgin to ask for her protection on the road!'

'I never would have imagined there were so many Christian drivers.'

'But they're not all Christians! Far from it! Even Hindus stop. In fact they're nearly all Hindus. This Virgin Mary is Our Lady of Travellers;

she protects everyone. As a matter of fact, you're about to see for yourselves.'

A truck has just stopped in front of the winking statue of the Virgin Mary. The driver climbs down from his juggernaut and is instantly transformed into a meek little lamb. He kneels before the Madonna and slides a banknote into the statue's side as he gets up.

Father Paul looks after four children: one was abandoned at birth and the other three belong to a neighbour whose husband is a violent alcoholic. He treats them like his own sons, not hesitating to be strict with them. He teaches them not only science and the arts but also plumbing, drawing, painting . . .

Dinner is served by Father Paul's cook. He doesn't sit with us, doesn't talk unless he's spoken to, and respectfully does what the priest tells him to: he serves the food, clears the dishes, does everything. The children eat sitting on the floor, with their plates on the ground while we sit at the table with the priest. All this seems a far cry from the spirit of Christian brotherhood but it seems I just don't understand and it's cultural. Anyway, we all eat with our fingers. And I find it so spicy that I start thinking less about my neighbour and more about how I'm massacring my own stomach. All of a sudden I feel very protective towards it.

The heat and humidity make physical exertion particularly difficult. We leave before sunrise, hoping to steal a march on the sun, but before long I get a puncture. The sun comes up, gently stewing us in its heat as I make the repair. It's my second puncture in two days. Six to me, four to Gabriel. I'm back in the lead:

'Lucky we bought "unpuncturable" tyres, eh . . .?'

'Marvellous! Give me a hand, will you?'

Even though it's so early, we're immediately surrounded by a swarm of intrigued Indians. In the middle of the huddle the temperature soars. Sweat pours down my face and my sticky hands are soon covered with grease. Then it slowly spreads all over my face as I wipe my forehead. When I finally look up there's laughter all round: I've got black grease smeared all over me. Every time we stop it's the same. Hordes of people appear out of nowhere and come running to watch us. Some want to touch us; others try to help us repair the puncture; most just stare without saying a word.

This last patch seems to hold. We finally head off. After about 50 kilometres we pass the town of Ongole. Now it's Gabriel's turn for a puncture. Another repair. Then another puncture 300 metres further on. He swaps his tyres around, to avoid putting the load on to the more worn tyre. A few minutes later, the chainwheels of my derailleur decide to go walkabout. They've broken off before I have time to realize what's happened, and the four screws that held them together have vanished into thin air. These parts are made in Europe; we know it'll be impossible to find any here. We pace up and down the road, our eyes glued to the ground, and finally retrieve two of them. But it's not enough because if the chainrings aren't attached properly, they'll slowly be bent out of shape and end up completely wrecking the whole mechanism.

We turn round and head back to Ongole. To avoid further damage to my trusty bike, I hang on to Gabriel's shoulder and he tows me. In the town centre we find a cycle shop with its wares laid out neatly in the window. They clearly don't stock the parts I need, but an employee straightens the damaged plates by hammering them with a mallet. I watch anxiously as this big, burly chap tortures my poor, innocent bike. Will it survive?

It's a makeshift repair. To replace the screws, the mechanic has bolted both sides together.

Thank heavens I have Gabriel as my travel mate. He's a real handyman whereas I'm all thumbs when it comes to fixing things. After giving the repair a quick inspection he makes his prognosis: 'If we tighten up the screws regularly, they should hold.'

I take his word for it because, frankly, I don't have the faintest idea. As far as I'm concerned, if something has been mended, I leave it well alone. But Gabriel seems to know what follow-up measures will be needed, the 'post-op care'. I'm sure if I'd gone on this journey alone I would have come back on foot.

We make our way through the hordes and come across a church. Another one. Since we left Chennai two weeks ago we've slept every night in a church, a presbytery, a school or a dispensary kept by nuns. Without ever knowing beforehand where we would find Christians, they just turn up, as if by magic, every evening. Even though Catholics only represent a very small percentage of the population of India, and we're not even travelling through the areas where most Catholics live (further south in the state of Kerala, for example), and although most of the time we're on the motorway, we end up sleeping in a bed beneath a bell tower every night.

We venture into the church courtyard. A serving boy explains that the priests are having a siesta and do not want to be disturbed. We park our bikes and take the time to update our blog in a cyber-café. When we return it's getting dark. One of the priests is up and about. He invites us to eat with him and offers us a bed for the night. Before retiring we pay a visit to the orphanage next door and meet the children. Father Anthony is in charge of the orphanage and the associated school – once again we find the Church working for the good of society.

What would happen if all the dispensaries, schools, hospitals, orphanages and guesthouses run by the Catholic Church across the world closed, even just for one day? How many poor, unfortunate people would find themselves abandoned or destitute? The Church is recognized as the second-largest social services provider in India,

**Some boys welcome us to their orphanage**

after the state. In reality it's probably the largest, since it runs 25 per cent of the youth training organizations (universities and medical schools included), 80 per cent of the leprosariums and 70 per cent of the social work. We Westerners only know about Mother Teresa and her Missionaries of Charity, who give their lives for others, selflessly, all over India and in many other countries as well. But they are far from the only ones. Nevertheless Christians are still disadvantaged: although they make up 2.5 per cent of the total population, numbering 26 million (15 million of whom are Catholics), about 15 per cent of the Dalits or Untouchables are Christians, and 70 per cent of those who have no caste are Christians.[2]

We're finding the going very difficult. The kilometres roll by too slowly. We've temporarily left the main road for a smaller country road. A young man of about 20, who punctuates all his sentences with 'Sir', accompanies us to the end of the road. He's extremely polite, considerate and chivalrous. Just like Edwin in Chennai, he wears a permanent smile, and his hair is neatly combed. We come across a bicycle towing two cows in a trailer. Suddenly our load seems very light. Further on several motorcyclists surround us, without saying a word. They can't take their eyes off our bikes. One of them suddenly accelerates with a roar, overtakes us, slams on the brakes, gets off his bike, and orders us to stop. From 25 kilometres per hour to zero within seconds. We narrowly avoid a crash.

'Hello, sir, I am a journalist!'

He asks us some questions. He doesn't seem to be listening to our replies but appears to be 'recording' them with a microphone that isn't plugged into anything. Then he thanks us, and we get back on the road. We come across him again a few kilometres further on: he stops us again, but this time he's brought reinforcements.

'This is a newspaper colleague. He works for a very big newspaper. You'll see.'

No doubt we'll see nothing at all, but no matter. The colleague repeats the questions his sidekick asked a few minutes earlier.

[2] Thomas Grimaux, *Persécutions antichrétiennes dans le monde: rapport 2005*, Paris: Hoëbeke/AED (l'Aide à l'Église en Détresse), 2006.

'Why are you here? What are you doing here? What cause are you fighting for? A humanitarian cause? Do you want to get into the *Guinness Book of Records*? You must have a lot of money to travel like this? How much would it cost for a bike like yours?'

When the same motorbike blocks our way again a few moments later, we start feeling seriously fed up. This time two television cameras film our answers! We both think of the same ruse spontaneously, without even consulting each other, and just start to say whatever comes into our heads, dreaming up some cause or other. They've no idea what we're up to. If they did, it would show that they at least understood English.

'We left Paris on 5 July to carry the message of love to the world. We believe we should love each other more. That's what the world desperately needs today. In our country, we say "make love not war". But despite our efforts, the population pyramid has never been in such a mess! So we always stop three times a day to recite our mantra and hug a few trees. We hug nature. It's our calling. Loving trees and people.'

We pull out all the stops. They lap it up. Clearly they don't understand a thing we say. Anyway, they don't bother us again.

After about 50 kilometres, stopping on the brow of a hill, I notice a six-storey tower. On a country road, out in the middle of nowhere, here's this mini skyscraper! As we approach we realize it's some sort of museum, an exhibition hall. Each floor is full of statues of Christ and Mary.

'What on earth is that?'

'It's weird.'

Leaving our bikes at the foot of the tower, we look around for someone to ask. We find a shop nearby; it belongs to Baby the sculptor, who shows us around his workshop.

'There are 42 statues in the tower. My father taught me sculpture. And now I'm teaching my son. Our family have all been sculptors, from one generation to the next.'

Baby's moustache, his rounded stomach moulded by his too-tight shirt . . . Everything about Baby is uncommonly friendly and good-natured.

'Where are you sleeping tonight?'

'We don't know yet.'

'Why don't you go and knock on Father Jesu's door?'

'Jesu? Yeah, good one, Baby!'

'No, I'm not joking at all!'

'Jesu's place . . . is it far from here?'

'It's just over there . . .'

Opposite the tower stands Father Jesu's retreat. Baby points out a stone stairway leading up to it. The yard below is full of beggars scrounging for small change from shoppers at squalid little stalls. We climb the hill and find a surprising collection of buildings in a well-kept park planted with soothing greenery. A young man calls out to us:

'*Bonjour, je suis le frère Ravi!*'

*Ravi* (it means 'delighted' in French)? He does seem delighted!

And we're delighted to meet Brother Ravi.

'If you want to sleep here, I don't think there will be any problem. Ask Father Jesu about it.'

He takes us along a little path to the pavilion where Father Jesu receives visitors. Father Jesu is a guru, so he has many people coming to see him – all day long in fact. That's normal for a guru! Some people just drop in; others have an appointment. He stands up when we enter. He too is all smiles.

'Delighted to meet you, Father Jesu.'

He wears a saffron-coloured cassock of fine cloth. At first sight he looks more like a Hindu monk than a Catholic priest. He has big, expressive, golden-brown eyes and a neatly clipped ash-grey beard. A rosary is wrapped around his neck, its beads made of round seeds. He's a short man; his head must only come up to somewhere between our elbows and our shoulders. He explains that this place is a 'Foyer of Charity', one of many around the world. The inspiration for these homes came from a French woman, Marthe Robin, in the 1980s. Her vision was to see retreat centres consecrated for prayer, meditation and teaching the resident monks and nuns. She also wanted men and women to live together under the same rule and pray for the world.

'It's beautiful here.'

'I established this home about 12 years ago. Thirteen brothers and sisters live here and lead retreats, including Brother Ravi, whom you've met. People can come here, receive counselling and discuss

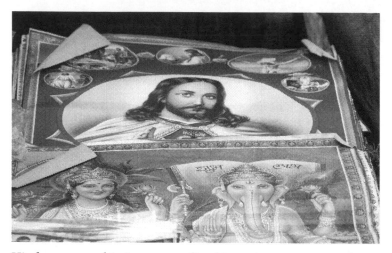

**Hindus can worship Jesus, regarding him as just one more god**

things that are on their minds. It's become known as a place of pilgrimage all over the region!'

'Given the number of Christians, it can't be very busy most of the time . . .?'

'We don't get many Christian pilgrims. But we do receive an enormous number of Hindus: hundreds every day! You know, for Hindus it's not a problem to worship Jesus Christ or the Virgin Mary. They regard them as just two gods among many . . .'

'What's another two gods when you've already got thousands?'

'You can put it that way. But whatever you do, don't tell them that Jesus is the only God. Then you'll have real problems!'

At this our little guru laughs heartily.

'Why do you dress like that? To get closer to Hindus?'

'Exactly. My rosary is made of the same beads that Hindus traditionally use. The same with this saffron robe. And here in the home, we only eat vegetarian food, like them. Besides, everyone thinks of this home as an ashram, a house of learning, a term that both Hindus and Christians understand.'

A young couple and their children interrupt us for a few moments – just enough time to greet the Father and ask him for a blessing, which he willingly gives them.

'You see, they're Hindus! Incredible, isn't it?'

Incredible – but I don't quite get the point of it. At first I feel as though I'm witnessing some sort of strange religious syncretism that's sidestepping the real issues in the name of interreligious dialogue.

'You know, in India, almost everyone sees the Church as a social "super-organization". It's involved in education, development, health . . . It does remarkable work, comparable to NGOs, but often with significantly fewer resources.'

'Yes, since we've been here, we've seen orphanages, schools, dispensaries everywhere, run by priests or nuns.'

'There you are. You've seen for yourselves. It's great that the Church plays this role; it's very important. Essential even. And here in our ashram we try to provide for people's needs as well: every day we provide a free lunch for hundreds of pilgrims. People are free to donate if they want to, according to their means. And thanks to several generous donations, this miracle keeps happening day after day.'

'Very impressive.'

'But you see, the unfortunate thing is that as far as most people are concerned, the Church is only that – just a social "super-organization", nothing more. When they need something material, they come to see us. But when they need something a little more abstract, they go to see their own spiritual guides. In fact what we're trying to do here is show them another dimension of the Catholic Church. We're not simply an enormous NGO; we're so much more than that! We have a wonderful spirituality that we must make known, and offer to as many people as we can.'

In other words, preach the gospel. Father Jesu also tells us about a vehicle his community has built, a colourful parade float set on the back of a pickup truck, from which he proclaims the good news by megaphone all around the roads of Andhra Pradesh. This at least has the merit of making the 'offer' clear and accessible to everyone. It's not exactly subtle, but no one could accuse him of keeping it to himself!

We realize straight away that his approach is quite bold, given that the Indian constitution provides for several years in prison and heavy fines for anyone found guilty of proselytizing. This law is applied more or less strictly, depending on the state.

Hearing him talk about evangelizing, I think back to a recent evening when we stopped at a Jesuit centre. Five kilometres before we arrived I was lying flat on the road in a pitiful state, splayed out between two potholes, to the thunderous applause of blaring horns as trucks calmly passed within a hair's breadth of my skull. Sending up a quick prayer of profuse thanks to my guardian angel, we rode on and ended up finding the Jesuit preachers. First there was Father Anthony (not all priests in India are called Tony but we certainly came across more than one), who is young and passionate. He has been preaching the gospel for two years in the surrounding villages and remote rural areas. And then we met Brother Billy, 30 years old, sporting a polo shirt and a jaw as square as his glasses. He spoke English with a British accent, which is rare among Indians.

We interviewed him in his little office with book-lined walls. In spite of his youth he was a contributor to some of these volumes. The cool evening air wafted through the iron mesh of the mosquito screen across the window. Perched delicately on a sort of rubber ring like a large inner tube, he said something I'll never forget – it completely dented my image of him as a young intellectual.

'Please do excuse me. I'm obliged to sit on this cushion. You see . . . I have just had an operation on my anus, only a few days ago, and it's very painful.'

Being totally immature, we both suddenly swung round towards the bookshelf and, trying not to look at each other, fixed our eyes on some random point in a desperate effort to contain a fit of the giggles. The very British Brother Billy, perched on his little cushion, is primarily a recruiter for the Jesuits. Today India has the highest number of Jesuits of any country (4,000 out of 18,000 worldwide), having recently overtaken Spain and the USA. Brother Billy, who is to be ordained as a priest in two years' time, goes into schools, seminaries and anywhere else he's invited to speak to young people about the Jesuit order.

In India, as in other developing countries, it is difficult to discern the real motivations of new believers. It must be said that from a purely practical point of view, the Church takes very good care of her members. It is one large family, and becoming a member can make life considerably easier in countries where many still die of hunger.

French missionaries to India in the nineteenth century – certainly not the first missionaries to India – used an apt expression for new Christians who were interested because of the material advantages: 'rice Christians', those who converted in exchange for a few cups of rice. This kind of abuse has occurred in the Catholic Church in the past. But although some excesses still remain today (for example, some parishes offer plots of land to their members), it seems that Catholic preachers are, by and large, preaching the gospel with the right motives.

Father Jesu, in his Foyer of Charity, recognizes the need for sincerity. He doesn't try to make a Hindu into a Catholic – like trying to fit a square peg into a round hole – just by preaching at him.

Brother Ravi returns. He's going to show us to our room.

'Give them the bishop's room,' Father Jesu calls to him, smiling.

The bishop's room – it's the ultimate! There's an immense, soft bed for each of us. Who would have thought a visiting bishop would need two beds? Plentiful running water flows from golden taps. Several huge armchairs covered in faux leather stand in the corners. And we can choose our ideal snoozing temperature – all we have to do is adjust a little slide setting on the air conditioner.

After a fantastic shower, we join the community to pray the Rosary[3] in the round church. Then, in the refectory, sitting at Father Jesu's table, we dine on the most fabulous food, which he's ordered especially for us (without too much chilli). The next day is a Sunday. Father Jesu is waiting for us at breakfast.

'I mentioned yesterday that Hindus like praying to the Virgin and Jesus. In India, visitors to Catholic churches are 70 per cent Hindus, 29 per cent Catholics and 1 per cent Muslims. You don't believe me? You'll see for yourselves very soon.'

Our little saffron-suited, smiling guru celebrates Sunday Mass at half past eleven. The empty church in which we prayed the Rosary the previous evening is now full to overflowing. You couldn't even squeeze in a Kleenex. However, with Ravi's help we get a good view from the back. It's a riot of colour, with every kind of veil imaginable. Families have come together, with their older relatives and children.

---

[3] The Rosary is a set of prayers, mostly Bible passages, used especially in the Catholic Church, in which a string of beads is used to count the component prayers.

Father Jesu preaches with great gusto. Everyone listens. We understand nothing of the local dialect, but we imagine it's a talk that's relevant and acceptable to everyone without diluting anything of the Christian faith. Only about 30 people stand for Communion – a few Catholics in this sea of humanity. With the Indians' love of pomp and ceremony, Mass is celebrated with a grandiose liturgy, with much incense and genuflecting. Father Jesu and the other celebrant look splendid in their red and white robes edged with gold. After the final sign of the cross, the congregation, Christians or not, rush to the altar to receive a blessing from the guru-priest.

When Mass ends, the congregation moves into a vast room, several steps down from the church, where they sit down at long tables. In the kitchen about 15 volunteers from among the day's visitors help the brothers and sisters of the community prepare the rice and dhal before serving it to the hundreds of hungry travellers. Each Sunday there are three services. Today 215 kilos of rice are cooked in immense pots.

We spend the night in a village with an unpronounceable name: Visakhpatnal. It's nevertheless welcoming. A community of Lasallians, followers of Saint Jean-Baptiste de La Salle, welcomed us in last night just as it was growing dark.

When we're on the point of leaving, this morning at eight o'clock, after breakfast and Mass, one of the brothers of the community advises Gabriel to pump up his rear tyre. Out of politeness Gabriel complies and – *pchhhhhhhht!* The inner tube suddenly deflates. The rubber at the point where the valve attaches to the tube is cracked: it's beyond repair – even I can see that.

This time we don't have a single spare inner tube and hardly any more patches. It's high time we stocked up. Problem: Indian valves are larger than French ones and won't go through the hole in the rim. The brother, feeling extremely embarrassed, sends us off to see another brother who, it seems, can help us. We ring the bell beside a heavy iron door and a young man in overalls invites us in. We find an immense workshop, which turns out to be a training centre led by the brothers of Saint John-Baptiste de La Salle. Dozens of young men are in training here for jobs in mechanical engineering trades, taught by professionals and nuns!

One of the young apprentices leaves immediately on a motor scooter to comb the shops for inner tubes. During this time we visit the adjacent school also run by the brothers, which educates 1,800 children.

In the director's office we witness a dreadful scene. We knock timidly at the door, and then enter. Ten or so young boys in uniform are waiting in line, looking intimidated. Their teacher has sent them to confess their wrongdoing to the principal. But they don't get off with a parent liaison card to be signed, or a warning . . . They must line up in front of the priest principal to await their punishment. The latter, impassive, takes a long wooden ruler out of his drawer. The first child holds out his hand, the priest strikes, the kid winces, and holds out the other hand. On to the next! While he strikes and strikes again, without the slightest sign of emotion, the good father looks at me and asks:

'Do you use the same methods in France?'

He wants me to give them a sermon on good behaviour, but his approach makes me uncomfortable and besides, I would have difficulty waxing lyrical about school discipline.

When our bicycle-spare-parts-hunting apprentice returns, he looks pleased with himself. He brandishes half a dozen boxes of inner tubes, only to be deflated by Gabriel's observation that they're not the right ones for our bikes. They go off together and return an hour later with inner tubes of the right diameter, though as I said, the valve stem fits only bikes made in India. The solution is to drill larger holes in our rims, which we do. But we won't be able to use our pump on these new tyres. Adding the weight of a new pump is out of the question. And if we have a puncture? Oh well, we'll see.

We ride off, swearing we'll never go on a bike trip again.

'Eight more months of cycling; two more weeks to Darjeeling!'

This morning we crossed the border into the state of Orissa, tragically famous for the massacre of entire Christian villages in 2007 and 2008. We passed abruptly from brand new bitumen to a dirt road. The government of Orissa stopped financing the road's construction before it was completed. About 88 kilometres into today's journey, my front tyre punctures. I look to the left and notice that we've stopped in front of a . . . convent! I sit down in the shade of the porch to make the repair, while Gabriel goes off on a reconnaissance mission. He comes back breathless a few minutes later.

'You'll never believe it! The diocesan centre is just across the road! You have a puncture between a convent and a diocesan centre!'

Monsignor isn't available but his assistant offers us something to eat and advises us to push on to the archbishop's house in Bhubaneswar, where they have a lot of visitors. It's on our route anyway.

'At the moment, the situation is quite calm . . . Last year the approaching elections meant that tensions were running high. Hindu extremist groups had been terrorizing Christians, who fled and hid in the bush. That meant they weren't able to vote . . .'

We get back on our two-wheeled chargers and head for Bhubaneswar. This city, capital of Orissa, is dedicated to the god Shiva and is famous for its numerous temples. We arrive at the archbishop's house well after dark. They offer us a bed each. In the morning, after a quick breakfast, we join Father Matthew. Following the anti-Christian persecution he was forced to leave the village where he was the priest. He recounts the events in a cold, detached voice.

'It started in 2007, on 24 December. We were getting ready for Christmas. All the other priests were away, visiting in the surrounding villages. Several parishioners were decorating the church while I was at the confessional. Suddenly I heard shouts . . . so I went outside. There was a huge crowd. Perhaps 500 people. They had forced the gate, come right into the church compound. Everyone fled . . . including me. Some parishioners took me to a neighbouring village to hide. Everything was destroyed. That was in 2007. And in 2008 they came back again.'

From what we can tell, Father Matthew is just an ordinary man – not a great hero or a fiery preacher. We feel that he's vulnerable, deeply wounded.

For many Westerners the mention of India immediately brings to mind Mahatma Gandhi, the Father of the Nation, who pioneered peaceful resistance to British colonization. He was able to stop the killing between Muslim and Hindu, and assumed the role of defender of the Untouchables. His message of non-violence and peaceful coexistence had a profound impact on the world, and one might be tempted to think that his fellow-countrymen were all like him. This would be a great mistake.

In India, the first persecutions against Christians were carried out by . . . other Christians! In the fifteenth and sixteenth centuries the navigators and explorers arrived, followed by missionaries who brought the good news. But to their great surprise they discovered that there were already Christian communities: St Thomas had been there 15 centuries earlier. Unfortunately for the indigenous Christians, the religion hadn't evolved the same way in Rome as it had in India. The European missionaries 'reformed' the first Indian Christians, and in their Inquisition they were quick to burn not only their prayer books but some of the dissidents as well.

This explains the situation of the Indian Catholic Church today. It is composed of a large majority of Latin rite Christians (12.5 million) and a minority of Syro-Malabar (3.5 million) and Syro-Malankar rite Christians (285,000). There are also Anglicans, Lutherans and several other Protestant groups.[4]

Only very recently has the situation of Christians deteriorated. The 1980s saw the foundation of the BJP (Bharatiya Janata Party), an ultra-nationalist party that promoted the idea of 'Indianness'. As far as the BJP is concerned, Hinduism is the foundation of the national identity; believers of all other religions cannot be anything but second-class citizens. In order to protect the disadvantaged, who could be tempted to change religious affiliation in exchange for financial benefits, the BJP attempts to curb proselytizing. Officially the Indian state is secular, and its constitution proscribes all discrimination (ethnic, religious, caste or sex). But in practice the laws on religious freedom and banning proselytizing only apply to minority groups: Christians and Muslims.

Although the central government in New Delhi rejects the ideology of Hindutva, which advocates Hindu dominance, some regional governments still adhere to this principle. In 1978 the first anti-conversion law was adopted in the state of Arunachal Pradesh. Baptizing a Hindu would henceforth be considered a crime. Similar

[4] René Guitton, *Ces Chrétiens qu'on assassine*, Paris: Flammarion, 2009.

laws are in force in other states: Gujarat, Madhya Pradesh, Chhattisgarh, Himachal Pradesh and Rajasthan. It's interesting to note that this legislation only operates in one direction and doesn't apply to christians converting to Hinduism – quite the contrary in fact. In 2004, for example, the BJP conducted a 'reconversion to Hinduism' ceremony for 200 indigenous Christians. The fact that before they became Christians, these 200 people had not been Hindus but animists didn't worry the BJP at all!

From 1998, when it came to power, until 2004, the BJP tried to reduce access to the resources supplied by Christian churches. Irrespective of the fact that church organizations were serving the needy of all sectors of society, regardless of their religion, the BJP disapproved of all funding from overseas. They toughened the law on the financing of religious organizations and increased the complexity of administrative processes, which made implementing social aid programmes more difficult. The BJP is particularly suspicious of the Church's work with Untouchables and the casteless. To be a Christian and an Untouchable is a double condemnation.[5] When an Untouchable converts to Christianity, he or she loses the right to public service posts and all civil rights.

Some states have gone one step further, adding violent physical persecution to their bureaucratic bias. The state of Orissa has the dubious honour of being the worst of the lot, and Father Matthew is one of those who have experienced this harassment first hand.

'I was the priest in a village that was divided between Christians and tribal animists. The latter are very simple people, easily influenced. They were manipulated by a few Hindu extremists who ended up inflaming the whole situation. They poisoned these people's minds against us.'

'What did they tell them?'

'They told them that the Catholic population was growing because people were being converted. But in reality, we didn't convert anyone. The population grew because of births in Christian families, that's all. In 2007, nine people were killed at Christmas time; 600 houses and 90 churches were destroyed or burnt. For several days, groups of thugs armed with swords and rifles attacked every Christian property they

[5] Guitton, *Ces Chrétiens qu'on assassine.*

could find. Nothing was spared: statues, crosses, Bibles, everything was left in ruins.'

Father Matthew pauses. Nervously he wipes his glasses with his shirt tail before he continues.

'In August 2008, it all started again, but this time it was worse. The violence spread all over. Persecution, killings . . . They burnt churches . . . and people. The rioters used the assassination of a Hindu leader as a pretext to escalate the violence. This time, it lasted several weeks, and over 100 died.

'The police did nothing. They knew but they didn't intervene. The persecution continued until the end of September. Some people even came from other states especially to "lend a hand" and kill Christians! Can you comprehend that? Christians fled into the forest and stayed in hiding for several days. Everyone was terrorized. The attackers organized hunts, beating the grass to flush them out. When they were found, they were tortured. Sometimes they were even chopped into pieces.

'The fanatics urged them to convert to Hinduism. Thousands of homeless were forced into refugee camps under government protection to escape the massacres. Everyone here grumbles that the state authorities aren't much help to them. The victims have ongoing problems with reporting crimes, speaking out against perpetrators, giving evidence and claiming damages. Out of the 2,500 grievances filed after the violence of 2008, only 823 were registered by the authorities.'

Shivers run up and down my spine. A few kilometres away, people are being killed for being Christians.

'All that is terrible, really terrible, it's true. But our parishioners have great faith and courage! Some convert to Hinduism out of fear but others resist and remain true to their faith. These latter cannot go home, as they are forbidden access. They live in camps, in tents, and wait for the situation to settle down. And we see the hand of God at work, the God who saves. For me personally, my faith has been strengthened. I don't rely on anyone. Not the police, not any man. I rely solely on God.'

The horns are blaring twice as fiercely; the traffic has slowed to a crawl. The kilometre markers are down to single figures. It's one thirty in the afternoon and we're finally arriving in Kolkata.

111

Since Bhubaneswar we've covered between 120 and 170 kilometres per day. We've just clocked up 1,700 kilometres in India. For quite a while now, cycling hasn't been much fun. It's time we had a break. We plan to stay in Kolkata for several days, long enough to get a visa for China and to rest our legs. We know nothing about Kolkata, except that it's where Teresa lived – Mother Teresa. She left many daughters behind her. We ask the way to the Mother House of the Missionaries of Charity, where we hope to find a place to stay.

We discover a sprawling city, colossal arterial roads, traffic as cha-otic as ever. The proportions of the whole seem exaggerated, but its components are human size: rickshaws, cars, pedestrians, little alleys. We turn on to a wide avenue, and there we find Mother Teresa's house. The city is alive. People everywhere, children begging, miserable, makeshift tents squashed in cheek by jowl, corrugated iron shacks cobbled together with scraps of rubbish, shops that are nothing more than a hole carved into the wall, vendors squatting over their piles of cheap junk, whole families sleeping on the footpath, sewers that throw up a thousand monstrosities. Some people have white teeth; others are ravaged by the effects of alcohol and tobacco chewing – faces that are striking because they're beautiful or because they mask a lifetime of suffering.

Mother Teresa chose to make this her home. The sisters can't have us to stay but they recommend several youth hostels and cheap hotels, as they do for the multitude of Western volunteers arriving every day. Faithful to our rule, we don't stay in a hotel. We try some of the churches nearby. At the first they close the door in our faces. The sec-ond agrees to put us up for the night. Our Lady of Sorrow.

We make use of this stop to have my one pair of shorts repaired; they're riddled with holes. We wander around the market streets look-ing for a tailor. Surveying the tide of humanity, my eye settles on a little man, half shaven, standing as straight as a board. A gob of spit shoots out of his mouth. On his head he carries a bundle that's almost as big as he is. Like a tightrope artist, he squeezes between stalls of vegetables and fruit. Between two tents, two women inspect each other's heads for lice. A little kid scampers around on all fours. Business as usual. Indians wander around happily between sellers of bananas, onions and vegetables we've never seen before. A smell assaults our nostrils. It's the smoke from the chapatti sellers' fires. Behind a fence, a goat snatches dry leaves offered by a child. Further on a man is plucking a hen with deft fingers, while chickens peck around his feet. We finally come across a tailor. He reinforces the seat and patches the holes. I've now got red and saffron coloured shorts. For under a euro.

We celebrate the feast of All Saints with the sisters of Mother Teresa. For this special day of remembrance, we want to 'play volunteers' just for a day. We lend a hand. We have no illusions about our microscopic contribution. We just want to get some idea of what really happens with these Missionaries of Charity.

At six in the morning we arrive at the Mother House for Mass. Having slept in churches almost every night for the last month, we've been able to attend Mass most days. In the great potpourri of Indian priests, we've seen them all: tall, short, fat, ugly, handsome, bald, hairy, charismatic and deadly dull. We've endured all kinds of preaching. Over the last few days I've felt just plain sick of them. It all seems so false. I've been forgetting about the culture gap (which does explain a lot of things), and I can't reconcile the way they preach the gospel while living the high life, as some of them do, with their cooks, chauffeurs and comfortable little presbyteries. I've felt as though I've been suffocating, had difficulty praying and, little by little, been sinking into indifference. Tiredness and a begrudging attitude haven't helped either. During Mass, increasingly I just let the words go over my head. I'd had enough of dragging myself out of bed every morning to get there. I've felt terribly disappointed – never thought I could have such an overdose. And yet slowly but surely, I've felt it happening: I've been becoming bitter.

But here it's different. The sisters' chants have magical powers.

Since its foundation about 50 years ago, the order of the Missionaries of Charity has attracted 5,000 nuns. An average of 100 new nuns each year! Some visit the poorest of the poor. Others live in seclusion and pray for the world: they're called 'contemplatives'. They're young, of all nationalities and all colours.

This morning's Mass is carried by their faith, which seems as pure and natural as that of a child. The sisters have a great love for the Virgin Mary and immense respect for their founder. They distribute 'miraculous' medallions to visitors to her tomb. Mother Teresa brought these back into fashion, giving out handfuls wherever she went.

'Blessed are the poor.' Today's Gospel reading. Just because you're poor doesn't mean you'll be happy or blessed by God. But poverty allows us to depend only on God. Poverty forces us to trust. The words of the American priest aren't earth-shattering but they linger in my mind. And yet I've heard this verse from the Gospel many times before – at least twice a year for 22 years. But today it takes on a new meaning. The word of God is like the best episodes of *Asterix*: they can be understood on several levels. With each reading you realize how little you really grasped the previous time. Today, no new revelation, but I feel a great inner peace. The nuns' chants have soothed my frustration and prised open a crack into my heart. Allowing the words to flood in, I feel brand new, sure of my faith again. Trusting. Everything seems clearer now.

The immense room is a sea of white saris. Hundreds of nuns are praying. A few European and American volunteers attend Mass, standing on the right. Through the window I can see a railway bridge. A train roars past making a terrible racket. Beyond the window, Kolkata is alive. The sisters sing on.

We eat breakfast with the day's volunteers, who have also come from all over the world to lend a hand for a day, a month, a year, some even 15 years. The sisters demand nothing of them – no CV, no reference, no experience, no skills. Each morning those who wish to do so come for Mass first, followed by breakfast in the basement of the Mother House, then to be assigned their service for the day. Gabriel and I are sent to the Prem Dan home which, they say, should be a good place to experience what happens here, because many of the volunteers have come for the experience, as well as to help. The sisters tell them straight out that they don't need them. But they do bring a little freshness and a little warmth: a fresh outlook and sometimes some skills.

At Prem Dan they look after men and women who have been brought in from the street in a critical condition due to illness, broken legs, malnutrition, among other things. They provide them with the necessities of life. We're struck by how simply and naturally everything happens – no fuss. The general philosophy is: 'We do what we can with what we have.' Over the years the Missionaries of Charity have become a veritable army, but in the beginning the sisters had nothing but their own hands and their faith to serve the poorest of the poor. That initial spirit lives on.

We talk with the sick, take them to the toilet, help with the laundry, which is washed in immense concrete tubs, serve lunch and help with the dishes. Nothing out of the ordinary. And we appropriate the beautiful words of Mother Teresa: 'We well know that what we do is but a drop in the ocean. But if that drop wasn't in the ocean, it would be missed.'

In Prem Dan the sick lie side by side in a vast hangar with rows and rows of beds. Nuns who are trained doctors and nurses pass from bed to bed tending to their needs. In a garden outside, some patients take, or are taken for, a walk. Others sit, waiting for time to pass. Each one has a terrible story to tell; in each heart there's an ocean of suffering that we can't begin to imagine. Many were rotting in wretchedness and despair before being found and brought here. The little sari-clad nuns care for the unlovely, with faces filled with deep compassion, their hands easing pain and healing wounds. They burn with a love that takes away the fears of the dying, most of whom know they have little time left. But in the twilight of their lives, someone is caring for them. As Mother Teresa said: 'They lived like animals, but here they die like angels.'

As I take a man in a wheelchair to the toilet, I think again of the homily that morning. I can hardly believe that Gospel reading has come today, the very day we're with the poorest of the poor. How she must have loved those verses, little Mother Teresa! She was one who looked at the poor with the eyes of Jesus. She knew how to look for Jesus in every person, even the dirtiest and the least attractive. For her, the poor man was a prophet, a hero.

Among the crowd of today's volunteers there are all sorts: travellers like us, here for 'the experience' for a day, old hands – and then there's Aymeric, 30 years old, a consultant from Paris. He's finishing a six-week stint as a volunteer, thanks to his company's financial crisis plan: in exchange for half salary, employees can take on a personal project. Our new friend takes us for lunch in the backpackers' quarter, where the volunteers hang out in cheap hotels. In the space of a few hours we see more Westerners than we've come across in three months. The local greasy spoons and cyber-cafés are full of *baba cool* types – odd-ball Europeans, perpetual hippies and other dropouts. It's comical to see them disguised as Indians. Some wear baggy trousers and Hindu bracelets; others go for the traditional sari. They look a bit awkward and seem worried about their health – wearing a sari doesn't protect them from Delhi belly.

I give my size 46 sandals to a little cobbler on the street to be reheeled. He has them for an hour and gives me a pair of size 38 flip-flops to use while I'm waiting. They protect my toes. Better than nothing.

# 7

## India: Kolkata to Guit Dubling

### In which we fish in our undies and pray without ceasing

29 OCTOBER, 3 MONTHS AND 24 DAYS AFTER DEPARTURE
After a few days' break, beneficial as much for our morale as for our legs, we leave Kolkata. Our departure is a saga: a thief steals some gear from Gabriel's panniers, a pathetic, emaciated man vomits on the steps of the church where we've been staying; another man whose forehead is split in two by a deep gash watches us sorrowfully as we pass. And we pass. Thanks to Pierre, who has joined us to film several days of our journey, we have new Marathon-Plus tyres – the Rolls-Royce of tyres, supposedly unpuncturable – as well as several new inner tubes.

We enter the fray, pitting ourselves against the traffic 'made in India'. Only a few weeks ago in Chennai we thought these good people in their motorcars quite exceptional drivers and considered their disorganized traffic rather delightful. That's past history. Trucks graze us, shave us and force us off the road. A driver's licence in India is a licence to kill. These crazy drivers are always dicing with death, swinging between homicide and suicide. The thundering concerto for horns and overheated engines could be our funeral march. Their bumper stickers say 'Good speed = 40 km/hr' but they drive at over twice that.

Sometimes it's David against Goliath. We're two little Davids, two wheels and no motor against thousands of Goliaths with four wheels and no brains. We see them coming hurtling towards us at top speed, on our side of the road as they wildly overtake the monsters in front of them. We spread out our arms and wave them about, extending their range with our batons so that we take up more space, in an effort to make them leave us more than a bare half metre. Often we end up careering off the road. We swear and rage and shout abuse at the driver, and then we get back on our chargers to do battle against the next.

Pierre B. bought a bike in Kolkata for about €30 and is travelling with us for a few days. He's wearing street shoes and winter trousers; the rest of his stuff is strapped to his luggage rack or divided between our bags. Pierre is an artist. His camera is always within arm's reach, mounted on the pannier attached to his handlebars. He films as he's going along; according to him, this footage will make the film more dynamic. Pierre's presence means a rest for us: when he's here we don't have to do any filming.

But the trouble is that Pierre is about 40, wearing dress shoes and not very fit – he won't win the yellow jersey. Nightfall takes us by surprise 40 kilometres before our goal for the day. We make do with a truckers' hostel, for the second time since we've been in India. But this one wins the prize, without any contest, for the worst night of the whole trip – make that of all time. Mosquitoes attack us non-stop, buzzing in our ears, around our eyes and up our noses. The atmosphere is depressing. The truck drivers are either drunk or high on hash. A bare electric bulb blinks on and off intermittently all night. And while men are wandering around smashed or stoned, and we're trying to get some sleep, a child is working. He's about 13, and he prepares chapatti dough, washes dishes, serves customers. All night long. At seven o'clock in the morning he's still there and he still finds it in himself to smile.

On this part of the journey the priests we come across are more pleasant than those we met in the south. One night, Father Samir, the spitting image of the actor Danny DeVito but slightly more sun-tanned, invites us to eat with him and his curate. They were preparing a meal for two but no matter – there'll be enough for four. He talks about his cook with great respect – quite different from some of his clerical colleagues in the south, with their high and mighty attitudes. In Bhadempur, Father Sebastian, a Salesian and old friend of Mother Teresa, opens his door and bursts out laughing when he sees our trusty steeds. Pierre leaves us to return to France. He gets rid of his bike with jubilation, gifting it to the parish of that same priest, making him laugh even more. As a newly ordained priest, Father Sebastian started his ministry when there were no Christians at all in this region. Some 20 years later he announces proudly that he's baptized over 3,000 Indians. It has almost cost him his life: there have been three assassination attempts.

Since our odometers were stolen in Kolkata, we've stopped being so hard on ourselves. No more obsessing about performance. We no longer keep our eyes riveted on the dial, counting every kilometre. Now we move along in the old fashioned way, working out how far we've come by roadside markers. Technology takes a back seat and our bodies call the shots. We soon reach Siliguri, the legendary town lying at the foot of the mountains, a hub for travellers en route for Bhutan, Sikkim and Nepal. It heralds the mighty Himalayas and the final kilometres of our journey through India.

The alarm clock failed. We leave an hour late, having filled our stomachs with a good solid breakfast of bananas with sugar.

An altitude difference of 2,000 metres, over a distance of 80 kilometres, separates us from Darjeeling. We glimpse two monks standing on the balcony of a Buddhist temple, blowing long trumpets. After several kilometres we enter the jungle, where we see wild fowl, monkeys, peacocks. The humid morning air sears our throats and lungs.

To the right of the narrow road runs the track of the mythical railway built at the end of the nineteenth century by the British to facilitate access to their newly built town and sanatorium. In those days the covered carriages were reserved for women – the men, who sat in open wagons, were covered in dust and cinders from the smoke belched out by the locomotive. The train follows a spectacular route affording dramatic mountain and valley views as it negotiates precipitous gorges and hairpin bends; passengers today still hide their eyes in horror. The scenery is magnificent. There's an awe-inspired hush. And yet there's a gentle murmur everywhere; all around us stand magnolias, banyans, orchids, oaks, rhododendrons, pines and colossal bamboos. On the forest floor, gigantic ivies intertwine, forming a carpet large enough to cover the rooms of a great palace. We pass some splendid banyans. Each one forms its own dense forest as it sends down numerous shoots from its branches. When they touch the ground they take root and form new trunks.

The slope is gentle and we stop at a lookout point to contemplate the valley, which comes into view little by little as we climb. Now we're riding through cloud; it seems to dissipate as we reach it. The cold becomes ever more penetrating. Steam rises from everything: our saturated T-shirts, the goats' breath, the porches of the houses. The staccato crack of our gear changes breaks the mountain stillness. All is calm.

The white and yellow milestones stand impassive along the road-side. They're reassuring but drive us to despair – it's such slow going.

We pass a home of Mother Teresa's Missionaries of Charity, a statue of the Virgin and, further on, a Himalayan Reformed church. Few Christians live in the mountains, but this area clearly shows the presence of French and Swiss missionaries in the past, and the work of local clergy. People smile when they see us. The women and children wave their hands, the men laugh out loud.

The slope drops off to our left. Huge tea plantations cover the land, another legacy of the British. Thousands of little shrubs, all pruned to limit their height, cover the hillsides as far as the eye can see. Apparently the first spring leaves are the best. 'The champagne of tea', we read on a roadside billboard. As the bishop of the area will explain to us later, the produce is destined for the clients of Harrods, the prestigious English department store, where it sells for an outrageous price, while the Indians who harvest it are paid a pittance.

On our right, the railway tracks are singing: a barely audible squeal that grows louder and louder, becoming an ear-splitting screech that shreds the silence of the valley. Here it comes! It's right on our tail – the little train of Darjeeling. It's grinding, groaning, grunting. We play along and soon we're caught up in the game. We overtake. It gains speed, overtakes, whistles and thumbs its nose at us. The passengers love it. They pull out their mobile phones and take photos of us. We pound on the pedals once more and battle on for a good 20 minutes. Then our legs give out. Our adversary vanishes into the mist. The cold hits us: we're 2,400 metres above sea level. We've made the saddle.

As night falls we finally reach Darjeeling. Since Chennai, in the south, we've covered 2,400 kilometres. We glide down to the diocesan centre, where we're offered two superb rooms. Apart from the cold, it's absolute bliss.

We've taken up residence with the bishop, Monsignor Stephen Lepcha. The house is a large Victorian stone building. We've barely been here a day and already we're wondering how we'll be able to tear ourselves away. It's so good. This morning we tucked in to a ten-star breakfast: toast, fried eggs, porridge, coffee, jam, pancakes, cheese, oranges . . . And what's more, we're seated at a long, wooden table, on thrones fit for the best English public school.

Darjeeling was the sanatorium of British India and remains a mecca for tourists from all over the world. Built on the foothills of Mount Senchal, its superb mountain setting is second to none. The town still boasts a few gracious villas from the British colonial days. Thanks to its altitude and proximity to the snow and ice, the temperatures here are milder than down on the plains. Tourists fortunate enough to be here on a clear day are rewarded with one of the most magnificent sights imaginable: the jagged, sparkling Himalayan peaks, floating over distant cloud under a blanket of eternal snow. Kanchenjunga and Everest stand out among them.

Our little Mont Blanc barely comes up to their waist.

Talking with a bookseller, we learn that Darjeeling used to belong to Sikkim. Then, one day in 1828, two Englishmen, Grant and Lloyd, were returning from an expedition when they discovered the tiny hamlet of Darjeeling. They recognized the potential of its enchanting position and its mild, healthy climate. After a series of twists and turns, the British East India Company finally bought the whole Darjeeling district from the Rajah. At the end of the nineteenth century another Englishman, Dr Campbell, was charged with the task of building roads, levelling hills, regulating the erratic stream beds, introducing a wide variety of plants, building churches, convents, barracks and law courts, constructing the railway . . . From that time on, Darjeeling became a magnet attracting Westerners of every ilk – English first, naturally.

We walk around the town, stopping at the market to buy some socks and long johns. Among the different market stalls there's a curious mix of all the peoples of the great Asian plateau: Limbu, Lepchas, Nepali, Kashmiri, Bhutanese, Tibetans.

We're struck by the strength and influence of the local independence movement. The people want a regional autonomous state, which would be called Gorkhaland. The inhabitants predict an absolute bloodbath if Delhi continues to turn a deaf ear to their demands. Even the bishop, who comes from this area, declares himself to be pro-independence. Everyone writes slogans on their houses, cars and shop windows. They want a border. I think of Robert Frost's poem, 'Mending Wall', which talks about the arbitrariness of walls – and their importance: 'Good fences make good neighbors'.[1] In Darjeeling, therefore, it doesn't seem absurd to build a wall, to draw limits, to divide in order to separate. For the inhabitants it would not make things more complex, it would make them simpler. They belong to the same ethnic group and they all speak the same language.

We plan to stay for three weeks in a local village. For the moment we're waiting for the bishop to point us to one of the villages on the map with his sovereign finger. After this village stay, our route takes us north to China. We've found an Indian colonel who is prepared to get us a pass for the Indian side of the border, but that still leaves the Chinese border. So we go to see Father Kinley, who might be able to help us.

He's the director of St Joseph's, the Jesuit school in Darjeeling. It's a fee-paying school, which finances nine other schools in the diocese. The children wear a uniform and the architecture is very British. If it weren't for the mountains in the background, you'd think you were in Oxford. In the hall, a display shows a summary of the sacred writings of the world's great religions: Christianity, Hinduism, Buddhism, Islam. Some 20 per cent of the students are Catholics, who are granted admission automatically. The vast majority of the others are Buddhists, who undergo a major selection process to get into the prestigious school. In his time, Father Kinley was one of these.

Above the priest's desk hangs an immense portrait of the Dalai Lama. Not a portrait of Benedict XVI, or even the Indian president. No. The Dalai Lama! Father Kinley smiles and confides that before he

[1] *The Poetry of Robert Frost*, New York: Henry Holt, 1979, p. 34.

was converted he was a Buddhist. He's from Bhutan, and is the only priest from his country. The number of Christians in Bhutan can literally be counted on the fingers of two hands.

'And you became a Catholic?'

'Yes! I'm a freak!'

He bursts out laughing.

He explains that he studied at St Joseph's and discovered that Christianity isn't like other religions. And then, having completed an MBA at the best university in India and worked for three years, he met Mother Teresa on a plane. She persuaded him that he had a vocation as a priest. Six months later he threw it all in and entered seminary.

'Other religions propose thought systems or a philosophy of life, whereas Christians follow a God who became a man. This is no abstract love: it's a personal relationship. What makes us happy is the relationships we have with others. So for me, having a relationship with God is the key to happiness.'

Since then he has become a Catholic priest while still continuing to practise the Buddhist method of meditation.

'Every day I practise yoga and meditate, using the techniques my old Buddhist masters taught me. It helps me to detach myself from material things, and the thoughts that plague me. I am able to empty myself inside.'

He puts his elbows down on his desk and leans towards us, as if to share a secret.

'When you throw an object into the air, it falls back down. That's the law of gravity. We all know that. Well, I think our heart has its own law of gravity; it cannot remain empty! That's what happens in my Christian prayer: I let the love of God come in. So I would say that my Buddhist roots help me empty my heart and prepare it, while Christianity enables me to fill it!'

He's bemused by the Americans and Europeans he's met in Buddhist monasteries searching for spiritual reality, who claim to have 'rejected Christianity'.

'But the Church has its faults. That's what they're rejecting, isn't it?'

'Yes, of course. But, in my opinion, the Church's faults don't constitute a reason to lose one's faith. Our faith is simply a matter of following Jesus. That's the important thing. Of course, we must condemn offensive behaviour, and strive for real unity in Church life, but the Church is made up of people, and people are not perfect. That's why the Church has its faults. That's just how it is.'

'What's your view of the Church in Europe?'

'I'm not very familiar with it. When I went to Paris, I didn't know anyone. So I went to see the Jesuits in the 16th arrondissement, to get some information. A woman opened a little window, asked what I wanted, and went off to get it for me. When she brought back the papers, she slipped them to me through the slot! Nothing like the warmth and generosity you experienced in India. I don't hold it against them at all. I wasn't wearing my habit. Perhaps she was afraid.'

Suddenly he looks more serious.

'What I do think is a shame, the real shame in France, is that the dominant philosophy is one that seeks to make you forget the roots of your prosperity. And its influence is everywhere. For 2,000 years the Church has opened minds, provided education, trained the elite of your country. In turning away from the spirituality the Church offers, little by little you're losing your culture from the roots up.'

We really enjoy our time with this priest, who strikes us as a real character; he's completely free and independent but also loyal to his faith. Unfortunately, he can't help us to enter China through Bhutan. We've left it too late to go through the proper channels, and anyway, officially tourists have to shell out €250 per person, per day in tax. Father Kinley refers us to his friend, one of the old hands who introduced trekking to India 40 years ago. According to him, our only option is to go from India to Nepal and from Nepal to Tibet. It would be a very pleasant detour.

We stay in Darjeeling for two more days, catch up on sleep and enjoy the comforts of the diocesan centre. Our bodies needed this stop. Now we feel completely refreshed. Finally, after much prevarication, the bishop tells us he's chosen the village for our three-week stay. After dinner he gets up and invites us to follow him into the hallway, where a large wooden panel hangs on the wall showing a map of the diocese and its parishes. You'd think it was a map of a military campaign, except that there are crosses instead of flags, marking churches and chapels. He presses his finger firmly on a spot, which seems to be close to a little town called Kalimpong.

'Guit Dubling! You're going to Guit Dubling village. It's wonderful. I adore it. I was a curate there, a long time ago.'

We leave Darjeeling in the late morning. Another Jesuit is expecting us for the night; the bishop has warned him we're coming. We freewheel down the valley and then climb again. Sometimes the slope is so steep that our front wheels lift off the road and we tip over backwards. We zigzag to keep the wheels on the asphalt. With no strength left, I end up falling at a bend. Unfortunately for me, although this mountain is sparsely populated, this happens right in front of a house. The occupants, who all come outside, watch me sheepishly picking myself up off the road. They burst out laughing. But three little boys earnestly rush to my aid.

'Sir, do you want me to help you?'

I don't refuse. I'd just been wondering how on earth I was going to make it all the way up to our destination. With the help of my three gallant little gentlemen, clothed in rags, the last two kilometres pass with no effort at all; they push me along with their hands on my backside, and I, the Lord of the Manor, have but to pedal lightly. They're adorable. Clothed in rags, and adorable.

'Do you know the Gandhi Ashram? That's where we're going. It can't be far from here.'

'Of course we know it. It's our school!' exclaims the smallest of the three. 'It's just around the corner.'

When they see us coming, other children come running to help push my bike. That evening we learn that they live in little huts with neither running water nor electricity. Most can't even afford a pair of shoes. Until a few years ago these children, whose villages are among the poorest in the Indian Himalayas, had a bowl of rice per day at best, and very limited prospects for the future. Today many of them are part of an orchestral group of stringed instruments that gives concerts in Europe and the USA. And when these little field mice play, the audience melts.

A young man wearing a white cassock greets us. He's a priest, a Jesuit. He settles us into our room and invites us to join them for dinner. We're amazed to find, among the fifteen children at the table, three young Europeans. They're German, and are taking a gap year. They wanted to do something to help others. All three are top students at the conservatory in their home city. The curate of their home parish sent them here to teach music, especially music theory, to these Indian children. Mike and Grita play the piano, Ludwig plays the double bass. They're extremely talkative, obviously delighted to come across other Europeans, and are happy to give us a rundown on the background of the school.

'This place was founded by Father Edward McGuire. He was a Canadian Jesuit who came here in the 1950s and started working in education. He had a feeling that music could become a formidable weapon against poverty. At the request of his superior, he opened the Gandhi Ashram Elementary School, which combines learning the violin with a demanding academic programme. The idea came to him when he was working in a school in Darjeeling. One day he invited the head of the Calcutta Symphony Orchestra (now defunct) to give a concert, and as he watched the pupils sitting in absolute silence, he realized the remarkable effect that music can have on children. Without further ado he bought nine violins, hired a teacher, and after three weeks of school, the students who played an instrument had the best academic results. That was the proof that his hunch was right.'

Ludwig, a tall young man with fair skin, chimes in, 'Isn't it fantastic? Unlike many Indian schools, the ashram is totally free. They don't have to buy a uniform or school supplies, which can often be prohibitively expensive for families. The school employs five highly qualified teachers and provides each child with a violin and two meals per day! How can you ask hungry children to concentrate on anything apart from their stomachs?'

The school's solid reputation is known for miles around. Even the rich want their children to attend. But if the child hasn't got hollow cheeks and dirt behind his ears he hasn't a chance of getting in. With its limited budget and, surprisingly, overstaffing, the ashram is reserved for the poorest of the poor. It's a place like no other. You only have to watch the children jostling to get into the school's auditorium. They hurry towards a cupboard to get out their violins. Some gather on the stage to rehearse a concerto, others go off into a corner to practise by themselves. A magical cacophony suddenly breaks out. And a certain sound of hope can be heard.

'Good evening!'

Another man in a white cassock appears on the doorstep.

'Welcome! The bishop told me you'd be arriving soon. Please excuse me for being late; I was visiting a family. Is everything going well?'

This is the new priest in charge of the ashram. Since Father McGuire died, he's the boss. The children have finished their dinner and go off to their various activities, while we stay on in the dining room. The priest sits down and entertains us with endless stories. True stories of the Gandhi Ashram.

'Take Sunita, for example. Sunita was eight years old when she joined the ashram. Before that she spent most of her time working on another family's farm, a family richer than her own. Like her parents, she was illiterate and on the brink of malnutrition. But after a year of schooling she could read and write in her own language, Nepali, as well as in Hindi and English. And above all, she could make her violin sing! She played with such dignity and determination. It was incredibly impressive, with such a tiny, fragile body. Believe me, when you see her play, positioning her violin precisely under her chin, you forget she lives in a mud hut with her parents, brother and sister. And the more she plays, the more confident she becomes. Her results and her relationships with the other children are improving each day.'

Tomorrow we leave at the crack of dawn, in order to reach Guit Dubling by nightfall. We say farewell to our German friends and our hosts.

## Second isolated community: Guit Dubling

Darkness overtakes us once more. We've been riding all day but haven't got far enough. We haven't got a map, and I have to say that when we ask people how far we still have to go, their answers really aren't much help. We gear up for the cold that we know will set in with the arrival of twilight.

The bishop has announced that we will be arriving this evening; they'll be waiting for us at Guit Dubling. And since we'll be spending the next three weeks there, we'd like to avoid appearing ill-mannered and unreliable before we even arrive.

We get back on our wheels, wrapped up to the ears. The road, which is no more than a series of humps and potholes, turns downhill. With headlamps on our foreheads, we let ourselves glide gently down. And then in our night blindness, we sense that the road begins to climb again.

'Fortunately it's downhill all the way from here!'

Once again we've been fed a load of nonsense. Or else – and it's quite possible – these mountain people don't have the same idea of 'flat' as we do. In the blackness we slalom between potholes – quite a delicate art. Not a sound for kilometres around. We find out the next morning that for the first time in human memory, bears are not hibernating this winter and are coming out of the forest to devour the harvest, and people. Already several have been attacked and wounded. But for the moment we enjoy a blissful and exasperated ignorance. We could be going for hours at this rate, with the darkness forcing us to go so slowly. I shout a prayer at the top of my voice.

'You know what would be great right now? If a car came by . . .!'

At that exact moment, the headlights of a 4x4 shine through the mist. Soon it reaches us and a happy band of tipsy travellers stick their heads out of the windows, jeering at us. The driver, even more drunk than his mates, confirms that we're going the right way, and that there's 15 kilometres of uphill still to go. Between two alcoholic sighs he finally realizes that we're asking him to take us on board. He's very reluctant. He gauges the opinion of the crowd, bellows and snorts, and finally accepts, to the applause of the passengers. He gets out to strap our bikes to the roof of his 4x4, a tricky operation at the best of times, and rendered doubly perilous now by the five grams of alcohol in his bloodstream.

We close our eyes and try to relax, for a full half hour, and by some miracle he manages to avoid sheer cliffs, ditches, potholes, trees and rocks. After the other passengers have been dropped off, and there's only the three of us left, he bellows Nepali drinking songs at the top of his voice, and insists that we sing along with him.

'Hic! Look, we've arrived!'

A short man with a troubled expression and of indeterminate age is waiting for us, hands on hips, at the bottom of a flight of stairs that leads to a natural terrace. The dampness of the night air strikes us as we get out of the big wagon.

'Are you the French cyclists? Here you are at last. I was very worried!'

'Er . . . We're so sorry.'

We're embarrassed. Just when we wanted to avoid looking like disrespectful young louts. We've blown it! But within a few seconds his grouchy expression gives way to a smile.

'Forget it! Welcome to our place! I'm Father Joachim.'

Father Joachim is to be our host, our guide, our Sherpa, our chaperone, our dad. In the picturesque little wooden chalet that serves as his presbytery, he sits us down at the table without further delay. The floor is made of packed earth and concrete. The dining room and kitchen are in a little building set apart. The dishes are washed outside. Next door, the cook is bustling about and the aroma of sizzling chapattis blends with the fragrance of the wood fire. Our first dinner with Father Joachim. We don't realize it now, but over these next few weeks this will become a very special time of the day. During these evenings we will get to know our host and, little by little, we'll come to feel more of a bond with him than anyone else on our whole journey. From the very first minutes, we both feel immensely fond of this wiry little man with laughing eyes that have a teasing twinkle.

'I was afraid you might have been attacked by a bear. Several men from around here have been wounded or killed already this season. You must be very careful!'

Many months later, and even now as I write this book, I can still hear the distinctive timbre of his voice; the sounds seem to come from the very back of his throat. The way he talks, chopping up his words into short, truncated syllables, and stopping all of a sudden, midsentence. When he speaks of his faith, his speech becomes halting and he swings his head from side to side with a look of great concentration. It's quite comical.

'Tomorrow we're going walking. Do you want to come? You don't mind? I think you'll find it's a great experience.'

The scene we discover when we wake the next day is quite different from Darjeeling. Almost all the houses here look like Swiss chalets. The ceiling, walls and floor are made of wide, irregular, wooden planks. Some are roughly painted in bright colours. Guit Dubling sits on the side of a hill. The houses are built on earthen terraces supported by solid wooden retaining walls. When you look down on a village from above, the main thing you notice is a big clearing in the vegetation, which is the school playground.

According to Church tradition, November is the month for remembering the dead. It's six in the morning and, as promised, Father Joachim is taking us walking. He puts on his worn-out imitation Nikes and we're off for a general tour of the tombs!

For a small man he's a great walker. We can hardly keep up with him. We walk for five hours, endlessly climbing one hill after another. We cross rice paddies, past feather-duster willows, luxuriant jungle and golden sun-ripened barley. When we come to a Christian home, Father Joachim always stops to greet the family. He likes to sit down for a few moments to catch up with the news of various family members, while sipping a glass of hot water. He invites the family to pray before he leaves.

The mountain scenery is superb. A river cascades down between each ridge, and here and there waterfalls explode on to the rocks below, making rainbows in the sunlight. The hillsides are covered with the most beautiful trees and the villages are hidden beneath the vegetation, only to be revealed at the very last minute. The tracks are rough; sometimes we have to swipe the branches in front of us away with our sticks. Father Joachim is a fine naturalist; he can name all the species we come across – oaks, willows, mangoes, red and white rhododendrons, magnolias, lotuses, sycamores, spiny holly, bamboos.

He's as fit as an Olympian. Gabriel and I had thought ourselves super fit – it teaches us a good lesson. We try to make ourselves feel better.

'Aren't you exhausted, Father?'

'I'm joyful!'

Great.

From time to time the priest sits down on a rock and pulls up his trouser legs to pull off some leeches that are sucking his blood and sapping his energy. But they don't seem to like us foreigners. Even though we're wearing shorts, they don't come near us. Our little group grows as we go. Young girls, men who've taken on the role of catechist to help the other men keep up their prayer life while the priest isn't there, grandmothers . . .

Here we are, in the house of an 84-year-old man; he actually looks about 20 years older. He clambers barefoot up to the family cemetery.

His face is covered with little brown spots and he has no teeth. He's wearing peacock-blue sports shorts and an old loose-knit, sleeveless jersey over a coarse linen shirt, and a scarf around his head. In his hand he holds a long cane that comes up to his shoulder. He says nothing, except one sentence, muttered between breaths.

'God is coming to get me, but he's taking his time!'

Each time we stop at a graveyard, Father Joachim kisses his white stole respectfully and puts it over his polo shirt. Then he recites the ritual prayers and one of the catechists holds out a basin of water as our motley little procession gathers around.

The priest then walks about among the tombs, sprinkling copious amounts of holy water over them. His head is bowed, his voice strong and confident. He seems to hunch himself over and retreat into his own heart in order to draw forth the words. With open hands, he prays, and his words are clear. The family can't remember exactly who is buried where, but it doesn't really matter. The prayer finishes with the Lord's Prayer, which we recite with our eyes closed. The cemeteries are generally sited not far from the family home, in a clearing or on a promontory. In the background the forest extends as far as the eye can see. The ridge lines merge and disappear in the mist.

Late in the day we arrive at the hamlet of Longshall, where we're welcomed into the home of the head of the Christian community. Sitting on a log, the father listens to his son recite his English homework. The women scuttle back and forth between the bedroom and the outside kitchen, where a terracotta pot sits over the fireclay barbecue table. Rectangular in shape, the table has two holes for pots to sit in and two where logs can be fed into the fire. Our tin plates are black but the food is tasty. A young man of about 20 comes home from school and feeds the pigs. He invites us to walk with him. He knows these mountains like the back of his hand and never tires of them. Every morning he walks for an hour to school and the same in the afternoon to get home. But, more importantly, on Sundays, with all the other inhabitants of his village, he walks four hours to church in Guit Dubling to help Father Joachim celebrate Mass.

We're in Lepcha country, very close to Sikkim, at the foot of the Himalayas. The origin of the Lepcha people is unclear. Based on their language they may have originated in Mongolia. They have flattened cheekbones, strong arms, large chests, slanting eyes, coppery skin. To our Western eyes, they look more Chinese than Indian. They are one of the Himalayan people groups. They don't have castes, just clans and families. Having been influenced by their neighbours they now speak more Nepali than their traditional language, Lepcha. Nepali is spoken at school and in church. They no longer practise their traditional customs, whereas their Nepali, Bhoutani and Tibetan neighbours remain very much attached to theirs.

A huge dinner awaits us. Night falls as we sit down to eat. There's neither running water nor electricity; they use candles or oil lamps for lighting. The colours are soft, the faces peaceful. Chicken, fish, rice, sauce, vegetables. It's fatty, hot and stunningly good. The villagers have pulled out all the stops because Father Joachim is passing through; it shows them that he doesn't forget them, despite their isolation.

The next day, before taking the return route and continuing the rounds of the tombs, Father Joachim celebrates Mass in a little chapel made of simple sheet metal and wood, materials that would have been carried up here on men's backs despite the altitude and the absence of roads. The church stands on the top of a hill, in the middle of the forest. It's called the Chapel of St Francis of Assisi. It's raining heavily and the children are at school, which explains the low turnout. When the bell rings, people take their places: a young woman with a club foot, an old man, mothers carrying their babies on their backs. They've walked a long way and climbed the hill to be here for Mass.

Very close to the church there's a rustic little school. It's break time and they're all outside, busy playing in front of the wooden building. When they see me coming they suddenly fall silent. Then a deafening hullabaloo erupts, with cries of joy and screams of terror. I don't understand anything they're saying, until one of them shouts out what everyone else is thinking:

'It's Jesus! It's Jesus!'

Jesus? I've never been taken for Jesus before. With my thick beard and dark brown hair I vaguely resemble the kitsch Jesus of the posters on their parents' walls.

We walk between the raindrops. Now and again we come across children walking home from school. As I'm walking, a little girl coming towards me calls out, 'Hello, Brother!'

Everyone here thinks we're monks or seminary students because of our beards and because we're walking with Father Joachim. When I ask her what she wants to be when she grows up, she smiles an angelic smile with several teeth missing, and replies, 'I want to be a nun!'

Simple as that.

Back in Guit Dubling we treat ourselves to a shower with the help of a large jug and a washcloth; the cook boiled the water ready for Father's return. She has a high-pitched, reedy voice, a shrill laugh and a sweet face. We decide to call her Barbie.

Later, by candlelight, we have a lengthy discussion with Father Joachim about vocations (his own and others'), his image of France (a country without any Christians) and Paris by night, his inability to put himself in the skin of French people and the complexities of our way of life, which is totally foreign to him. At his request we show him our camera. He confesses that he adores photography, but he gave his little camera to his niece, who enjoys it even more than him. I resolve to send him a new one when I get back to France.

He also talks about how the Lepchas were reached with the gospel: they were 'accidentally' evangelized. Indeed, the missionary priests only settled here in order to access Tibet via India, having failed to get into Tibet through China. The first missionary priests, from the Paris Foreign Missions Society (MEP[2]), arrived in Pedong in 1882. They ended up staying there for 60 years and never managed to get established in Tibet. The mission was called the South Tibetan Mission because they were so sure it would lead to the establishment of a mission in Tibet. But here in this region they built so many presbyteries, churches, schools and orphanages that it ended up becoming its own diocese.

'Do you know, 100 years ago these jungles were inaccessible because there were no roads and no transport? Those missionaries braved the jungle, and gave their lives to make Christ known!'

At the end of the nineteenth century Father Durel tried unsuccessfully to open a mission outpost at Guit Dubling. Thirty years later, in 1935, Father Gratuze obtained government permission, which had been refused to his predecessor, and set himself up with another missionary in Guit Dubling. They cut down bush, levelled the land,

[2] Missions Étrangères de Paris.

collected all the necessary materials and built a church and a presbytery. Saint Joseph was made the patron saint of the mission. The
priests took care of the only two Catholic families in Guit Dubling as
well as Catholics from surrounding villages. In 1937 they handed over
to two Swiss missionaries. Today there are over 200 Catholic families
in Guit Dubling.

'The Swiss! That's who introduced this great cheese!'

How come we hadn't thought of it before? Every evening Barbie
puts before us a magnificent cheese, Tomme de Montagnes, which
bears no resemblance to the rest of the local cuisine. Ah, so that's why.

Father Joachim really takes his mission to heart. He's in charge of
showing us the Church in the region, and he's going to do it properly.

He hands us over to Namsing, the head of the little community of
Dublin, which is an hour and a half's walk from Guit Dubling. Along
with some other villages, like Longshall which we've already visited,
Dublin is one of the stops that Father Joachim relies on as he does his
rounds to encourage the Christians' community life. Namsing takes
us to his home, a pretty little house right out in the middle of the forest. It's made up of several buildings with bamboo and thatch roofs,
and a packed-earth floor. It's idyllic. We're received royally by his parents, his wife and his adorable children. The next day, Namsing hands
us over to Marcus and Gilbert.

Marcus and Gilbert are fearless.

Marcus is 20. His mother has passed away and he lives with his
father and grandmother. He's the youngest in the family and works in
the fields when he isn't at school. With his big smile, white teeth and
shaggy forelock, he reminds me more of a Japanese pop singer than
a Lepcha. Gilbert is 26. His long hair falls down on to his shoulders.
He looks like a Confucian sage with his moustache and goatee beard.
Given the low level of male hairiness in the area, I imagine that these
few, straggly, yellowish blond whiskers are the fruit of an endeavour
that began in the very first days of his adolescence.

We follow Marcus and Gilbert through the rice paddies and millet
fields, under an immaculate blue sky. Marcus speaks a little English,
which enables us to communicate.

'We're going to show you our valley.'

Each family has its own field. The system of agriculture is rudimentary but well suited to the people's needs. In the rice fields the irrigation canals are cleverly combined to maximize the space available for planting. Lepcha people are peasant farmers: they cultivate wheat and barley during the dry season and rice, maize and millet during the rainy season. Some also grow potatoes and buckwheat. After walking for a while we come out on to a flat terrace of bare ground on the hillside. An old man sits in front of his house weaving baskets. A woman is feeding pigs in an enclosure to one side. Hens peck the ground.

Marcus and Gilbert greet the family and introduce us.

'*Jesu barai!*'

We're not used to this. In Lepcha land, they don't say, 'Hi, how are you going?' or 'How do you do?' When they greet each other they call out an enthusiastic '*Jesu barai!*', which means 'Praise the Lord!'

Marcus and Gilbert say a few words to them in Nepali, of which we understand nothing. Everyone immediately stops what they're doing to gather inside the little house on stilts. We follow like sheep. We have to bend right over to get through the doorway and into the dark little room.

In the dim light I make out something blue on the wall. It's a laminated poster of Our Lady of Lourdes. It's pinned up above a little hanging chapel decorated with flowers and covered with pictures of saints. Pope John Paul II is there, among others – *Habemus papam* is taking its time to get to Lepcha land.

We meet other members of the family sitting around this pretty little prayer corner. Altogether there are nine of us in this tiny, cramped space. We sit cheek by jowl; I can feel my neighbour breathing. Gilbert signs himself with the sign of the cross, the rest of us follow. Marcus prays in Lepcha or in Nepali, I'm not sure which. His eyes are closed, his voice faint. As his prayer comes to an end we're spellbound; and taken aback, because praying together, to the Lepchas, is as natural as our having coffee with friends in France. As the little chapel bears witness, the family is clearly in the habit of praying together. Because prayer is taken so seriously, all other activities can be interrupted to consecrate a few minutes to it.

We continue on our way, still on our two friends' heels, and come to another family's home. We pray once again – and at the next house, and the next. We're astounded. They must be doing this especially to impress us – the whole valley can't be this devout!

That day and over the following days, we continue from house to house in the same valley. Each time it's the same ritual, the same confirmation. The same joy shows on their faces.

'Greetings! We've come to pray!'

Once we get over our surprise we feel deeply moved. They are a people of prayer. They pray continually. You only have to walk with Gilbert for five minutes before you hear him murmur his Hail Marys. Having spent time with them, I find myself quite lukewarm in comparison. I'm no longer so sure that I take my own prayer very seriously.

Last night, when we were warming ourselves by the fire with the whole family, I timidly asked about the river, using gestures and noises to get my meaning across. Having successfully mimed 'fish' and 'fishhook', I finally made myself understood: do they sometimes go fishing in the river?

No sooner said than done. After visiting three families and, therefore, after three good prayer times, we dash off down the hill with about ten Lepchas for a grand fishing and bathing expedition. Our friends carry crowbars on their shoulders, an enormous mallet and a large bag with some tin plates clattering about inside. I ask if we're going to fish with hooks or net. They look at me lovingly.

When we get down to the river the Lepchas strip off without saying a word. We do the same. A few moments later, we're in our underwear wading in the icy water. We haven't washed for several days, and the river cops the accumulated grime. Mind you, compared to our Lepcha friends, we're as clean as two new pennies. And then, still in our undies, we all head upstream to catch some fish. Or rather, they go upstream to fish and we follow. The most macho among them carry a crowbar or a mallet, which clashes somewhat with the nudist ambience. The youngest are equipped with strange-looking baskets, elongated with a narrow opening at one end. In Lepcha land there are two tried and true techniques for catching fish.

The first, which we christen the 'brute in briefs technique', consists of hammering an enormous mallet down mightily on to a flat rock in order to daze the fish hiding peacefully underneath. Then they simply lift the rock and collect the stunned fish. The second technique consists of 'blocking the holes'. First a young Lepcha rushes into the forest with a sickle or machete, and promptly returns with a pile of branches. They strip the leaves and use them to meticulously block all the holes around the sides of a rock, between it and the riverbed, so that the fish sheltering beneath it find themselves trapped. Then, with the help of the crowbar, the rock is jiggled around to make them panic. Finally they unblock one little hole, taking a little bit of foliage away, and with the help of a basket placed over the orifice, catch the fish as they swim into it in an attempt to escape. So that's why they laughed when I talked about nets and fishhooks.

Today the fishing has taken a long time and produced meagre results. We only caught about 20 tiddlers. We light two fires on the riverbank and sit down to eat. In spite of our cries and protests, we're given four each – 40 per cent of the booty for less than 20 per cent of the party.

Just as night falls, Gilbert comes to collect us. Gabriel drank some river water earlier without boiling it; he's now stuck in the toilets. A wise man could have said to him, as I did myself an hour ago, 'Whoever drinks this river water has great faith in his stomach.' Sitting on a rock, I contemplate the moon intently, making various profound comments. 'We all look at the same moon. I wonder if our Iraqi friends are looking at the moon tonight? Hey, what time is it in Iraq?' Gilbert stands beside me, murmuring almost imperceptibly. He's praying. Again. Without ceasing.

We've never prayed as much as we have since we've been in this valley. We pray almost all day; the least mouthful of water is subject to a blessing. The Lepchas have brought God into their daily lives. It's beautiful. But I'm slowly reaching saturation point.

Marcus and Gilbert take us to the village chapel, where the other young people are waiting. The walls are made of concrete, which means that sacks of cement and buckets of water must have been carried up here on men's backs. The little church is built on a terrace. The land for it was given by one of the villagers to the whole community. When you know how very poor these people are, you can well imagine that, even for the richest among them, such a gift would have represented a major sacrifice. I regret having heaved a weary sigh when I entered the porch of the chapel. I'm moved and Gabriel is too. They wanted this chapel with all their hearts.

Inside there's hardly any furniture, just an altar and a few chairs for the celebrant and the old people. The walls are bare and grey. A little cross stands on the altar. Two candles are burning before a statuette of Our Lady of Lourdes. The few young people present sit on a rug on the floor. Gilbert leads the prayer in a melancholic voice, then Marcus takes over. A young woman, an English teacher, intones a chant to Mary and then prays in English, for us.

We don't know much about their customs and nothing of their language. We wouldn't last a month in their shoes. And yet we're brothers in the faith. These aren't just empty words. It means that we call on the same Father and we feel we belong to the same group, the same family, where we're accepted and understood. There's something instinctive about this brotherhood. The Church is a delicate reality that we experience first hand. And it's precisely because it's fragile that it's so moving.

We've been travelling for four months, especially so that we can experience this church unity. We've heard people speak about it but it seems so abstract and ill-defined. And then the Lepchas give us the greatest of gifts. They're the first community to take us into their hearts, to take the initiative and allow us truly to share their lives. Until now we've had to make the first step. Not this time. It means they understand why we're here – that they're in true communion with us, united with us, that we really are talking about the same thing, that we believe in the same God. What began as an intellectual and spiritual exercise has, thanks to them, become very concrete in this time of prayer together. I'm moved to tears. It's so clear, here before our very eyes: the universality of the Church, Christian unity – the Jesus of the Gospels, present among us here when we pray together.

When the prayer ends they sit us on two chairs and Marcus shyly brings out a scrap of paper from his pocket. He's prepared a speech.

To top it all off, he thanks us and hopes we've enjoyed our stay with them. They will pray for us; they promise to. There's a lump in my throat. They put a traditional scarf around our necks, a sign of respect and friendship. They smile from ear to ear and shake our hands with great warmth.

Back at Namsing's house, they've killed the fatted hen for our departure.

We're back in Guit Dubling. After morning Mass, Father Felix, the other priest in Guit Dubling, who is in charge of the village school and the youth of the diocese, introduces us to the pupils. They're between 3 and 16 years old and come marching into the playground two by two – 600 children from all the surrounding villages, in spotless uniforms: smart red V-neck jerseys, flannel skirts or trousers, black ankle boots. Many of these children are from very poor families, but today they could be Princess Kate's children.

Today, as on every Monday morning, the band is playing. An athletic-looking boy with an impeccably straight parting sets the pace and leads the procession, twirling his baton. The orchestra follows. The others march in time. This very military parade stops opposite the platform on which Father Felix is standing. The sign of the cross. Prayer – for all, even those who aren't Catholics. The priest reads out some short words of wisdom from a book. The 600 voices repeat them. It's a well-oiled machine. I wonder what these students are thinking as they repeat everything parrot fashion like this. The Indian education system is being modernized but it still seems to be based on rote learning and corporal punishment. The school children, some of whom walk several hours each morning to come to class, all have a very clear idea of how lucky they are to come to school while so many others are toiling for long hours in the fields.

The good Father Felix asks us to mount the platform and introduces us to the children. By way of introduction, he treats the little soldiers to a rendition of the *Song of Roland*.[3] Embarrassed by so much praise, we don't know where to look. Suddenly we seem to have become

---

[3] *La Chanson de Roland* is an heroic poem about Roland, the universal ideal hero, based on the Battle of Roncevaux in AD 778, during the reign of Charlemagne.

'handsome' and 'adventurous'. To hear them, you'd almost think we'd slain bears ourselves, barehanded.

'Isn't that right? You're very proud to welcome our two French friends?'

'Yeeeeeees, Faaaaaather Feeeeliiix!'

The Church in India is the second-largest social services provider after the state, and what is true for the whole is also true for the part: at Guit Dubling, Father Felix is continually searching for new financing to build new schools in isolated villages and pay for new teachers. For €80 he can pay a teacher for a month. At the moment his teachers are paid half that, and stay only until they can find a better employer. Their salaries are paid from school fees and several external donations. Only about 60 per cent of the pupils' families can afford the fees, even though they are very low.

'Finding a sponsor for a teacher allows a whole class of students to study free. It's a lot more efficient than sponsoring a single child.'

The school staff consists of Father Felix, the salaried teachers and three nuns. And not just any old nuns – they're Sisters of Cluny in fact. We've had occasion to meet them several times before. After our first lunch with them, when we tasted some marvellous *momos*[4] and succulent vegetables, their Superior plucked up the courage to ask if we were travelling with much baggage.

'No. We're travelling light! The Bible says to throw away anything you've doubled up on, doesn't it, Sister?'

'I see. If I understand rightly, you have only one T-shirt. Is that right?'

'No. I've got two or three.'

'And have you got two or three pairs of trousers as well?'

She seemed to be hoping that this was the case.

'No, just one.'

She looked appalled.

'But your trousers are quite worn, aren't they? Would you like me to buy you another pair?'

'No, I don't need any more. I'm fine with just the one pair. I don't mind their being shabby. At least no one wants to steal them!'

That really made us laugh, but the nuns were not amused.

---

[4] Ravioli stuffed with meat and vegetables.

'Yes, quite.'

'What's the matter, Sister?'

'I'm going to send you to see our tailor in the village. He's very nice.'

'No, I assure you, there's no need. Anyway, we don't have the money for a new pair of trousers.'

'Well, we'll buy you a new pair. I insist. Do you understand?'

'Understand what?'

'The children. They mustn't see you dressed like that.'

Looking like tramps, we weren't showing the children a good example. If the nuns or Father Felix introduced us to the children dressed like this, they would be giving the impression that they tolerated scruffy outfits. Appearance and cleanliness are very important in India and we weren't respecting their values.

So Sister Mathilda sent us out to get ourselves spruced up, which we did with good grace and, obviously, at our own expense. Gabriel had a pair of trousers made at the village tailor for €5, and I found some second hand ones at the market.

Another day, the saintly Sister Joanna took me under her wing. She has run the dispensary for years and trained first-aid workers in each of the surrounding villages. Despite its being beyond the range of their skills, these women are responsible for visiting the families regularly to check on the health of each member, giving advice on hygiene, checking that the children are going to school and looking for signs of malnutrition. In the dispensary at Guit Dubling there's a never-ending stream of people coming for care and advice from the old nun. Very often she takes care of the heart as well as the cuts and scratches, because she exudes an immense peace and a deep motherly kindness. Everybody loves her.

The reason I became acquainted with Sister Joanna was because I wasn't feeling 100 per cent. I was perpetually getting stomach aches, nausea, headaches, and my crotch was itchy, red and covered with strange little spots. Whenever I moved, it felt as though I was on fire. So I limped awkwardly to the dispensary and, feeling extremely embarrassed, revealed my privates to Sister Joanna. The diagnosis didn't seem clear. Thrush? Scabies? An allergic reaction? She dusted me with a kind of disinfecting powder and gave me a little medal of Saint Alfonsa, a recently canonized Indian. Shock treatment.

The next day I was already feeling better. Three days later, I was a new man.

It's Sunday, and our last day in Guit Dubling. This means it's our last Mass with the Lepchas. The church is full again this time: the people have walked for between one and four hours to be here for Mass. Marcus and Gilbert are here. Namsing and his family as well. All the villages are represented.

I feel quite overcome. We sing one chant after another, songs that we've sung almost daily for three weeks. We know them all now. Our favourite is a Nepalese chant to the Virgin Mary, *Mata Maria*.

> *Mata Maria Harpal Timi Nai*
> *Mero Sahara Ho,*
> *Andhyaro Mero Jiwan Ko,*
> *Timi Diyalo Ho.*
> *Timi Nai Mero Mata Ho,*
> *Timi Nai Mero Asha Ho,*
> *Timi Lai Sumpe Sampurna Jiwan,*
> *Patha Pradhar Shak Timi Ho.*

### Translation

> *Mary my mother, every moment,*
> *You are my protector and my help,*
> *When my life darkens,*
> *You are the light that guides me.*
> *You are my mother*
> *You are my hope,*
> *I have offered you my life,*
> *You are the way, you are my guide.*

At the end of Mass, Father Joachim invites us up to the altar and we offer them the 'gift' – the rosary given by the Syrian villagers of Tal Arboush. And the Lepcha, in turn, give us a little cross made from coconut wood, which we will pass on to the next village – in Tibet, if we ever get there.

They want us to make a speech, and the honour falls to me. I struggle to put a few words together.

142

'Thank you for how simply and naturally you live out your faith. You have renewed us in our faith.'

Hundreds of faces are riveted on us. Sometimes with benevolence, sometimes with no expression at all. Hard to know if I've been understood. Difficult to know how *really* to say thank you. In these few seconds of eternity, my eyes linger on each of them, knowing I will never see them again.

After Mass the sisters arrange for those who want to to come and share the French dishes we'd prepared for them the previous day: *mousse au chocolat, crème pâtissière, sablé* (shortbread). They find our dishes rather good; we find them absolutely extraordinary. And we stuff ourselves.

We're dining with Father Joachim for the last time. These past weeks, we've shared some wonderful times with him at this magical time of the evening. His mimicry, his expressions, the way his eyes crease up when he doesn't understand, the way he makes a little half-smile when he's about to tell a joke. We take them all in. The atmosphere now is strained, our feelings barely contained.

'Thank you, Father.'

I can't say anything else. It's all been so marvellous. We thank him for everything, for his way with people, for who he is. He, in turn, thanks us; he says that he's loved these days we've spent together, that he has had a lot of fun. The electricity fails and we shower each other with compliments by candlelight. The warm light accentuates the kindness of his words. I listen, I taste, I savour. I already miss Father Joachim. I remember his great faith, his desire to give God first place, his sense of duty, his simplicity, his dodgy humour, his tactlessness, the way he teases the kids.

We see him again one last time at five thirty the next morning. He suggests praying together before he leaves us. In his office there's a large painting of Jesus, which he commissioned himself. Quite an unusual Jesus, because he's smiling.

'What's wrong with that? Do you think Jesus was boring?'

And there he is laughing, in front of his joyful Jesus.

We pray the prayer of Lauds in English. Priests all over the world use this prayer – the prayer of the Church. A Church that unites us, makes us brothers. We thought we knew it. Having been with the Lepchas, we *feel* it.

# 8

## Nepal

## In which the Church has only just come of age and is not yet vaccinated

1 DECEMBER, 4 MONTHS AND 26 DAYS AFTER DEPARTURE
'Tourism in Tibet is a rich man's game. That's what he told me! What a mongrel!'

Kathmandu – city of the great white trekker. Gabriel storms out of the travel agency, furious. The man who for years has fired the imagination of the French with the dream of trekking in the Himalayas has, in one short sentence, shattered our hopes of entering Tibet from Nepal.

'It's $500 minimum to cross the border by land. And, as a bonus, you're saddled with a guide and a bunch of tourists.'

'So? Once we'd crossed the border we'd just go off on our own, wouldn't we?'

'No! Because the guide keeps the entry permit for Tibet until you return to Nepal. They've got you over a barrel.'

Between India and China there are two border crossings; both are closed to travellers and only partly open for freight. An Indian army colonel we met in a church we visited had offered to pull a few strings to get us across the Indian side – but that would still leave the problem of the Chinese border. In the end we decided it would be simpler to go via Nepal, and we'd come to Kathmandu to sort the whole thing out.

'Oh, that's great! We've come all this way for nothing.'

'Yeah. And the flight to China only costs €170.'

Not as romantic as trekking, but a whole lot cheaper and more straightforward. Oh well, at that price we'll have to kiss the trek idea goodbye.

We left Guit Dubling several days ago and have just arrived in Kathmandu. We rode the dreadful road through the hill country all the way to the Nepalese border. Then, pushed for time, we loaded our bikes on to the roof of an old beaten-up bus to get to Kathmandu faster. That meant spending 16 hours on an overnight bus, with a driver who apparently had no need of sleep; 16 hours of constant prayer and appreciation of the virtues of two-wheeled vehicles, while this reckless road hog threw the bus with gay abandon around hairpin bends and over precipitous mountains at breakneck speed.

'That terrifying trip – all for nothing.' The thought of dismantling our bikes all over again and packing them up safely for yet another flight doesn't thrill us.

'Damn it.'

We're freezing. The streets are wide and clean, with large shop-window displays on either side. We mope about for a bit, tired and disappointed, before heading for the cathedral. We planned to spend very little time in Nepal so that we'd have time to go to Tibet. But we find Nepal fascinating. It's one of the Himalayan kingdoms, bordering China to the north and India to the south, east and west. The further north you go, the more rugged the terrain becomes. Its inhabitants are mountain people; eight of the ten highest mountains in the world are in Nepal, including Everest, which we've already seen from Darjeeling.

Not knowing much about Nepal, I grab a tourist brochure from a trekking agency's leaflet rack. I find out that the country has 30 million inhabitants, of whom 80 per cent are Hindus, 10 per cent are Buddhists and 3 per cent are Christians. The vast majority of the Christians are Protestants.

We leave the wide, open avenues and plunge into a labyrinth of narrow lanes. On the far side stands the cathedral, Our Lady of the Assumption. We notice armed guards at the entrance. Strange. We're interested to find out why.

After centuries of rule by absolute monarchy and more than ten years of civil war between the army and Maoist revolutionaries, Nepal adopted a new constitution that ratified the transition from the Hindu monarchy to a democratic regime. This was naturally followed by the abolition of the caste system, a legacy of Hinduism, and the establishment of religious freedom for minorities, especially Muslims and Christians. While on the one hand the constitution prohibits all missionary activity or proselytizing on pain of imprisonment, it does allow personal conversions. In press interviews, the Apostolic Vicar of Nepal doesn't hesitate to say that Nepal is very tolerant towards Christians, who generally feel safe here. So why is this church surrounded by high walls? Why the big, heavy gate? Why the intercom, surveillance cameras and professional security guards?

We're greeted by a priest, Father George, who sports a little charcoal goatee. He offers us a small room with everything we need. So we decide to stay in Kathmandu for a few days with the three priests from the cathedral, before flying to the south of China.

Each morning we accompany them to church. Mass here is not just 'low Church' but exceedingly low Church. At ground level, you could say. The altar is a low table around which the celebrants kneel or sit cross-legged. The congregation also sit on the ground on square cushions. It's a striking contrast to the liturgy at Guit Dubling. Here no one stands up at any time; they get up only to kneel for the consecration.

As the bishop will explain to us later, the church displays features of the four great religions: Buddhist-style paintings, statues made by Hindus, sculpted pillars made by Muslims. A great leap into cultural integration. And their Jesus has fat cheeks, a shaved head like a Buddhist monk, and slanting eyes.

Rakesh is one of the faithful few who attend Mass daily. Even if the church had been packed, we wouldn't have missed him. It's difficult not to notice this strange little fellow with his shaved head, wearing a Franciscan habit.

We can't help wondering how he got the strange scars on the right side of his face.

Straight after making the sign of the cross at the end of our first Mass in Nepal, he comes to welcome us and offer his help. He accompanies us during our time in Kathmandu.

He's not Nepali but Indian. From a Protestant family in the north of the country, he became a Catholic as a teenager. It was while in Nepal that he first felt attracted to the life of a hermit. But then he did an about turn and created a Catholic community in Kathmandu, the very first in Nepal. He was 29 years old.

'The bishop strongly advised me not to wear my habit, thinking that it would cause problems for me.'

'And . . .?'

'I've been wearing it for several years now and I've never had any issues.'

We have a wonderful time with the young monk. One day when we're talking in the church courtyard, we ask him to explain why there's so much security around the church. Usually all smiles and enthusiasm, his face suddenly darkens.

Paradoxically, although the amendment to the constitution guarantees the rights of minorities, the months that followed its ratification saw an increase in attacks against the tiny Catholic community. While Christians represent 3 per cent of the population, Catholics represent only 0.3 per cent; they number no more than 7,000. The wave of violence started in 2008 in Sirsiya, in the east of Nepal. A group of four armed men killed a Silesian priest, who was a school principal. This was the first assassination attempt by terrorist groups in the history of the Nepalese Church. Over the following months terrorist threats spread to other priests and lay people. Suddenly all Catholic schools were told they had to close.

The police were directed to guard religious buildings, such as the cathedral in Kathmandu.

Rakesh points to his cheek. He shows us his scars. His stigmata.

'Last May a bomb exploded in the church, leaving two dead and thirteen wounded, including me. I spent several days in hospital.'

We could feel, with his every word, what a terrible shock it was for him; he still has not really taken it in.

'It was a Saturday. The church was full. Mass had barely begun when a young woman sitting just in front of me said she needed to go out to the toilet. She gave her bag to her neighbour to look after and went out. And while we were singing the Gloria, the bomb that was in the bag exploded. There was a lot of noise, a lot of blood, lifeless bodies. A woman and a child were killed.

'That was on 23 May 2009. The young woman's name was Thapa Shretha. She was 27 years old, a member of the Nepal Defence Army. When she was arrested a few days later she spoke of her deep hatred for Christians and other religions'.

'Are Christians persecuted in Nepal? Is that why guards are stationed in front of the entrance and the walls all around the compound?'

'Security has increased since the attack, yes. But I don't know if it's true to say that Christians are persecuted. As in other Asian countries, there are sometimes tensions between the Church and fundamentalist Hindus or Buddhists who, for various reasons, don't like to hear of people being converted. This attack was the act of a Hindu extremist group. Their leader, the brains behind the attack, was put in prison and, believe it or not, barely a week later sent a letter of apology to the victims! From prison he asked Catholics and Muslims to forgive him for what he did!'

'Was it sincere?'

'Difficult to say. Perhaps he did it to get a reduced penalty. But who knows?'

'How did people react at the time of the attack?'

'Everyone agreed it was sad that politics should interfere with religion. Even the Hindu and Muslim leaders, who called for attacks on sacred places to stop. It brought the Catholic community closer together. The bonds of brotherly love have become even stronger as we've prayed together.'

Months after the attack the atmosphere is still strained. The church has been cleaned and repaired but you can still feel the impact among the community.

The following day, after Sunday Mass, Brother Rakesh introduces us to another victim of the attack. He's a man of about 40, with deliberate movements, smiling, calm. Joseph lost his wife and six-year-old daughter. As with the Christians in Orissa, who said they bore no hatred towards their persecutors, Joseph affirms that he has been able to forgive.

How can we make sense of the unspeakable anguish he has suffered? Confronted with his story, I realize that what we're really facing is the problem of evil. If God is good, why does he allow suffering? How can he allow the death of innocent people when at that very moment they were singing his glory at Sunday Mass? How can we understand it? How can we accept it? Nevertheless, we can see that Joseph himself has clearly accepted it. When we search his face, we find neither distress nor anger, neither fatalism nor rebellion. His eyes are full of tenderness. His face shines with that same light I've seen before in monks and devout believers.

Joseph is radiant. He speaks Nepali and Rakesh interprets, not without a certain amount of emotion because he admits to having experienced a great spiritual crisis himself, after his hospitalization. For Rakesh, the attack is still an extremely sensitive subject.

'In some ways,' Joseph says, 'this terrible event is a mercy because since then I have understood the meaning of life better. It is a gift. All is grace. If God asked me to, I would be ready to sacrifice again the two children he has left me. The body is not important; it is our soul we must make ready.'

There we are, the four of us, in the church where six months earlier his whole life was turned upside down. And he comes back here every Sunday. At the site of the crime, he prays for his wife, his daughter and their murderers.

A sweet little lady approaches us.

'We are having a little show. Would you like to join us?'

Suddenly we're the guests of honour at a concert put on by the children of the Legion of Mary. Some little girls perform a dance. They're charming, with their immaculate white dresses and floral crowns. Their hands and feet twirl delicately to the rhythm of the Nepalese songs. Brother Rakesh whispers in our ears, 'They're adorable aren't they? Adorable . . . and all HIV positive since the day they were born.' The nuns look after them and their mothers.

We make use of this stop in Kathmandu to stock up on winter clothes to prepare ourselves for the Chinese mountains, higher and colder than the mountains surrounding Darjeeling. This time, one pair of long johns won't be enough. We'll need more layers. We go to Thamel, the part of town that's famous for its alpine sports shops, cyber-cafés and numerous tourists. After hours spent noting the prices of the various items we've got our eyes on in several of the shops, we go for the one that seems to be the cheapest. Armed with a list of their competitors' prices, we're able to negotiate unbeatable deals. We leave with two complete outfits for less than €100 each: walking shoes, a fleece jacket, a top-quality goose-down jacket in fire-engine red (so we'll be setting the trend on the slopes), socks, gaiters, long johns, beanie, mittens and rucksacks as well.

Brother Rakesh takes us to an immense, magnificent Buddhist monastery. With his brown habit and shaved head, he could easily be taken for a Buddhist monk, except that their robes are maroon. He confides that he really likes this place and comes regularly to talk with his 'brother monks', as he calls them.

He likes sharing with them about his life, his vows, his joys and difficulties, and about Jesus.

In the midst of all these Asians we see a tall European monk with very pale skin and, amused, we think of Father Kinley, the ex-Buddhist priest from Bhutan we met in Darjeeling a few weeks earlier. Hundreds of banners and prayer flags flutter in the wind as the faithful come to turn the prayer wheels and prostrate themselves. Brother Rakesh reveals the trick to telling the marriage status of the monks.

'Look at these monks. You can tell if one is married simply by looking at his habit. If the hem of his habit is wide, he's single; if it's narrow, he's married.'

The monk takes us to his home, the newly established Alleluia House. It's clean, tidy, sanitized . . . to the point of obsession. We meet the monastery's only other monk and the three orphans they look after. When it was opened in 2004 he was the only one there with the children. Since then, little by little, others have come forward. Today the Poor Servants of Jesus the Master have two monks and one postulant.

'It's best to start small! If it's God's will, others will be called!'

The fledgling community received its accreditation from the bishop in 2006. It's the first and only Catholic community to be founded in Nepal.

The brothers make a vow of obedience, poverty and chastity, like Catholic monks all over the world. They also make a fourth vow, to give 'totally free service to the needy'. That's the distinctive feature of their vocation. They consider themselves followers of Saint Francis of Assisi and Mother Teresa, and their desire is 'to wash the feet of the poor and needy'. They want to make themselves available to the most desperate.

'Ah, but how do you prioritize the needs? Don't the street children need you more than Gabriel and I do this afternoon?'

'Oh, we never have to decide like that. These things just happen naturally.'

The morning of our departure, we finally meet Monsignor Anthony Sharma, first Bishop of Nepal, first Nepali Jesuit and the first bishop we've met who tells jokes virtually non-stop. For a week we've heard people talking about him wherever we go; we're pleased finally to put a face to the name.

'You know, it's incredible, but our Church is not yet 20 years old!'

'But there must have been missionaries in Nepal?'

'No, not really. In the seventeenth century some Capuchin monks came, then Jesuits who built schools at the king's request. But Nepalese Christians have always been part of the Indian Church! Up until today, we have never had an autonomous, indigenous Church!'

He became bishop in 2007. Nepal got its first cathedral and some 7,000 Catholics have been proud to be involved in the birth of their Church since then. I use the word birth, for it really is a completely new Church, one of the newest in the world. A Church that has barely even come of age.

Monsignor Sharma is a little comedian – he really is small – and he livens up his conversation with religious jokes. Ecclesiastical humour can be rather heavy, but our little bishop brings it to another level altogether.

'Did you know that in the Bible there's a brilliant description of constipation.'

'I beg your pardon?'

'Yes, constipation, the bowel problem. There's a very long description of it in the Bible.'

'Really? Whereabouts?'

'All through the Bible!'

He squirms with delight. We can't help smiling too. It's contagious. We can't help it! And here's the punchline.

'Cain was not Abel, so Moses took two tablets, which made David sit on the throne for 40 years. For 40 years! And the lot fell on Matthias.'

He cracks up. We crack up. To think that on Sunday he walks around with a mitre on his head.

Monsignor Sharma's life began 12 hours after his father passed away. He was brought up by his mother, to whom he's still fiercely devoted.

When she left Hinduism to convert to Catholicism, Anthony and his sister followed her. Like other young privileged Nepalis, he was sent to India to pursue his studies. In Darjeeling he came into contact with the Jesuits. When he finished school he decided to join the Society of Jesus and entered seminary.

'Do you know, I was the first Nepali to become a Jesuit! When I came back to Nepal, the Church still had quite a low profile. In 1951 the grandfather of the then king invited the Jesuits to come to Nepal to open schools. Before that it was thought that educating ordinary people would make them into rebels! So they had no access to education and only a few had the means to send their children to other countries to study. We were invited to Nepal to educate the children, although with certain restrictions: we were forbidden to convert anyone and we could only work in the Kathmandu Valley. Today there are 31 schools, with a total of 21,000 students, including 11,000 girls!'

He explains why it's so important for the Church in Nepal to be engaged in education. According to him there are four good reasons. The first is that education is the reason Catholics were called here. The second is that Nepalis have a great thirst for knowledge because they've been deprived of it for so long. Third, the caste system is very powerful. Catholic schools open their doors to children of every caste in order to create a mix that doesn't exist elsewhere, and they teach children to accept each other. The last reason is particularly interesting: the empowerment of women. The Church wants to give a voice to this half of Nepali society, viewed by men as second-class citizens. The bishop explains why this last reason is very close to his heart.

'My mother was given in marriage to my father when she was seven years old! That's the custom in Nepal. Women are men's property. When she was a little girl she had a great desire to learn and improve herself. But when her father was teaching her two brothers, he locked the door and she had to listen from outside and try to catch fragments of the lesson. One day the inevitable happened. My grandfather caught her out and beat her. By way of punishment, he sent her into the forest to gather wood and cut grass, teaching her a lesson she has remembered all her life. "You have committed the gravest mistake! Your calling is to collect wood, cut grass and do the cooking. You don't need an education to do that."'

We could sense that he felt moved just remembering his mother's sufferings, even though it was so long ago.

'One of my Hindu cousins was also married off at the age of seven. But her husband died the day after the wedding. Her relations accused her of causing his death. So ever since then she has had to atone for her "wrongdoing". She's not allowed to eat food prepared by others, she cannot wear a coloured sari, she must bathe in the sacred river several times a year, take a full bath every day to purify herself. If she accepts all that, perhaps she will be united once again with her husband, at the hour of her death, and enter paradise with him.'

He assures us that these kinds of situations are still going on today.

The little man quickly perks up. The Church in Nepal is a service Church, a discreet Church. In accordance with the King's wishes, the Church doesn't seek to convert people. There are two million Christians in Nepal, of which the vast majority are Protestants, who employ more direct evangelistic methods, which the bishop doesn't endorse. However, he recognizes their zeal and that they're capable of getting access to the most remote parts of the country, where the Catholics don't reach.

'The Church in Nepal is primarily involved in social work. It's certainly true that we are just a little group, with 65 priests, 174 nuns and 7,515 Catholics, but we have 31 schools and 40 other charity projects. Our Church is orientated towards service.'

We get up and accompany him back to his car. As we walk along the beautiful, shady colonnades, Monsignor Sharma tells us one last story. This story, the gift of our very last minutes with him, strengthens our faith in the Providence of God.

'You know, when we finished building this beautiful church I had a moral dilemma. I said to myself, "Some people will come here every day, some will come once a week, but most will come only about three times a year. What should we do with this superb place that's just crying out to be used for something worthwhile?" Without really knowing why, the idea just came to me quite naturally that we should open a school for street kids. One week later, I received a call from a family friend in Italy. "Come back to Italy! A godly old man says he has just had a vision. It seems that the Virgin is asking a family of rich industrialists here to establish a school for boys in Kathmandu." I flew to Italy to meet the family. They gave me $59,000 to build the school, which now has 70 boys enrolled. They continue to support us, providing students' uniforms, teachers' salaries and one full meal per day for each boy.'

He climbs up into his electric blue 4x4; it's too high for him and he has to clamber up into the leather seat. Above the roar of the engine, he calls out one last message to us . . .

'The Lord never ceases to shower us with blessings. *Bon voyage!*'

We spend several hours preparing our bikes for the flight, dismantling them piece by piece, wrapping each in brown paper, taping nuts to bolts, bolts to the frame, chain to the frame and so on. Gabriel is much quicker than me. Every time we have to go through this palaver, I wind up feeling angry and frustrated. I just can't seem to do it. My package is too big. I have to re-do it. I switch around two parts that don't fit together. Then the paper splits and bursts open on the other side. The box explodes. I'm going to have to find another. Gabriel places his wrapped package against the wall and calmly watches me pounding on various bits of broken cardboard. He ends up giving me a hand, but when I finally finish, I glare furiously at his compact, neatly wrapped package, comparing it with my enormous, misshapen bundle of string and cardboard. It's humiliating.

We load our two enormous parcels on to the roof of a tiny little taxi. The main thing now is not to lose them on the way; we give the order to drive very gently and not to use the brakes. We realize that with the purchases we made in Kathmandu, the weight of our bags has increased considerably. With 12 kilos of bike per person, we've only got 5 more kilos each for the rest of our baggage. Although we're travelling light, it's not light enough. When we flew from Iraq to India we were already over the weight limit, but we were able to negotiate without too much difficulty. This time we'll be *well* over the limit.

We approach the Chinese airline's check-in counter feeling a little flustered. Stay cool. Don't let it show. They say the Chinese are impassive; Chinese we will be.

We smile insistently at the hostess and place our packages on the conveyor belt. We should be allowed 20 kilos each.

'Gentlemen, we have a problem.'

'Really? What could that be?'

'Your baggage weighs 100 kilos.'

'Oh! Are you sure?'

We gamble on what we hope are charming smiles, jokes, distractions, long-winded explanations. Nothing works. She's incorruptible.

'That will be $500. How would you like to pay?'

We try to arouse her sense of pity. But that doesn't work either. No warmth, no sense of connection, no empathy. She's a cold, heartless monster. And her patience is running out.

'I'm sorry, but it's the same rule for everyone. How do you wish to pay?'

We keep on pleading. No response. We have to pay. We ask for a little time and move away to prepare our counterattack. We need a more convincing strategy. Discreetly taking our two already full carry-on bags, and stuffing as many clothes into them as we can, we reduce the weight to 60 kilos. That makes only ten kilos each extra. Ten miserable little kilos.

We try again.

'You are still 20 kilos over. You must pay $200.'

Doom and despair. An iceberg would have melted. But not her. She's made of cold, hard rock.

'Could you call your manager, please?'

'I am the manager.'

'Oh!'

We play our final card. Double or nothing. Even if it means dying of embarrassment in front of the other passengers in the queue.

'Madam, since you can't seem to understand us, we're going to have to throw some of our things into the rubbish bin. You do understand that we can't pay more to transport something than the cost of the item itself, don't you? But it would be crazy to throw away things that are virtually new. You could take them yourself. We'll give them to you. Or maybe some of your colleagues might be interested? This adjustable spanner, for instance. It's brand new, but really heavy. We'll leave it. Take it, I insist! And this screwdriver. And these inner tubes. And ...'

The hard commercial exterior is cracking. Embarrassed, our implacable hostess squirms like a worm on her chair. She has no idea how to react.

'Wait, wait! We can give you ten kilos free. But you will still have to pay for the other ten – $100. That's all right? $100? Can you pay $100?'

You'd think we were bargaining at the local market. 'Roll up, folks, ten kilos, a bargain at one hundred dollars.'

'Impossible, unfortunately. We can't just fork out $100. But how about we give some of our baggage to other passengers?'

'Er, yes, all right. But be careful – you can't give them to Chinese passengers. You must not upset them. You can ask other foreign passengers.'

To this day I still wonder if I heard this last sentence right.

'Not upset Chinese passengers?'

'Yes, but there are other nationalities. You could always try to sort it out with them.'

We survey the queue looking for passengers who might not be Chinese, to palm off our ten measly kilos of bargain junk. But the world being what it is, there are a lot of Chinese on a flight to China. In fact, apart from us, we have a grand total of three other foreigners on the flight: a young French couple, who have just checked in and are no longer in a position to take our luggage, and a businessman, who agrees with a smile. We're saved.

We finally check in, relieved. Our hostess seems just as relieved.

But we're not quite in the clear yet. There remains the customs problem. We have four pieces of hand luggage, not to mention our little rucksacks that contain the audio-visual material. If all the officials in the airport are made of the same stuff, we're not going to get through. Quick as a flash, without anyone noticing, we pass two bags to Laure and Nicolas, the two young French passengers, who don't turn a hair.

The inevitable happens: Nicolas is chosen by the security officer for baggage inspection. One by one he unpacks and unwraps all our things and, improvising with panache, he answers the customs inquisitor's questions.

'What is that?'

'Look, I'll show you. Here, I'll help you open it. It's, er, it's a washbag.'

The officer seems convinced by Nicolas' act. We breathe again. We've made it! We relieve our new friends of our heavy bags before boarding the plane. But as we walk out on to the tarmac we recognize the team who were on check-in. They're waiting to greet the passengers as they board. She's going to eat us for breakfast. Our hostess eyeballs us angrily. We shrink down into our seats. We catch sight of her coming down the aisle. She takes a long look in our direction. I hold my breath and look down at my feet. When I look up again, she's gone. We take off. Soon we'll be in China. I hope we won't have to negotiate with her fellow Chinese very often. China's inflexible approach to doing business? All right – now I understand.

# 9

## China

## In which the Church has one head and two bodies

Our arrival marks a turning point: for the first time since we left Turkey three months ago, we're not living amid a state of anarchy – on the roads, the footpaths, the narrow lanes, where might is right and a bicycle is of very little consequence. The streets here are broad and clean. Huge grey buildings tower above us, and I savour the relative silence of this Chinese city.

We have a contact by the name of Aliocha.[1] He's a young Frenchman, a friend of friends who is working for an NGO in China. When we emailed him a few weeks ago he advised us to stay in the city of Cachei for a few days before going to meet him at his home, in the mountains further south. In his last message he also indicated roughly where the Bishop of Cachei would be celebrating Mass this morning, at this very moment. If we don't want to miss it, we'd better get moving. I leave Gabriel at the airport with our baggage and race off to see if I can catch him after Mass for an interview.

The bishop is one of the last of the Chinese bishops chosen by the Communist Party who haven't been recognized by Rome. Over the last few years the Vatican has expressed its desire to see the end of the current situation in which there is a division between the 'official' Church, supported by the Party, and the 'underground' community, faithful to the Catholic faith and to Rome. Many 'official' priests have since been recognized by Rome. The last diehards are hard nuts to crack. And despite the progress so far, there are still 18 bishops and 19 priests locked up in Chinese prisons. The Catholic

---

[1] The names of people and places have been changed.

community is divided in two – 60 per cent in the official Church, 40 per cent in the clandestine Church. To complicate things further, some Christians attend services of both Churches. The situation of the Church in China is extremely complex. It's not just a simple confrontation between good and evil, the faithful on one side and the traitors on the other.

When we arrive the situation still seems confusing to our European minds, and I'm really hoping to meet this bishop so he can shed some light on it. But no matter how hard I search, I can't find the place. The taxi drops me at the intersection that Aliocha described, and I try to get my bearings. I survey the streets in the vicinity, asking passers-by the way. In vain. No one speaks English. I mime praying, making the sign of the cross. They take me to a temple. Further on, I try to force my way into a building past security men – the ensuing panic makes me quickly bail out. In China, finding a 'room that's serving temporarily as a place of worship on the second floor of a building', within a radius of 500 metres, is not as simple as I had thought.

Aliocha has also put us in contact with two young French teachers living in Cachei for a year. I rejoin Gabriel at the airport and call them from a mobile phone borrowed from a passer-by: they're keen for us to stay the night with them. The taxi drops us in front of the imposing entrance of a drab, grey apartment block. We look for an ultra-modern online gaming centre, which Claire described to us on the telephone. We guess it's the room on the right with dim, yellowish light shining through the windows. That's where we're supposed to meet them. A uniformed security officer, whose bulging belly hangs out over his belt, raises the barrier and lets us in. A young woman comes to meet us. She's European. It's Claire. She left work early so she can let us into her apartment.

Sitting in the living room, we chat with Claire like old friends. The sun pours in through the bay window, bounces off the parquet floor and floods the room. We French people may be complaining, individualistic, cold and rude to tourists visiting Paris but, as we demonstrate here once more, if nothing else we love our country and are never happier than when we meet up with other French people overseas.

We hit it off immediately with Claire, sense the common bond and feel right at home.

'Do you know Aliocha very well?' she asks.

'No, we don't know him at all. Just through email.'

'Oh, I see. He's got a nerve! He gave you a glowing recommendation and talked as though you'd been friends for years.'

'Surprise!'

'Oh, it's not a big deal. Make yourselves at home, anyway. I live here with Adrien. He's French as well. Did Aliocha tell you what we're doing here?'

'He said you were teachers.'

Claire must be in her late twenties. She has blue eyes and long blonde hair. When she talks, her lips have a slight ironic curl.

'Yes, that's because all emails are read, controlled – there are certain words it's better not to use.'

'Pardon?'

'"Christian", "church", "priest", "missionary" or "Tibet", for example. If you use words like that you can be sure they'll be picked up by the police. And if you want to be absolutely sure, type "Tibetan Christian". I guarantee it'll work every time! Some emails just never turn up!'

In the People's Republic of China, emails can be blocked and numerous websites are inaccessible. The largest communist country in the world doesn't tolerate the expression of divergent opinions. And although the constitution recognizes freedom of worship and conscience, notably forbidding all kinds of discrimination, it's only a façade. In living memory, never has a Catholic, for example, been allowed to join the Communist Party, which means Catholics are unlikely ever to hold senior posts.

'We are teachers, as Aliocha told you. We've been sent here by a Catholic organization. We teach French and English to adults.'

'And is that so secret?'

'Some of the students are Christians but they can't say so. They're "underground". There are also "normal" students who aren't Christians and come to take classes in English, French or Spanish, without knowing who their classmates really are. You have to be very careful what you say.'

'Yes, I can imagine. But why do they need to learn English, French or Spanish?'

'So they can further their studies in Europe, of course. They go on to study philosophy, theology, the Bible. Sometimes also to become part of a religious community, in order to become a nun or a monk. In China the clergy of the underground church obviously can't be trained in the open, which makes things complicated. It's better for them to go overseas for training.'

We can't believe our ears. The organization Claire describes seems to be a real, structured resistance network in opposition to the atheist regime.

Before we left home we met the missionary Father Georges Colomb at the Paris Foreign Missions Society (MEP) headquarters in the Rue du Bac. He had recently been made Superior General. We sat in comfortable leather armchairs, enjoying the Indian cigars he offered us. A great expert on Southern China, he gave us the background we needed to understand what Claire is telling us now. Fortunately, all I had to do was remember the fragrance of the cigar and it all came back to me.

At the beginning of the 1950s, when the People's Republic of China was born, the government expelled virtually all foreign priests. Chinese Catholics were forced to give their allegiance to the new regime. The churches were henceforth answerable to a 'patriotic association', which was committed to breaking off relations with the 'foreign capitalist imperialists' and the Vatican, as well as to the Religious Affairs Bureau, whose function was to oversee the autonomy of the Catholic Churches and ensure that they renounced the Pope's authority. This was part of the famous 'Three-Self Movement' – self-governance, self-support and self-propagation – that became the basis of the development of the Church in China for the following 60 years, right up to today.

The clandestine Church spread as the majority of the Catholic hierarchy refused to break with Rome. In 1957 the government decreed that only those clergy who were members of the 'Three-Self Patriotic Association' would have the right to exercise their ministry and celebrate Mass. Those who refused were hunted down and sent to forced-labour camps.

During the 1960s some priests – appointed by the Religious Affairs Bureau and not by Rome – were ordained bishops of the 'Patriotic Church' by other bishops who had themselves been appointed by the Pope. From the point of view of the sacrament and apostolic succession, these bishops were therefore in line with the Roman Catholic Church. But their ordination did not comply with canon law. The underground Church developed during the 1960s. The existence of the current underground church is simply the logical result of the government's policy on religion and the total lack of religious freedom at that time.

When the Cultural Revolution broke out in 1966, members of all religious groups suffered. Until 1976, the year Mao died, all places of worship were closed and made into meeting rooms at best, factories or pigsties at worst. Religious life was stifled, crushed.

The arrival of Deng Xiaoping in 1978 marked the beginning of a period of openness and reform. And although Christians continued to suffer major repression, places of worship were reopened, public worship resumed and numerous priests were freed. And the market economy finally arrived in China. It makes you realize how terribly far behind China was compared to Taiwan, Hong Kong and Singapore. It's ironic that the political regime only survived thanks to the market economy. The government opened up to foreign investment, and managed to survive thanks to the tax benefits.

It was also during that period that the Chinese elite were trained: students were sent to study in foreign universities and foreign experts were brought to China. That's how missionaries got back into the country: as university professors or engineering tutors they were able to enter China and get in contact with the underground Church. Young seminary students, official and clandestine, were among the students who went overseas to complete their religious training in Europe, in Rome and, notably, Paris.

Since the beginning of the 1990s there has been an unprecedented phenomenon, which has made things even more complex for external observers: some official bishops – that's to say, appointed by the Religious Affairs Bureau – have written to the Pope to ask for recognition from Rome. In the majority of cases the Vatican has accepted, secretly. So now there are official bishops who are recognized by the Catholic Church.

'It must be frustrating for you never to be able to say that you know, and for them not to be able to say that they know that you know.'

Claire smiles.

'Yes, that's the hardest thing. Sometimes we meet in an apartment for Mass. But that's all. We have to limit contact so that they're not spotted, if they haven't been already. For example, I had an appointment to tutor a student. When I told him you would be here, he decided to cancel, saying that something had come up. But actually he was just scared.'

Night has fallen. Neon signs light up all over the city. Large Chinese characters wink in the darkness. The video-games centre on the ground floor of the apartment block is still crowded. Claire and Adrien, the other volunteer, take us to a bar for foreigners in the foreigners' quarter. First Thamel, the backpackers' quarter in Kolkata, then the trekkers' quarter in Kathmandu, and now here we are in the foreigners' quarter in Cachei! We see more Westerners in one evening than we'll see over the next two months.

On my left, two young Chinese women are flirting with a pot-bellied American; he's having a great time. Claire explains that that kind of thing is very common and that the town is full of Westerners who've come to take advantage of the cheap charms of young Chinese women. We order one beer after another, but we're not used to drinking. When our friends suggest finishing the evening at a karaoke, we decline. Too drunk, too tired.

Before leaving for the mountains, we make the last of the visits Aliocha organized for us by proxy. The address is at the other end of town, in a residential quarter where the absolute calm contrasts with the bustle of the streets the night before.

In front of the door, on the ground floor of a building that's the same as all the others with its grey, angular, functional architecture, stand three armed and uniformed policemen. They're not in the least interested in our arrival and don't even interrupt their discussion as we approach to ring the doorbell.

The clatter of dishes comes through from a half-open window. We ring the bell. There's a little knot in our stomachs; we're not sure why.

Behind the door we hear hurried little footsteps on the floor. A tiny little woman of about 60 smiles at us and without saying a word, leads us to the living room. It's a modest apartment – three rooms, perhaps four. The floor is grey lino; the walls are covered with wallpaper with childish motifs and decorated with a calendar of imitation parchment. In the central room there's a small, low table protected with transparent waxed material. A television screen takes centre stage opposite the sofa and three tiny chairs. Behind the living room, in a dark little room, I can make out a red glow of light. Impossible to mistake it – it's the light used in all the temples. The little room is a chapel.

A very old man is sitting on one end of the sofa. Seeing us, he tips his head slightly to one side and smiles.

'What can I do to help you?'

'We're the French guys, friends of Aliocha. We'd love to meet you, that's all. And talk a little, if you have time.'

'I have time. Come. Sit down. Would you like a cup of tea?'

He says a few words in Chinese and our tiny hostess hurries away, scuffing her slippers along the ground, and returns a few minutes later with three bowls of tea. Father Bao speaks impeccable and very precise French. His back is broken and his hump prevents him from sitting straight. His jaw cracks with each word he utters. His cheeks are hollow and his face is dotted with age spots. His body is shrunken and gaunt. In spite of all this he is radiant. His eyes shine with great tenderness and kindness. I get the camera out from the bottom of my bag. Today, I'm filming and Gabriel does the interview.

'Father, would you tell us . . . about your life?'

'Pardon me? I don't understand.'

He is almost totally deaf. Gabriel gets out a little scrap of paper and scribbles his question in two words: 'Your life?'

'My life? You want to know about my life? Is that it?'

'Yes, only what you would like to tell us.'

'It's a long story . . .'

'We've got plenty of time.'

He bows his head and closes his eyes, as if he's dipping deep into his memory to find the right words.

'I was born in 1918, into a very fervent Christian family. We lived in a little village. Very early on I knew I was called to be a priest. I went to a Catholic secondary school and then straight on to seminary. That's where I learned French; our teachers were members of the order of St Sulpice in Paris.'

He was ordained a priest in 1944. After the communists took over in 1950, he felt he was being watched. His comings and goings were observed by minions of the new government.

'I had some freedom, but I wasn't allowed to leave town. I knew they didn't like me meeting with foreigners, but I didn't know what else to do other than continuing to work with the missionaries.'

In April 1957 he was accused of being a 'running dog' for the capitalist imperialists and arrested. After a year's detention he was finally judged and condemned to ten years' forced labour. It was to be 26 years.

'When I was first in prison, I started off complaining about my lot. I grumbled to myself that I had always been faithful to God, and I didn't understand why he was treating me like that. Why had he allowed me to be imprisoned while I was serving him and serving his people? I went through a period of very painful doubting. But quite quickly I realized that in his great goodness, he was protecting me. Outside, everyone ended up denying their faith. The Party manipulated the media, which spread messages against our faith. Many Christians could not bear this persecution and lived with fear in their hearts, tormented with intolerable lies and threats.

'Certainly I could no longer pray as I used to – they had taken my rosary, my cross, my devotional books – but I kept my faith completely intact, safe within me. I started praying the Rosary, counting on my fingers, and I made use of reduced surveillance on national holidays to sing – discreetly – the Latin hymns the missionaries had taught me. But I was unable to celebrate Mass for 26 years because there was no way of getting wine or bread; I received the Holy Sacrament spiritually. When I got out of prison, a priest gave me an Order of Mass written in Chinese! I was amazed! Before my incarceration, they were all in Latin! I had never said Mass in Chinese!'

Father Bao is very restrained about the conditions of his imprisonment; he doesn't give any details about the treatment he was subjected to. However, he doesn't have to say much for us to feel moved with pity for him and awed by his heroism. But he's not one to seek the praise of others.

Gabriel and I have both read books in the past about the persecution the Church in China suffered. They give a very accurate picture of the horrors of torture, interminable interrogation sessions, the jailers' shouting, spitting, routine beatings, the cells and solitary confinement, prisoners being kept awake for days on end to break their will, the insults, the unfounded accusations, the false confessions they were forced to sign, the courses of re-education and indoctrination. Detention in Chinese jails was an assault not only on their bodies but also on their reason: they were brainwashed to spout communist ideology, the only acceptable philosophy.

'Communism is a virus that threatens the fundamental values that Christianity has given to mankind, to the extent that the very existence of Christianity and every other religion is threatened.'

While the situation today is immeasurably better than in the time of the Maoist Cultural Revolution, the fact remains that at least 20 or 30 bishops, priests and lay people are still detained, under house arrest, or kept apart in isolated parts of the country. And some have not been heard of for years. They have disappeared.

When he came out of prison in 1983, they forced Father Bao to go back to the church where he had been the priest.

'That was a shock. I was astonished because the church was no longer Catholic but Patriotic. It had become a government church. I said that I would rather go back to prison than stay there, but they gave me no choice. Since I had no ministry in the official Church I had to earn a living doing little jobs. At first I was a nightwatchman. I had to watch over a parking lot with 100 buses. Then, after a few months, I went to work in a factory. My salary was very low, the equivalent of $40 today – hardly enough to survive on. When I was sick, I couldn't buy medicines or go to hospital.'

After four years some Catholic families took pity on him and begged him to let them take care of him.

'They told me this wasn't the right job for me. That I was too respectable! They said they were going to provide for me and I would no longer need to work. So I was then able to take up my ministry as a priest. I began visiting Christians again. I even travelled to other provinces because there was a shortage of priests everywhere. But

I always refused the government's offers, and I always refused to talk to the heads of the Patriotic Church. I'm very stubborn!'

At this he gives a mischievous giggle.

'Once, during an interrogation, they told me the government knew I was very stubborn, but since I wasn't doing anything wrong they couldn't put me back in prison! Still today I'm under surveillance and constantly guarded. When I go away to meet with Christians, I always run a slight risk of being arrested again. And as I can't walk, I need a car to drop me at the front door of the church! It's quite complicated!'

He laughs heartily.

'Young priests write to me and come to visit me. In this region there are four dioceses but there have been no bishops for a long time, except here at Cachei. But that bishop is not in communion with Rome! The Pope secretly appointed me Apostolic Administrator of the four dioceses. The apostolic representative on whom I depend told me that I must stay on, whatever happens, and that it was my duty. But he added: "Just do what you can, because I know it's difficult. The Holy Father is asking you to do your best." Since the consecration of the official bishop of Cachei, I'm no longer allowed to leave the city. It's a way of keeping an eye on me.'

He is extremely endearing and we listen very carefully to his clipped speech. Father Bao confides that he's extremely happy to be a priest. He says that it's a difficult task but a great honour at the same time; that he's not worthy of it but he knows God has called him. For him there is no greater joy than working for his Church and seeing people turn to God.

'Doing the will of God is a great joy for me. I will honour my duty towards Christians until the end! In the last five years I have had two car accidents. The first time it wasn't serious, but the second time I should have died on the spot. Several ribs were bruised and the bottom of my spine was broken. At the hospital a nurse said to me: "It's a wonder you didn't die at the time of the accident. It's a miracle! Your God is powerful!" I think the Lord spared me so that I could continue my work. The Church's situation in China is very difficult and Christians still need me!'

In spite of all the difficulties he's not fatalistic.

'I have great faith in God. The Church in China is going to flourish, more than anywhere else, because here in China we've had a lot of martyrs! And there are still priests and bishops in prison today. I still have the hope of seeing a radiant Church in China. I'm very optimistic about the future. This is the paradox at the heart of the Christian view of suffering: suffering doesn't have the last word, it can be a trampoline to joy.'

The jovial air of this man who has been bruised and battered by life, wounded a thousand times over, expresses it better than any catechism. His story is one long series of sorrows and sufferings; it's also a story of joy and lasting peace. Difficult to explain and yet undeniable. We can see it for ourselves.

Since our meeting with Father Bao there have been further developments in China. Pope Benedict XVI, in his letter to Chinese Catholics in 2007, pleaded for greater unity within the Church in China and assured the openness of the Pope towards the official bishops who want to be in communion with Rome. His letter, passed illicitly around all the Catholic communities in the country, met with an overwhelmingly favourable response among both lay people and clerics. But the Patriotic Church has again recently ordained illegitimate bishops, thus directly and openly opposing the will of Rome. There are still some who remain uncooperative. The situation is far from being resolved. It has even been called a 'great leap backwards'.

Meanwhile, I make my own great leap forward: while preparing to write this book, almost two years after we returned from our journey, I met Father Charbonnier at the Rue du Bac. He's a former missionary with MEP in Singapore who has made numerous trips to China. I asked him some questions about the situation of the Church in China, and his answers gave me some new insights.

'The real problem in the journey towards reconciliation is the bishops' lack of authority. The priests are the ones who have authority over their community, the people who know them and follow them. Some of those priests abuse their position. They don't always obey their bishops, and some of their behaviour is quite unbiblical. Among the underground clergy, some are completely opposed to the idea of reconciliation with the Patriotic clergy.'

The opposite is doubtless true as well. He explains that the bishops' lack of authority is, in the end, a natural consequence of the government's behaviour towards the Church since the birth of communism in China. The appointment of official bishops has always been either by direct appointment or under very strict control: they were never expected to be leaders. In the eyes of their community, therefore, they lack credibility.

According to him, the current danger has arisen from the most recently appointed bishops. Many of them are real priests, popular with the Christians and doing a good job in their calling. They think that what's happening in the Chinese Church is better than what's going on in Europe, and therefore feel they have nothing to learn from foreigners. So some willingly accept being appointed by the government while persuading themselves that they're in line with the gospel. They're the ones who directly threaten the unity of the Church.

'In spite of everything, I am optimistic. There have been rifts before in the history of the Church. We will succeed in surmounting this difficulty as well! But we must at all costs avoid definitively cutting ourselves off from each other. I think it's essential that we maintain contact with both the clandestine Church and the official Church, and work with what's happening in practice. We must not conjure up an image of the Chinese Church as we'd like it to be, but rather see what is actually being done there, what is really happening. And apart from that we just have to wait for a few years, and be patient! We have to have a vision of the whole lifespan of the Church and the faith of the believers, which is very solid, and not interfere in a situation about which we understand very little. We're foreigners. It's a Chinese problem that must be sorted out by the Chinese. The Pope's letter is certainly a step in the right direction. They must find unity for the Church in their country for themselves.'

We leave our bikes with Claire and Adrien in Cachei and take an overnight bus for the long trip to the city of Shangri-La, where we'll finally meet Aliocha. It's a night coach fitted out with 40 mini-bunks with duvets and pillows. Unfortunately it's difficult for our large frames to adjust to Chinese proportions. Apart from spending the night in the centre aisle, all we can do is curl up with our knees under our chins. We dreamed of having a sweet peasant girl sitting next to us, but what we get is a stunning transsexual who makes eyes at Gabriel. All night our room companions smoke, drink, play cards and spit huge gobs of phlegm into the aisle. We bury our heads between the mattress and our polar fleeces and get what sleep we can.

On a short stop in the middle of the night we discover an unfortunate invention: an open-air septic tank. A real treat. The structure is long and narrow and the smell is acrid, as you might expect. No door. The user squats and the excrement drops four metres down into a ditch. The experience is made all the more charming by the howls and belches of the Chinese as they go about their business. Enough to turn you off everything. As I make a quick getaway I hear a nasal voice shouting. It's the little woman who looks after the toilets, sitting in her little grey hut; her head barely reaches the counter. Soon I realize she's actually standing up! She advances, treating me to more of her expletives. Fifty centimes per visit. Perhaps it's her attitude that's upset me; anyway, I vomit before getting back on the bus.

Our bus drops us in Shangri-La. We wander the city streets. The centre is full of stone houses with exposed wooden beams; nothing like Cachei and its great, wide, soulless streets. Aliocha rents a room in a guesthouse perched high above the town. His landlady greets us. She isn't Tibetan but Lhotse, and has some broken English.

'Aliocha not here. Come back tonight. Often go walk alone.'

She takes us to the wooden veranda in front of our host's room so we can relax there. Anticipating our arrival, Aliocha has been kind enough to put our Christmas presents, sent by our family and friends, outside his room. A month ago, through our blog, we started a major campaign: Operation Christmas. We launched an emotional appeal for goodies, giving our loved ones Aliocha's address so they could send them to us there.

The biggest hardship of the trip so far isn't the distance we have to ride, the dirt and grime or the hunger. In fact it's the desperate lack of chocolate, Comté cheese, camembert, bread, pâté and Pimm's that hurts the most.

We can't believe our eyes. There aren't just one or two packages waiting for us, but ten! We unwrap them feverishly and find all kinds of goodies: champagne, a bottle of Jurançon wine, foie gras, pâté, calissons (candied fruit and almond sweets), letters, books. Christmas promises to be a right royal banquet!

I nod off to sleep on the terrace while Gabriel updates our blog on the landlady's computer. It's disturbing that we're able to connect to the internet wherever we go. The idea of being isolated is romantic; imagined, but quite imaginary. With one or two clicks I find out that my little sister is in love, the President is at an international summit, our friend Antoine wants to join us, and the college students' election campaign is underway. It's very tempting to slip back into what we're used to in France, and worry about what other people think. Whereas the whole point of this trip is to focus on something other than ourselves; to become 'others-centred'; to free our hearts and minds so we can see new possibilities in each discovery, each new encounter. I had dreamed of making a leap into the unknown, an initiation year in which I would be changed. But I realize increasingly that if we're not careful, the internet, like an elastic band, will snap us back to our point of attachment as soon as we move too far away.

Aliocha arrives when it's already dark. He's adopted the suave adventurer look with a thick woollen khaki military jersey and Indiana Jones-style felt hat. Black glasses frame his gentle, blue eyes. He's not very chatty and likes his solitude. But even the toughest bear enjoys company sometimes, especially when Christmas is coming. He takes us for drinks and dinner at a bar where he knows the waitress. Aliocha works for an NGO. He walks from village to village looking for new children for sponsorship. The day after tomorrow, he's leaving for a 'tour of the villages' and taking us with him. Theresa, a young Tibetan woman who speaks broken English, is coming as well to interpret for him.

And, surprisingly, many of them are Christian villages.

# 10

## Tibetan borders

## In which we celebrate Christmas in a church with no priests

12 December, 5 months and 7 days after departure

### Third isolated community: Tibetan borders

An old lady, whose face is covered all over with wrinkles, pours each person a glass of wine. Grape wine. Real wine. It's made from the vines we saw lower down the valley. Nothing like our Bordeaux, but still, it's pleasant, sweet and alcoholic. I'm in heaven. Clearly it doesn't take much to keep me happy. Since we left Shangri-La with Aliocha and Theresa,[1] we've gone from one village to the next, welcomed everywhere like VIPs.

We're gathered in a dark room lit only by the fading light of day. The walls are black with soot. Perched on tiny stools around a brazier, we stretch out our hands to its heat. Peter, the head of the household, carries himself with quiet dignity; we fall silent in his presence. On top of his black hair he wears a scrap of shapeless grey fur, tattered and worn down to bare skin in places. He's a thin man, quite tall given the average height in these parts. His face is twisted out of shape, his left eyelid droops.

Peter gets up from his stool with great effort and from a shelf takes a dusty old album. It's full of photos, yellowed with age, of men with muscular physiques and dark clothing. They look like soldiers of the French foreign legion. Others resemble absent-minded professors with their bushy beards and pipes hanging from their lips. These French missionaries arrived in the mid nineteenth century. In 1952

---

[1] The names of people and places have been changed.

the communists kicked them out of China and sent the few indigenous priests to the *laogai*, the infamous Chinese gulag. They left behind thousands of converts. And over 50 years later the flame of the faith still burns in the Salween Valley, the gateway to Tibet, even though there are no priests left to administer the sacraments.

Peter gently caresses the pages of the album. He's wistful, full of respect for these men. He is one of the last surviving members of his community who lived through that era. Little by little, through these pages, these unknown men, long since dead, come to life again through Peter's words.

'Look! Here's Maurice Tornay, the last curate of the little Tibetan town of Yerkalo. He was killed by the Lamas, zealous Buddhist leaders, as he fled in 1949. He was on his way to visit the Dalai Lama to request a decree of religious tolerance to protect Tibetan Christians from persecution.'

Maurice Tornay stands with his brothers in arms, other hardy priests who came to live in the mountains, voluntary martyrs. On the following pages, Peter shows us some of the picturesque little churches built on the banks of the Salween River; they're very plain, some have one bell tower, some two. In the foreground of one of the photos we spot Father Bao, whom we met earlier in Cachei.

'That church is one of many built at Father Bao's instigation,' Peter remarks, his voice muted, full of admiration.

In the early 1950s, when Maoist China closed itself off to the rest of the world, darkness descended on these already isolated valleys – the passes are closed for several months over the winter and the terrain is brutal, punishing. The few remaining missionaries were expelled, their churches destroyed, and the local Christians were forbidden to gather for worship. Some faced 20 years in the *laogai*, others a dangerous escape through the mountains to India, most often on foot: the Way of the Cross on the path towards freedom of religion for all Tibetans.

'When he was young, my father fled to India to avoid imprisonment. He's considered a hero, an absolute legend. He escaped with several friends, taking some hunting rifles left behind by the missionaries. Some went on to India while others chose to head for Burma. The journey took over a year. It was fraught with danger: they were attacked by bandits, by wild animals. One of his companions died on the way. My father eventually managed to leave the country. He was taken in by missionaries. For 20 years he couldn't give any sign that he was still alive. When he was allowed to return home, about 15 years ago, he hadn't seen or heard from his wife and children for 30 years. Since the missionaries had all been permanently driven out of the valley, my father became the patriarch of the Salween Christians. He died last year. Now I've taken over the role.'

Surrounded by dizzyingly steep mountains whose peaks are perpetually snow-covered, the Salween River flows parallel to the Tibetan-Burmese border. The 30 million inhabitants of the region form a mosaic of ethnicities and religions: the Dulong, Lisu, Loutse, Tibetans and Han Chinese, of whom 4,000 are professing Catholics. We can make out, through the distant mist, little churches standing proudly along the flank of the valley.

Peter drives us in his big black jeep. Smiling, he brings it to a gentle stop on the roadside. He takes several steps to a hollow in the rock underfoot. Here lay the body of Father Durand, an MEP priest, killed by some Lamas as he fled, crossing the river with the help of a Tyrolean woman. His corpse was fished up out of the water by some Buddhist friends, who laid him to rest here under these cliffs. A few kilometres further on we stop outside a newly built chapel. The wall frescoes are the work of Michel, Peter's son, who is renovating the sacred paintings in all the churches in the area. Here we find the grave of the legendary Father Genestier, whose memory hovers over the valley. He was also an MEP missionary, and his enormous beard still fires the imagination of his beardless followers today. He was also a great hunter.

Peter stops his 4x4 in a village for the night. Officially we're all accompanying Aliocha as he visits the villages to check on the children sponsored by his NGO. He has to give them some money to cover their school fees and find out how their families are getting on. So there are six of us: Peter, Aliocha, Theresa, Jacob (who is a seminary student), Gabriel and myself. From here we're only a few hundred metres from the route that leads to the forbidden Tibet, so close now that we're sure nothing will stop us from entering. What seemed to us only a few months ago to be the ends of the earth is now only a few minutes away, as the crow flies, and what seemed only a short while ago to be an extreme adventure has become, through the simple unfolding of everyday events, a natural extension of our journey. Each day is certainly different from the one before, and from what we've always known, but for these people it's simply everyday life. In a few days' time we'll enter the legendary land of Tibet, and it will all seem completely normal.

The little village church looks out over the alpine valley and the silvery mist that engulfs it, little by little, as evening draws in. There's another grave behind the church, the resting place of a Chinese priest, Father Li. The story goes that when he learnt that the communists were on their way to arrest him he prayed and said Mass for a week. At the end of the seven days, he died of natural causes. It seems to us that every corner of the valley has been the scene of extraordinary happenings. If they now told us that the trees had been heard to sing in the night-time or that the animals could talk, we'd believe them. We're welcomed by Dawa, the local *huizhang* – the head of the community, in charge of the village parish. The Salween Christians have no priests but there's no shortage of pastors. They've managed to keep the spark of faith alive, as it has been handed down to them. Each village has its own church and Bible teacher. Peter, as the head of the mother parish, is the coordinator, or patriarch. Dawa is dubbed Double Thumb – his right hand has two thumbs. He has a round face, a cigarette drooping from his lips. He wears an old army jacket stiff with dirt. On his porch I notice a crossbow and a quiver full of little wooden arrows with straw vanes, which I imagine must be fast and deadly. Their tips are dipped in poison.

'Father Genestier used similar arrows in his combat against the Lamas. These days they're used more for hunting,' says Peter as we enter our host's house. Dawa's wife wears a pink hair-slide. A fire is burning in the middle of the room, giving a cheerful warmth.

We gather around the fire, where a pot of water is boiling, suspended from a tripod. The excitement is palpable. After we've eaten several bowls of rice and a few tasty scraps of meat, dripping with fat, we'll have earned the right to taste their mythical chicken claw wine. You absolutely must taste chicken claw wine before you die. We had a hot soup fortified with the chicken claw grain wine, with little scraps of chicken bobbing around on top. The sight is enough to turn our stomachs. We adopt a tried and true technique: positive digestive

**The dawn mist rises from the church belfries standing sentinel over the valley**

thinking. 'Yes, Gabriel, it's delicious. I can assure you, it's really good.' Meanwhile Aliocha is attempting to update his files on his sponsored children. But the family are already half-drunk and they give the most ridiculous answers to his questions. And no matter how many grandparents, neighbours and family friends they ask, they cannot come up with the baby's date of birth. Sitting on my right, Theresa is totally drunk, alternating between bouts of vulgar coughing and hiccupping. She mews, giggles and hiccups some more.

We move to another house and enter in strict single file. Our host stirs up the fire, throwing on a pile of branches, and from a dark corner he brings out a jar full of a clear yellow distillate. Sitting around the flames, we help ourselves as best we can. This time the alcohol is made from maize and everyone takes a swig before passing the bottle to his neighbour. I summon up every ounce of willpower I possess. The aim is to hang on until we get to the last family; it's not every day that Peter and Aliocha come up to the valley, and it would be unthinkable for them not to visit every home. It's going to be a long night; a hangover is inevitable. An old man, dressed in rags stiff with grime, splutters droplets of liquor over my face as he pours Gabriel more drink. Peter drags deeply on his bamboo pipe while Jacob, the seminary student, explains to Gabriel that refusing a drink would be a terrible offence to our hosts. Hic!

Jacob is in his twenties. He has slightly buck teeth and a mischievous look in his eyes. He's wearing a light blue tracksuit and imitation Nikes. His situation is sadly ironic: these people have been denied a priest for several decades and yet young men like him who feel called to the priesthood can't be ordained.

'I have finished my studies in seminary, but my bishop is not in communion with Rome. Jesus showed us the way – the succession of authority since St Peter. A bishop appointed by a government isn't a disciple of Christ! I don't want to be ordained by the government, so I just have to suffer in silence.'

In the meantime, Jacob serves the community and assists with Mass. He lives with Peter's family, helping him in all his activities. For Jacob there are only two possible ways out: the bishop's death or his appointment elsewhere. Late in the night we bed down on the floor of the parish hall with our bags for pillows. In spite of the sub-zero temperature outside, we don't need a brazier to keep us warm, thanks to the chicken claw wine.

The next morning we temporarily separate from the group, leaving Aliocha and Peter to continue their rounds while we spend a few days with a family from another village. Noah, a friend of Aliocha, is expecting us. We part, promising to meet up again just before Christmas. With no telephones, it's important to make an arrangement and stick to it.

'On the evening of the twenty-fourth, in Pi,' shouts Aliocha through the window as the 4x4 hurtles off with Peter at the wheel and Jacob smiling and waving from the back seat. 'You'll see what an amazing family Noah has.'

We walk for an hour along a dirt road and cross a footbridge over a river. The track widens and we're soon picked up by a beaten-up truck going in our direction. It's laden with equipment. We squeeze into the cab with the driver on one side and a lady with big rosy-red cheeks and a mentally handicapped man on the other. The woman talks and laughs loudly. She opens a packet of sunflower seeds and tips a handful into my palm. We strike a pothole, the truck lurches, and half of them fall on the floor. Roars of laughter from my companions, who poke fun at my clumsiness. The road peters out and the truck continues its rodeo ride across a wide, open prairie. Finally we stop in front of a miserable little wooden cabin, which we understand serves as a sort of base camp for workmen in the surrounding area. But we're in the middle of nowhere, far from anything that bears any resemblance to a construction site. They tell us that Noah will be arriving soon. While we wait, we drink tea, again, and eat, again. In his father's arms, an adorable little tot chews on a one-yuan note.

Noah finally appears, followed by a whole team of Chinese engineers who are bringing electricity to the valley. He's acting as their guide and we join the procession. Noah contrasts with the drunkards we've met since we arrived. For one thing, he's sober, which is quite rare in these parts. His hair is dishevelled and he has a thin moustache. When he sees us he breaks into a broad smile and a peal of silvery laughter. He is dignified; his face is intelligent and full of goodness. Noah is 35 years old but looks ten years younger. He carries a machete in his belt and when he speaks his voice is assured and warm. He doesn't waste words.

Noah is married to Catherine, and they have a little Joseph and a tiny Mary. No, I'm not making it up! And in this season of Advent, a few days before Christmas, the family gather around the fire in the main room each evening. They pray to the Virgin, reciting the Rosary, and we all say the Laudate Dominum, from Psalm 117, which is taught by the missionaries and made all the more delightful by their Tibetan accent.

The Chinese engineers continue on their way early the next morning and we leave with Noah, who wears his machete in his belt and holds Mary's hand as she trots along after him. It's 24 December, and it's Noah's responsibility as the village Bible teacher to get everything ready for the celebrations in the church this evening. There will be no Mass, of course, because they don't have a priest, but that doesn't mean they won't celebrate Christmas joyfully, in the proper way. We follow long, winding roads through dense forest before finally entering a clearing that overlooks a superb little chapel. With the rain and the cold, the wood has worked loose; Noah gives the hinges a good kick and the door shudders before reluctantly opening.

We discover a well-kept interior, carefully decorated. The altar is dusty; it hasn't been used for many years. Noah steps outside again, draws his machete and chops down several leafy bay-laurel branches, which he lays around a stage to the right of the altar. Then he rings the bell, to Mary's great delight. A procession of men and women appears out of nowhere. Their baskets, which hang down their backs from their foreheads, are full of branches, leaves and lichen to fashion a nativity scene. The result is certainly worthy of the name. Noah carefully positions the nativity figures while others are busy polishing the stone floor of their little church. It's going be a great celebration.

We head back down to Pi to keep the arrangement we made with Aliocha several days earlier. As we pass the houses on the outskirts of the village, three women with toothless smiles stop us. They're blind drunk. They try to make us swallow a glass of fire water in one gulp. Fire water? That's new. Somehow we manage to resist but they cry, beg, bat their eyelashes, spray us in the face with their not particularly fresh breath, and grab hold of our clenched fists, forcing a tiny glass into our hands. Well, 'a woman's will is God's will', as the French saying goes. We comply. It's not called 'fire water' for nothing.

We find Aliocha eating with Bonne-Maman's family. Contrary to all expectation, 'Bonne-Maman' ('grandmother' in French of course) is a young woman with fine features. She's the perfect hostess, attending to her guests' every need. She's also an excellent cook and good company. Every time Aliocha visits, he stays with Bonne-Maman for several days. Sitting down to the leftovers from a sumptuous lunch, Aliocha, Bonne-Maman and the rest of the family invite us to join them for one more drink.

'Come on, you Frogs, it's Christmas!'

We nibble some sweets and raise our glasses without noticing the time pass. Bonne-Maman brings out a sort of Tibetan blood sausage cooked in pork fat. The conversation becomes passionate; they hammer their fists on the table, loll their heads backwards and laugh more and more raucously. With bleary eyes, and vocal chords well oiled by the chicken claw wine, they burst into song. Then it's our turn. We sing French songs. No one is bothered by the eclectic mix: drinking songs, Christmas carols, bawdy choruses, Christian songs. The ambiance is electric; they're all as excited as puppies and bursting with happiness.

It's seven o'clock. Time for the first service. We make our way together with slightly unsteady steps towards the village church, our cheeks rosy and our lungs lightly scalded by the glacial evening breeze. The church in Pi fills little by little. The ground is bare earth, the walls are of stone. The roof is supported by thick octagonal timber columns, painted in pastel tones. Rustic wooden benches are arranged in rows on each side of the central aisle – men on the right, women on the left. In the middle, an altar covered with bouquets stands on a raised platform overlooking the nave. A nativity scene, set in front of the chancel, takes centre stage, and behind it hangs a painting of the nativity. The lighting is soft and the colours warm. Some are praying with all their hearts, others stand at the back of the church talking a little too loudly. Some are out cold from an excess of alcohol. They failed to limit their intake enough to enable them to make it through the night. They're dozing, propped up against a wall. The chapel is jam-packed and the bells ring out joyfully around the valley, joining those of Noah's and Dawa's villages, and those of the 4,000 other Tibetan Christians who are celebrating Christmas tonight.

At the end of this first service, Aliocha and Gabriel head off to rest for an hour while I stick my head into icy water in an attempt to control my nausea. I pace back and forth reciting the Rosary under the stars, in the silence of this unique night on the roof of the world.

Midnight. The second ceremony begins. It seems to be exactly the same as the first, but that's probably because we don't understand everything. The women are dressed in their traditional headdresses and some wear a fur belt over their brightly coloured outfits. An older man preaches – it's his turn to speak on Christmas Day, but he too seems overcome with tiredness and alcohol. He goes on, though no one's listening any more, and the master of ceremonies and village catechist signals to him that he's talked long enough. Frustrated, he frowns and sits back down.

I think of my own family attending Mass in our parish in Paris. Every Easter Vigil, my father sings the old Easter songs at the top of his voice – no matter if he bursts his neighbours' eardrums.

The catechist leads the worship with a clear, strong voice, singing a hymn that we know very well: *Il est né le divin enfant* ('The holy child is born'). Of course! A hundred years ago the missionaries taught their flock our French songs and translated them into Tibetan. Now they're part of the heritage that has been passed down from generation to generation. This celebration, which brings these families together, takes us back to our own families far away and yet so close. And now, singing heartily like my father, we pronounce the words of the song in French, which amazes our neighbours. They can't believe their ears.

When Gabriel and I were children, expatriates in Japan with our families, we sometimes went to Mass with the Franciscan community in Tokyo. After each service the celebrant would welcome newcomers and remind the congregation, composed mostly of foreigners, that this was their 'church home away from home'.

Visiting church after church over the last six months, we've dined and talked with hundreds of priests, monks and lay people. We've experienced several forms of worship, some of which didn't do much for us, prayed in dozens of languages and encountered cultural differences that have demonstrated a huge gulf between us and our hosts. The Tibetans are no exception and, in spite of our curiosity and numerous questions, we don't really understand much of the day-to-day reality of their lives.

And yet every time we enter a church and every time we meet a priest or monk, the same minor miracle is repeated: we feel at home. Beyond the enormous differences that separate us from this community on the other side of the world, we're at one with the Essence. We're far from our families, but this evening, at Christmas time, we feel somehow at home.

After the celebration, everyone gathers in front of the doors of the church. I can't understand why everyone is looking up at the stars. Suddenly a boom shreds the stillness of the night, and then a second, followed by dozens more. The sky lights up with plumes of fire and bursts of multi-coloured shooting stars. With every new skyrocket, the villagers' faces shine and the children squeal with delight. These families are poor but, at Christmas time, they treat themselves to a superb fireworks show.

Suddenly bells ring all around the valley. Jesus is born!

We creep soundlessly out of Bonne-Maman's house so as not to wake the sleepers exhausted from the festivities of the day before, and make our way on foot to join Peter, Jacob and their community.

The town of A. is the rallying point for the Christians of the Salween Valley. It's the largest Christian community living in a town rather than in shacks in the villages. When we arrive, Peter and Jacob are finishing their preparations for the ceremony. Peter has a little blue book in his hand.

'This is the book of daily readings for the year. It tells us which reading to use every day.'

Peter leads the service. He preaches with passion. We recite the readings for the day, sing a few hymns and pray. Without a priest, there's no Eucharist; we finish with a prayer to the Virgin Mary. The rhythmic, toneless chant reminds me strangely of Buddhist mantras.

The church in A. lacks the charm of those in the surrounding villages. It has three towers of imitation grey stone, each topped with a gold cross. For Christmas, streamers have been strung between the

**Boxing Day at the gateway to the Himalayas**

bell towers. The women are sitting together on the steps. The men stand chatting in groups and some pull out cigarettes. Most wear workers' caps of khaki or navy blue. Grandmothers keep an eye on the children playing. The little girls are gorgeous, dressed in mauve dresses with fur cuffs, and thick headbands of red, black and yellow wool. Jacob lights a big fire over which they boil up litres of chicken claw wine. A young woman passes by with a large pot of rice.

When everyone is well fed and watered, they make a circle around the fire. The men echo the women's actions. They don't sing, they shout, as if to outdo each other. The circle turns and they start to sway. They dance passionately, with Jacob in the lead.

We're touched by the faith and tenacity of these people. In 2002, when the construction of the church began, there were fewer than a dozen Christians in A. They have no right of assembly and each community needs at least 60 believers before they can apply to build a church. Conscious of the importance of having a place of worship, Peter, through sheer persistence, obtained the necessary authorization and carried out the work. Seven years later, over 200 Christians meet

**The Tibetans give the Karen people a magnificent Virgin Mary – truly unique**

together in the church each Sunday. Perseverance and boldness pay off: the number of Christians is growing despite the lack of priests and the expulsion of the missionaries.

The men who were supposed to pick us up at seven thirty this morning arrive half an hour late, but at least they've come. We sit in the front while the other passengers pile into the back, on top of lots of parcels and boxes. It's very cold. The road is rough but impressive. Not a soul in sight, not a sound, apart from the throb of the engine, which stalls from time to time. Sometimes we have to stop and clear the road of the debris from recent rock falls.

The Salween flows through chaotic terrain. The water is grey-green, the beaches black. The silence is absolute. Our truck drops us at Tsa at three in the afternoon. This is the last Chinese town before we reach the part of Tibet they call 'Autonomous'. When Pierre left us, he warned us to be careful. There would be police checkpoints on the road. But so far, nothing. Now we just have to cross the border and then the rest will be on foot.

We want to get to Yerkalo, the only Catholic parish in Tibet, where Maurice Tornay was the last curate before he was assassinated by the Lamas in 1949. There are now only three of us undertaking this long march. Theresa has gone home and Peter and Jacob stayed in A. Aliocha sets the pace; we follow. Multi-coloured flags float in the wind and carry the Buddhists' prayers to the heavens. We pass through a village; the houses are a brilliant white with brightly coloured window frames.

We come across a Buddhist nun, then a second. Their monastery is just a stone's throw away; they welcome us very naturally. One nun is sitting in the temple. Reading from little square pieces of paper, she recites prayers with a muted voice, to the rhythm of an enormous drum. The nuns, whose heads are shaved, laugh good-naturedly. Hens strut around in the courtyard: there's no killing of animals here.

Seated on a cushion inside a tiny wooden cell, I'm writing page after page in our journal – 'writing up the day' as Gabriel and I call it. Tomorrow it will be his turn. Our little nun friend can't believe her eyes. She leans over my shoulder, trying to decipher the strange hieroglyphics. She laughs at herself and out of a drawer she pulls a few old dog-eared photos of her family. I take some of my own out from my pannier. We exchange photos and make comments each in our own language, with lots of oohing and aahing. We're both delighted. I mime my place in my family, showing with my hand that the others are smaller than me. She understands and giggles. I laugh too.

Our hostess makes up three beds on the parquet floor and we share a meal of rice, fried bacon and potatoes from our provisions, before blowing out the lantern. I have to say that it's the first time we've slept with a nun.

The next morning we reach the first pass, at 3,300 metres. A tangled confusion of flags awaits us on the other side. We're on the trail around Kawa Karpo, a holy mountain and place of pilgrimage that lies between the Salween and the Mekong rivers. Looming ahead of us is an enormous mass of rock. It's covered in dust and scree. Rising to over 3,000 metres, it stands with its feet in the water and its head in the clouds. We savour the beauty of creation: everything around us is spectacular and totally astounding. There are a few lonely pines growing on the peak; the Tibetans, who are expert craftsmen, cut them down, prune them and throw them, end over end, down to the valley.

The further we go the fewer Westerners we see on the trail. The welcome we receive differs dramatically from one village to another. Some people slam the door in our faces, some are constantly after money. Others offer us bed and board without hesitation. Tibetan houses are enormous – as oversized as the scenery that surrounds them. They're built of stone, with several stories and a flat roof covered with earth to insulate them from the cold and conserve heat. Inside there are several large rooms, including a living room with colourful designs on the walls. The animals are kept on the ground floor in a stable that opens out on to an enclosure attached to the house.

Darkness will soon fall and we haven't seen a single soul for several hours. Aliocha quickens his pace. Without a tent there's no question of sleeping outside in these temperatures. If we don't find somewhere to stay we'll have to keep walking all night, stopping only for short periods so that we don't freeze to death. It looks as though the weather's going to be particularly bad overnight. My legs are stiff, my muscles are aching; I'm so tired my head is throbbing. I'd give anything for a bed, two litres of water and a hot chocolate. The valley is oblivious to our struggles, insignificant little beings that we are. 'When I am weak, then I am strong.' I ponder this verse nearly every day. It rises up from deep within me while my brain is in sleep mode for an hour or so, and I try to forget my aching back and my too heavy pack. Once again we feel small, vulnerable, at the mercy of the next downpour. We're reduced to dust before the immensity that is Tibet. It's when I'm weak that I turn to God for help. When I'm weak I am most able to allow God to guide me. And above all it's when I'm weak that I let myself be filled, by others and by God. My mind, foggy with tiredness, frames a barely coherent prayer, 'Please . . . a house, somewhere warm . . .'

It happens again and again. Over the last six months we've hardly ever had to sleep rough and never had to pay for a hotel or hostel.

'Look! Over there! There are two houses!'

Suddenly Aliocha, who is well ahead of us, turns to shout the good news.

*Alhamdulillah* – God is great, as Muslims say. Just when we're feeling tiny, insignificant, here we are revived, energized, invincible.

'Damn. No one here. That's impossible . . .'

The first house is empty but a wisp of smoke is rising from the chimney of the second. We rush towards the door. The man of the house is not yet home but the wife and children smile benignly at us and signal for us to sit down. They had prepared dinner for four. Now there are seven of us but it doesn't seem to worry them. The husband arrives a few minutes after us and, after an initial look of surprise, lets us know that we're welcome, with much smiling and bowing. Gabriel and I go off to wash our feet, tired and sore after this long walk in inadequate shoes. The low wall around the well is covered with snow. We let the metal bucket down and pull up pure, fresh – albeit glacial – water.

By way of an aperitif our hostess serves us the traditional yak's butter tea. In a hollow tree trunk about a metre high she mixes hot water with yak's butter, stirring it from top to bottom with a huge wooden spatula. Like zombies we watch her without batting an eyelid. The result is startling the first time we taste it, but we get used to it and end up asking for more. After the meal our host taps Gabriel on the shoulder and starts making shrill braying sounds. He waves his hands above his head and taps his feet up and down on the ground. We stare at him, speechless. The children burst out laughing. Ah, so you want to play a game of charades!

'A donkey. You're a donkey. Right?'

'You have a donkey?'

He keeps on miming.

'Ah, you've lost your donkey?'

Now we've got it. Our new friend is asking if we've seen his donkey, which has been missing for several days. In fact we saw it a few hours earlier, wandering around much higher up the slopes, and we draw a diagram to show him roughly where it was. He's delighted.

We all sleep in the immense communal living area around the wood burner, they under their fur rugs and we in our sleeping bags. Without worrying the slightest about our presence, the wife strips down to the waist, stirs up the fire, blows out the candles and lays down to sleep between her daughter and her husband.

Early the next morning we leave our 'family for an evening', profoundly grateful for this providential hospitality. Ever since we started our trek we've been crossing our fingers that the final pass wouldn't be too deep in snow for us to get through. It's the final obstacle separating us from the valley where our goal lies, the village of Yerkalo. The information we're given varies depending on the time of day: 'You won't get through; the snow is up to shoulder height', or 'No, it's waist high, but you won't get through'. We cross our fingers and uncross our legs. *Inshallah*. God willing.

After three days of fast walking we finally reach the foot of the dreaded pass. A family invites us to have yak butter tea with them before accompanying us for the first part of the ascent. We climb and climb. As the altitude rises, the cold becomes more and more penetrating. The skin of our hands freezes to the straps of our rucksacks. The stream no longer flows: it's frozen solid. Our steps become less and less confident: we're now walking on a carpet of snow that is growing deeper with every kilometre. At 4,200 metres it's up to our knees. At 4,500 metres we reach the pass. We make it over the top and the joy of our success overcomes any sensation of pain. We make a slow descent, partly because we're tired but also because we want to savour this victory, mixed though it is with apprehension. Checkpoints have been incredibly rare up to this point. We don't have permits and, so far, we've managed to avoid inspection. What will we find below?

We make a very long detour to avoid the police control at the entrance to the town. Yerkalo is the one and only Catholic parish in the Tibet Autonomous Region. We cross a bridge and clamber up the hill on which the village is perched. We choose the side that's furthest from the houses. Discretion is paramount; Chinese police officers aren't known for their sense of humour. Among the seemingly abandoned ruins we come face to face with an old man digging in a paddy field. He smiles at us and points out the way to the village. We just need to keep going straight ahead . . . Once we get to the top we steal cautiously between the houses and catch sight of the church in the distance. It's not quite where we thought it would be; it's on a different hill. To avoid being spotted and making difficulties for the Christians we wanted to meet, we try to keep a low profile. We retrace our steps down the hill and climb up the other side.

The valley extends below us with its salt mines and Buddhist villages which, only a short time ago, persecuted the Christians of Yerkalo.

The tiny Christian community of the Tibet Autonomous Region

It's four in the afternoon when we finally arrive. We feel excited to find the church open and a handful of elderly Tibetans praying. Their voices united in prayer fill the brand new church. After prayers, a nun dressed in ordinary clothes serves us tea and offers us a juicy nashi pear. We dig out of our pockets the trinkets and religious knick-knacks that Aliocha collected from his relatives in France: crosses, medallions, tiny chains and images of saints. This causes an absolute free-for-all, right there in the courtyard of the church on the roof of the world. Our saintly nuns are transformed in a flash into little kids with mischievous smiles. They compare their loot and negotiate exchanges with each other. One of them takes a postcard of John Paul II with both hands and presses it to her forehead several times, just as Buddhists venerate the portrait of the Dalai Lama.

As well as the difficulties of isolation, it seems that the community has been traumatized by its leader. There used to be a priest here, one sole Tibetan priest. In Cachei, Father Bao's voice was full of sadness as he talked about him; the young man had been his disciple. He still lives in Yerkalo but he left the ministry to marry a nun. We try as hard as we can to find him, but with no success. He still has a hold on the fragile community and generally refuses to meet Westerners. We're no exception. He remains invisible. When we communicate with mimes and gestures that we'd like to stay the night, the old ladies frown. They smile and bow but not one of them invites us to stay. Not even the nun, who is quick to shut the church gate and asks us to leave. They're scared, for sure. How can we blame them? We visit the tomb of Maurice Tornay anyway, and then we have no choice but to turn back. With night approaching, we agree that we should hitchhike. We position ourselves above the checkpoint at the entry to the village, hidden from the officers' sight by a bend in the road, and leap out on to the roadside whenever a car approaches. Few in number at the best of times, they're particularly rare at this hour. Every time someone stops, they tell us that Denchin, our destination, is too far away.

A sedan in rather better shape than the others appears around the bend. It approaches slowly.

'This time! This one will take us. Surely!'

I stand out on the road and the car stops. The windows are tinted. I can't see who is inside. I tap on the front passenger window. It slowly opens. Suddenly my heart races. Horrors! The eyes of five policemen are staring at me. It's an unmarked car; I feel naive and stupid. But they seem as surprised and lost for words as I am. Mechanically, I smile and ask if, by any chance, they might be going to Denchin. I understand by their gestures that they've finished their shift and are just going a few hundred metres down to the police station; they almost apologize for being unable to help me. The window closes and the car moves off. I bolt back to join Gabriel and Aliocha, who are hiding behind a low wall. Could these policemen not be bothered checking my papers at the end of their shift? Did they just assume I would have a pass? Were they so surprised that they failed to respond? We don't discuss at length the reasons for this miracle; we're happy simply to attribute it to Maurice Tornay. We decide not to tempt fate, and make a quick getaway in case the policemen change their minds and return.

Aliocha books us into a cheap hotel for the night. He's paying. Our golden rule still stands: we don't spend anything on accommodation. We dine at a restaurant that offers pasta, as much as you can eat. Before we arrived, the record was 60 bowls in one sitting. Aliocha clocks up 30 bowls while I reach 54. Gabriel, however, downs 61 bowls and sets a new record. The waitress hails his performance and seems pleased that she doesn't need to make any more trips to and from the kitchen.

From Denchin we return to Shangri-La, where we leave Aliocha and head back to Cachei, where we left our bikes.

'Put out into deeper water.' This was Pope Benedict XVI's exhortation to the Church of China in his letter of 2007. There in Yerkalo, the church stands, unshakeable, looking out over the valley into the distance. In spite of the sometimes adverse winds, the breath of faith still caresses the mountains and valleys of the Tibetan borders, and always will.

# 11

## Thailand

### In which we make the sign of the cross as we spit between the floor slats

After a break of several weeks, most of it spent walking with Aliocha, we get back on our bikes. We leave Cachei and head due south towards the border with Laos, in order to reach Thailand and our next stopover.

There are now three of us. Paul is an old school friend of Gabriel's. He joined us at Cachei, where he bought a bike. He'll be riding with us for a fortnight. Apart from Pierre, it's the first time we've welcomed someone else into our partnership. At first I had been very open to the idea of inviting good friends to join us for a few days, but the further we went, the more I realized that I was going to struggle to accommodate these cyclists, now that we'd found a rhythm, an understanding and everything was so straightforward with just the two of us. However, I realize that having received such marvellous hospitality from all sorts of people over the last few months, we now have an ideal opportunity to put what we've learnt into practice. And too bad if they take three biscuits instead of two or if their stomachs take several days to adapt.

All I remember of these days is the endless hard grind and aching thighs. For nearly two weeks we push ourselves to the limit, cycling like madmen to get through this mountainous region of southern China. We have an appointment on 15 January at the airport at Luang Namtha, in Laos, where we'll say goodbye to Paul and meet Gabriel's parents. So we race at breakneck speed towards the south, through regions that are doubtless incredibly scenic and which, at any other time, we'd stop to appreciate.

Every morning we stock up with bits of sugar cane from the fields to chew on after each hill, and replenish our energy stores. To avoid the endless hills, we end up cycling on the motorway. When we come across policemen, they politely ask us to get off, which we do. We get back on a few kilometres further along the road. The construction of the motorway must have been a mammoth undertaking as it is both straight and level, thanks to tunnels through the mountains and bridges across the valleys. The tunnels pose us a few problems. Many are several kilometres long and don't have a hard shoulder for break-downs or emergencies; opposing traffic is separated only by a white strip and we're repeatedly forced against the enormous tunnel walls. It's dark inside the tunnels and to make things really user-friendly, nobody thought to install any lighting. We've set up a protocol which we repeat every time we enter a tunnel. I go first, Paul follows and Gabriel takes up the rear. I turn on my headlamp and Gabriel sets his on flash mode, facing backwards. This way our convoy is visible to vehicles going in both directions. We ride as fast as we can and as close to the wall as possible. I always feel as if I'm going down a mine. My headlamp allows me to see my front wheel but nothing more. I can't even see two metres ahead. When the sound of an engine announces a vehicle's imminent arrival, our hearts start beating wildly and we redouble our concentration. The main thing is not to fall off. When a car is approaching Gabriel shouts 'voooooiiiturre!' ('car'). When it has passed and isn't followed by any others, we hear, '*C'est boooon!*' ('all OK'). But '*C'est boooon*' and '*caamiiooon*' ('lorry') are easily confused. We engage in absurd tunnel-yelling discussions in Chinese tunnels:

'*C'est boooon!*'
'*Pardon? Bon or camion?*'
'*Bah, c'est . . . on!*'
'*Huh? Un camion?*'
'*Non, un camion!*'

Apart from the Chinese tunnels, we discover another local wonder – the hospitality. As good as what we experienced in the Middle East. Every time we need a bed for the night, a family invites us to stay, and every time we're confronted with the same alcohol the Tibetans introduced us to. One evening we're attracted by the bright lighting of a building site. The project manager and his family invite us to stay and put their kitchen at our disposal. We sit down at the table together with glasses of *baijiu*. Paul, who hasn't tasted this poison before, says 'You can't really taste the alcohol at all,' and confuses it with his glass of mineral water. Before long he's drunk, to the delight of the family, who keep on topping up his glass. The drink lubricates the discussion and the two children, identical twins who nod their heads and laugh in unison, ask us dozens of questions with the help of their English exercise book.

After nine days of this kind of carry on we eventually cross the border between China and Laos. Most intrigued by my fulsome beard, a Chinese official spends a ridiculous amount of time inspecting my passport, examining the photo in which I appear clean-shaven. With a look of intense concentration, he scratches it with his finger, trying to see if there might be another photo concealed underneath. He inspects me from every angle, visibly frustrated. Then, after thinking for a moment, he calls an interpreter to ask me an extraordinary question:

'Are you Pakistani?'

Turkish, Romanian, Iraqi, Italian, Corsican, Basque, Syrian and even Indian! I've been told that, judging from my looks, I could be any of these. But Pakistani, no one has ever said that before. If my transit across the border didn't depend solely on his goodwill, I would have died laughing. But I simply reply, looking perfectly innocent, that I'm none other than a Frenchman. Just a boring old Frenchman.

The next day we finally reach Luang Namtha, where we leave Paul and meet Gabriel's parents, who've also come to have a good workout in the mountains. We ride across the north of Laos in three days and then meet another border. We load our bikes and ourselves on to a little ferry boat and cross to the other side of the Mekong. This river, which we've already met further north, in Tibet, serves as a natural border between Laos and Thailand.

'You can't *not* visit the Karen!'

Before we left France we met Father Georges Colomb of MEP,[1] to talk about China. He also mentioned the Karen people. He told us that they're an ethnic group who have been recently evangelized, and that the first individuals to respond to the gospel, in the Mae

[1] See Chapter 9.

Sot region in the north-west of Thailand, are under 50 years old. The first converts to be baptized are still alive. We also learned that, although they're not actively persecuted in Thailand, they are nevertheless extremely isolated. First, they're geographically isolated, which has shut them off from modern society and caused them to retain their own identity. And they're also isolated culturally because they're a religious minority, almost overwhelmed by the Buddhist majority.

That night, as we emerged on to a snow-covered Rue du Bac, in Paris, with noses red from the wintery cold, we made a decision: our fourth stop would be with the Karen. The prospect of thawing our frozen bodies in the furnace of South East Asia probably had a lot to do with our unanimous decision.

The landscape is nothing like what we saw in Laos. There we rode through a succession of hills and valleys with lush vegetation, and huge forests that had been cut down and partly replanted. We were constantly surrounded by groups of children who gathered around our cycle convoy with great excitement, and there were obvious signs of poverty. But here in Thailand, rows of modern houses line the roadside, numerous private cars vie with trucks to overtake us on smooth, well-maintained roads. Towns jostle for space with the countryside. Everyone dresses Western style. We could almost be in the suburbs in the west of Paris with all the detached houses. Thailand's economy is booming – it's clear to see, even from our bicycle seats.

Since we descended from the mountains to the plains, we're finding the heat and humidity stifling. We stop for the night 50 kilometres from the Burmese border, in the little town of Fang where, by chance, we come across a church run by three Italian missionaries. We dine on a large bowl of pasta with the 30 or so children who are boarders at the Church school. Father Massimo, recently arrived from his native Milan, tells us he's joined a class studying Thai language and culture, but can still hardly put two sentences together. With their charming Italian accent, the priests show us around the mission and share their knowledge of the country and its people who have embraced them so warmly.

They explain that Thailand is a predominantly Buddhist country: 94 per cent of the population practise Theravada Buddhism.[2] It's not uncommon to see a procession of monks in the street. There are 250,000 monks in the country, spread between 30,000 monasteries. Buddhism is the basis of the cohesiveness of Thai society, which is very religious. Catholics are a very small minority: 0.5 per cent of the population, or 340,000 people out of 64 million Thais. A drop in the ocean.

'It's a very small Church, but it's very visible thanks to the organizations it has established within the society, notably among the minority groups.'

The missionaries' school, which is a good example, opened 30 years ago. One of its purposes is to prepare young people from tribal minority groups to go through the Thai state-school system. The school's first objective is to teach the students Thai, because until they start school they speak only their own dialect. We find out from one of the three priests that 15 tribal villages have recently turned to the Catholic faith thanks to the work of the mission.

'These tribes were originally animists, but this belief didn't satisfy them. They were searching for something more.'

We spend a very enjoyable evening with the missionaries, and the sun has long since set when we turn in. Night hits us like a cold shower: Gabriel is doubled over with pain. He wakes frequently, groaning in agony. In the morning he's unable to get up for Mass. He just lies there on the mattress, semi-conscious, with a blank expression on his face and severe stomach pain. The thermometer shows he has a temperature of 41 °C. He's suffering from violent diarrhoea. The normal treatment has no effect. The first thing to do is to stem the tide; it's only possible to treat the illness itself once this has been achieved. However, our little bit of knowledge doesn't seem to help. Gabriel is still in agony. Seeing him so sick is worrying, especially knowing we're two days away from the nearest town.

I ask his parents' advice but they're reluctant to stick their oar in. They prefer to let me handle the crisis. So I decide to accept the help

[2] Theravada is a form of Buddhism that developed mainly in India. It teaches that only monks can attain salvation. According to Mahayana Buddhism (China, Korea, Japan), salvation is obtained by the merits of the follower.

of one of the Italian priests, who is going to Chiang Mai this morning. We sit Gabriel in the front of the pickup and put his bike and bags in the back. The priest drops Gabriel at the diocesan house in Chiang Mai, where we find him two days later. When we arrive he's deathly pale, worse than when we last saw him. He's lost five kilos. No one has been looking after him and he wasn't capable of getting himself to the hospital on his own. When I finally take him, a doctor in a white coat diagnoses salmonella. It's a nasty intestinal bacteria, but very simple to treat. In a few hours Gabriel is on his feet, weak but on his way to recovery. The following day you'd never know he'd been unwell.

The hospital is large, modern and full of Westerners. It's the best in town, in the whole region. It's expensive to be treated here but our insurance takes care of it. Every time we need to fall back on our insurance we're reminded that even though we're only staying in private homes, rather than in flash hotels being served fabulous meals, we're still incredibly privileged. If we fall ill, we can access good care. And if tomorrow we decided we'd had enough, we could go home. What proportion of the population in the countries we've visited these last few months could say the same? We have a choice; we're free. That makes us extraordinarily rich.

In Chiang Mai we divide our time between the diocesan house and a Jesuit centre where we are sleeping. There we meet several nuns who take the time to talk with us. We learn that sharing the gospel among the Thai Buddhist majority is extremely tricky; to them everything can be explained without the God we Christians believe in. For the numerous Theravada Buddhists in Thailand, the Christian God is simply inconceivable: the very idea that he could enter into a relationship with living beings calls his divine nature into question. To them it seems ridiculous that God would be imprisoned in a finite and transitory world. Also, how could they believe in a God who endured so much suffering and who therefore had such bad karma? How could he be the Son of God? Finding common ground for dialogue between a missionary and a Buddhist who has a good knowledge of his religion is thus very difficult. That's why missionaries naturally gravitate towards the minority groups, who are animists. The Karen ethnic group is an example of this dynamic.

We set off in the early morning. Two days ago we left Chiang Mai and Gabriel's parents. We know this last lap will be long and arduous. At first the road climbs slowly but then the gradient rises to a gruelling 15 per cent. The mountains around us signal our arrival in Karen territory. A good sign. But soon we're panting, groaning and grilling in the hot sun, all the more so because sweat, an effective magnifying glass, pours down our arms and legs. Trucks overtake us slowly, shuddering under the strain. Suddenly we're at the top. Then there's a long descent. Then a climb. Then a descent . . . Dog tired, we stop for a break in the town of Mae Sot, and finally we push on to the little town of Mae Ramat. There we should find Father Nicholas, MEP priest of the mission to the Karen.

It's already dark. Some passers-by point out Saint Joseph school, which is run by nuns. We enter the school grounds and head for the only building with lights on. Just as we roll to a stop a car pulls up beside us. A tall man with a fair complexion gets out. He has ginger hair, buzz cut, and he's wearing clerical robes.

'Hey! Are you the French guys who sent me an email? Welcome. Go and have a shower and then we'll eat!'

I feel like hugging him! His name is Father Nicholas Lefebure. We've finally arrived!

After a good scrub in the shower, we find him in the dining room. He moves the table out of the way and unrolls a carpet, which we sit on with some French volunteers who are staying for a few months, some young Karen and two Burmese refugee girls who are also staying here. One of them is very beautiful and we immediately decide to call her Pocahontas. Father Nicholas uncorks a bottle of rum. We drink to the health of the Karen.

'You've come at just the right time. It's a good thing you didn't arrive a day later – you would have missed everything!'

We look at him quizzically. He's satisfied with the effect his words have on us.

'Tomorrow we're all leaving to go to the village of Mae We, in Father Bourdery's area. He's the other MEP priest posted here. They're holding the inauguration of their new church – it's going to be a big celebration. Karen people from all around the region will be there, and the bishop as well.'

Once again we hadn't planned a thing. Someone has done some planning for us.

Father Nicholas celebrates Mass for the nuns and school students. As soon as Mass is finished we pile into the back of the pickup with 12 of the Karen. Another vehicle follows us, also loaded to the gunwales. It's a long way and the sun beats mercilessly down on us. We leave the tarmac and take an ochre-coloured dirt road. Every turn of the wheels stirs up clouds of dust; eventually we're draped in a drab sheet of yellow powder. We penetrate deeper and deeper into the jungle, thick with drooping vines and trees with gigantic leaves. The pickup suddenly stops. We look up and notice other vehicles parked in front of us. The bishop, who has come to bless the church, is blocking the way; we've disturbed him right in the middle of getting dressed. He dons his clerical garb before he arrives, so that he's all ready to go when he gets there. He explains that the garb is extremely important to the villagers and it would be unthinkable for him to turn up in his ordinary priest's robes and a clerical collar. Everyone would be disappointed. He climbs back into his 4x4 and we follow the long convoy, our weight gouging out furrows in the track, which normally carries only the odd motor scooter.

After several kilometres we reach the village of Mae We. Everyone rushes to welcome the bishop. Dozens of villagers gather around his car to shake his hand or receive a blessing. The men are short, thickset and lean, with olive skin and unkempt hair. Women carry their babies in a sling on their backs, wrapped in the swathe of fabric. Everyone wears shirts and dresses made from hand-woven material[3] embroidered with traditional designs.

A villager approaches, holding the end of a rope. And attached to the other end is an elephant, which calmly moves its massive frame into this atmosphere of feverish excitement. For Gabriel, it's love at first sight; he loves to sing the praises of this amazing animal. There

---

[3] We would learn later that the Karen weave their cloth in pieces 40 cm wide, in squares or rectangles, which they stitch together to make sleeveless shirts for the men and sarongs and skirts for the women. Some fabrics include clever designs, interweaving flowers and symbols.

are still 4,000 elephants in Thailand; the prestige and respect accorded them by the people guarantees that they're treated well. Their life expectancy is about 80 years, but they must not be worked once they reach the age of 60 – the working life of a typical Frenchman. Within seconds, Gabriel has whipped out the camera and started filming the new object of his affections. They hoist the bishop, wearing his white cassock and purple skullcap, up on to the elephant's back, while a man sits on its wrinkled neck to direct it. Tradition dictates that the villagers must welcome an important guest at the entrance to the village and carry him so that he doesn't set foot on the ground. Slowly, slowly, to the rhythm of the pachyderm's swaying gait, the procession moves off. The men blow into buffalo horns and beat the tom-tom drums. It's a magnificent sight.

In Karen mythology God the Creator first conceived Karen man and entrusted to him a little white book containing the secret of life; then, after that, he made white men. But the Karen man was not studious and he went off gallivanting around the countryside, leaving the little book at the foot of a tree. One of the white men picked it up. So when missionaries came to the Karen with their Bibles, the Karen saw them as the descendants of the white man who had gone off with their book, and had now come back to explain it to them! They welcomed them with open arms.

Fifty years ago, several MEP priests came to this minority group. Father Quintard, Father Guillou and Father Tygreat travelled all over the Thai and Burmese mountains, each in the area allotted to him. They say that in a village in the Mae We region, many years before the arrival of the missionaries, there was an old man who was interested in Christianity but died before he could meet a priest. On his deathbed he said to his son: 'If you meet a man dressed all in white, follow him and listen to him!' When the young man met Father Quintard wearing his white cassock, he followed him and converted to Christianity, with all his family, without further ado. This man started a significant movement that led to many conversions.

With no roads, the missionaries would often walk for several days to reach the outlying villages, which were surrounded by dense, hostile jungle. In Father Quintard's area, where we are now, the villagers remember that it was he who opened up the route to Mae We village to mopeds and

4x4s. In the region he's considered to be the father of the Karen. He gave himself to the people and they adopted him and gave him great happiness. In fact he concluded his will with the magnificent words:

'The Karen have been my happiness and I die for them.'

Since his death in 2003 in a car accident, another MEP priest has taken over from him – Father Alain Bourdery. During these two days of celebration, he's the Master of Ceremonies.

The procession crosses a stream and stops at a clearing, where the bare earth forms a natural hollow. This is downtown Mae We. Houses on stilts nestle between the trees on the banks of this natural amphitheatre. Father Alain shows us the school and the brand new church.

When it finally grows dark, all the villagers gather. Everyone is given a little paper lantern. The girls and single women wear long white dresses. A statue of the Virgin, carried by four men, leads the procession. The people light their candles and begin to sing, their voices silencing the murmur of the jungle. We're carried by the strains of the Lourdes *Ave Maria*,[4] which fill the night. Candles light up the children's adorable little faces as they sing with all their hearts. I'm quite taken aback. It's astounding to discover such a pure cult of the Virgin Mary here, something we French understand very well. Pinch me, I must be dreaming! Here we are in deepest, darkest South East Asia and yet even here they pray to Mary. Under the gaze of the crowd, several young Karen hoist up the statue of Our Lady of Lourdes: they're going to put her into a niche in the rock. From now on she will look down over the village.

The next morning the bishop consecrates the new church. It's small but very beautiful. Father Alain has decorated the interior in a clean, simple style; it's all angles and built with solid, neutral-coloured materials. The walls are off-white, the wood is dark and glossy. The result is soothing and conducive to prayer. Dare I say it: a touch of the contemporary in Karen land.

The bishop concludes the celebration with some advice for the villagers. Many of them have lifelong debts, having taken out loans from Thaksin[5] several years ago.

[4] A hymn to Mary, sung to a traditional French tune, mainly used in Lourdes.
[5] Thaksin Shinawatra is a Thai businessman and politician. He was Prime Minister from 2001 to 2006, when he was overthrown in a coup d'état.

**After Mass in a jungle village**

'Not all money is good to take! Flee from luxury! It makes you self-centred, it makes you forget about serving others. Don't try to imitate town people! The government has released money for you. We need to train people who will ensure you actually get the funds.'

Before returning to Mae Ramat we pay a visit, with Father Nicholas, to the Mae La refugee camp. There must be about 300,000 Karen on the Thai side of the border, who inhabit the mountainous north-eastern part of Thailand. On the Myanmar side there are over three million Karen.[6] But over the last 20 years, many refugees from Myanmar have crossed the border and ended up in refugee camps on the Thai side: there must be 150,000, from various tribes, including 100,000 Karen, who have fled from persecution in Myanmar.

The camp lies beside the road, behind bamboo and wooden fences. Hundreds and hundreds of huts stand packed in cheek by jowl. The refugees are crammed in like caged hens, with no privacy. They are looked after, educated and well nourished, but they have no prospects for a better life. The camps, which should be only a temporary solution, have become overpopulated towns with an uncertain future.

---

[6] Estimates vary from three to seven million.

Father Nicholas has come to see a man named Joseph. We follow him to the young man's hut. He became separated from his fiancée in circumstances that we don't really understand, but he tells us he finally found her yesterday, in the camp. And he's even more emotional because he's also just discovered that he has a one-year-old son. Because his fiancée had a child out of wedlock, the two of them and their son were rejected by their respective families. Joseph receives us in his miserable little hut; from his manner it's obvious that he feels honoured by this visit. The young mother is very happy to see the priest. Father Nicholas prays with them and blesses the baby.

Then he leaves to meet the head of the Catholic community in the camp. We find him beside a church built on piles, which is only slightly bigger than the houses around it. It's urgently in need of renovation, without which it will soon collapse. He fears that the floorboards will cave in if too many people come to Mass at the same time. Father Nicholas comes here as often as possible. He tries to communicate life, a breath of the outside world to this prison community.

It's quite touching to see the young priest, tall and fair with ginger hair, among these small, black-haired people. He's different from them in every way. And when you think about it, it seems crazy to send a foreigner to tell the good news in a country he doesn't know, whose people speak a language he can barely understand. Even after a lifetime of devotion he will remain a foreigner. After three years of intense study, he can finally make himself understood in Thai. But he still has to learn to speak Karen! Seeing him so weak, so vulnerable, we can't help wondering whether he would have more of a voice and, therefore, be more useful in France where, as we are continually reminded, we don't have enough priests.

'Jesus spent the first 30 years of his life sharing in the daily life of his people before three short years of ministry!'

Father Nicholas reminds us that the missionaries are following the biblical way: in the Bible, the good news is always brought by a foreigner – the Acts of the Apostles is the best example. And he points out that, contrary to popular opinion, rather than being imposed, the good news is offered. To suggest the opposite is to confuse evangelization with colonialism. The gospel is offered, and offered in all humility; it's not man who converts, but the Holy Spirit. In making himself vulnerable, the missionary leaves room for God to work through him. And so when he is weak, then he is strongest.

And that's nothing new! In 1659 the Apostolic Vicars sent to the kingdoms of Tonkin and Cochin China[7] were given the following instructions from Rome:

> *Don't advance any argument, or be zealous to convince these people to change their behaviour, customs and mores, unless they are obviously contrary to religion and morals. There's nothing more absurd than taking France, Spain, Italy or any other European country to the Chinese! Give them not our country but our faith, this faith which doesn't repulse or harm the rites and customs of any people, provided that they aren't detestable, but on the contrary, let us guard keep and protect them.[8]*

That evening, sitting down with Father Nicholas in the dining hall at Mae Ramat, we put the world to rights. He's an interesting person, a very good listener. He asks us about the Christians we've already met and seems to like our slightly ad hoc approach to travelling. I think of those words written on the seat of Gabriel's bike by little F.-X. (see Chapter 1), one July day, six months ago. Tomorrow, Father Nicholas will take us to the village for our next community visit. After that it will be difficult to communicate with him; so this evening we chatter on and on, in the good old language of Molière.[9]

We learn from Father Nicholas that the Karen people are descendants of the Tibetans, which explains their physical and cultural similarities, such as their costumes and various traditions. Forced from their home by another ethnic group, they must have migrated from the south of China to Burma. We ask him about the mission. What good is it really doing? What difference does it make for the people, who were probably quite happy before the missionaries came? Why did he become a missionary? Why did he come to live with the Karen?

'When I visit the villagers, I'm always surprised to see how similar their way of life is to the times of the Acts of the Apostles: the sharing of possessions, joining together in prayer – *all the believers were one in heart and mind*,[10] the fact that we go up to the "upper room"

---

[7] Kingdoms situated at that time in what is now northern and southern Vietnam.

[8] Quoted in J. Guennou, *Missions Étrangères de Paris*, Paris: Fayard, 1986, p. 75.

[9] Revered French playwright.

[10] Acts 4.32 (NIV).

in their houses, correcting each other in brotherly love. I find a lot of parallels between the village life of the Karen and the example of Christian community life that we see in the New Testament. As John Paul II often said, throughout his pontificate, there's a trace of Christ's divinity in each person, Catholic or not. He called it "the seeds of the Word". The missionary tries to extend God's kingdom, by practising love and teaching forgiveness, which is not easy in Asian societies and Thai society in particular.'

Father Nicholas confides that he felt the call to the priesthood in his teenage years, but he didn't listen straight away. He started off working in insurance for eight years, before starting seminary.

'I just naturally started thinking about going to serve in Asia. I had spent holidays in Laos and Myanmar and took to these people straight away. It was like a revelation to me at that time. For some missionaries, the desire to go to Asia springs from some historic event, such as the Tiananmen Square massacre or the plight of the Vietnamese boat people. For me it was very simple. I had the opportunity to get close to these two peoples for a very short time, but it was long enough to know that I wanted to live with them and serve them.'

According to their motto, the priests go *ad extra, ad gentes, ad vitam*, that is to say, 'far away, to be with people, for their whole life'. They serve the local diocese in the host country; they're under the orders of the local bishop. The seminary students preparing for mission at the Rue du Bac in Paris don't know where they'll be sent before the day they're ordained as deacons. That requires a good dose of faith and it's quite hard to come to terms with in a world where we take out life insurance when we start our first job.

'We don't choose where we go! And I really like that! We don't just organize something for ourselves on the basis of what we want; the Church gives us a job to do, people to serve. I didn't choose the work, the people or the place.'

## Fourth isolated community: Mae To

It's now five days since we arrived in the little village of Mae To, which Father Nicholas chose for us. He introduced us to everyone and left us in the hands of Kanpon and his family. The house we're staying in is built with rough-hewn wooden planks. It stands opposite the church, which is also built of wood. Ever since we arrived we've been trying to make sense of what's happening around us, because here in Mae To, everything is different – completely different. There's no common reference point, no grip to hold on to. We just go with the flow, depending totally on our hosts.

Today a man died. Night has long since fallen when we meet for prayer in the dead man's house. Out of respect for the family, we try to look serious, meditative. But our friends burst out laughing. Candlelight fills the bamboo hut; the man had obviously been very poor.

Kanpon (his Christian name is Jerome) makes the sign of the cross and opens the time of prayer. With a cigarette dangling from his bottom lip, he flips through his songbook, like a doctor trying to find the best treatment for an illness. An old man belches nonchalantly. Another clears his throat and spits through the gap between two floor slats. After the prayer they chat in groups. Some play draughts on a board drawn with charcoal on a scrap of cardboard. Everyone is smoking, drinking and chatting, putting the world to rights. Some chew on leaves, the sap of which contains a stimulant that will probably keep them up all night.

In the area allocated to Father Guillou, one of the original three missionaries, 35 Karen villages now have a number of Catholic families. In Mae To, out of 40 families, 20 are Catholic. We find their faith disconcerting; it's very new to them, simple, and evident in every action, every part of life. It's not the object of endless analysis; it just is. The first to be baptized are now grandparents, and they have passed their faith on to their children. But although faith nowadays is primarily handed down within families, people continue to be converted: more families are leaving their animist or Buddhist traditions, to which the majority of people in the region adhere.

As it grows, the little church is working out how to structure itself and find its bearings within the culture. The local clergy are progressively taking over from the missionaries. Meanwhile, since Father Nicholas can't be everywhere, he relies on catechists and the Christian leaders of the villages in his sector to help him carry out his ministry. Kanpon, who has just orchestrated this unlikely vigil for the dead, is one of the catechists.

Every morning Kuang comes to pull us out of bed. She knows a few words of English, including 'breakfast'. Her shrill voice drags us from the arms of Morpheus.

'Blek-fest! Blek-fest!'

She bangs on our bedroom door then goes back to her own home, knowing that we're awake and we won't be late for breakfast. Kuang is Kanpon's wife. She's not yet 30 and already has five children, each as beautiful as the other. Still bleary-eyed, we climb down the stairs of our little house and cross the school playground on the earthen path that runs from one end of the village to the other, to Kuang and Kanpon's house. She welcomes us with a huge smile, wearing a grey hooded sweatshirt and a pretty purple sarong.

The jungle that surrounds the village is bursting with teak trees; teak is so common that they even use it, as well as bamboo, to build their houses. Only the best for the Karen! Kuang and Kanpon's house is a good example. We sit with the children in a circle on the floor, like good little Karen boys. Before us Kuang sets several billy cans of rice and some dried fish, which Father Nicholas gave them when he asked if they would look after us. The menu is the same for every meal of every day, or almost, but I enjoy their rice so much that I never tire of it. After a family blessing we attack our breakfast with spoons, because the Karen don't use chopsticks. And then Kanpon appears. Kanpon is *the* man. And, as usual, he's got a cheeky grin on his face and his hair is a mess.

From day one we idolize Kanpon, just like little kids. No matter what the situation, he's the man to deal with it, the man who can handle anything. He always knows what to do. He's about 40 and has been a catechist since he was 20. He's a Pierce Brosnan lookalike, with bright, intelligent eyes. He is both shy and proud; he hardly ever smiles and doesn't say much, but when he does, everyone listens. He grabs his machete, which hangs from a nail in the wall, ties it to his belt and signals for us to follow him. Karen men are the heroes that we wanted to be when we were little boys. First and foremost, they have a sword – their machete. They also have a charger – their motor scooter. Furthermore, they live in little cabins in the forest. We accompany our friend to the school playground, about 30 metres from his house. There we find about 20 men of the village, each armed with his own machete and a smile on his face. The children need a new dining room and they've come to build it. The whole operation takes three days, including the finishing touches. The dining room is made completely of bamboo, with the exception of the roof, for which they tie together large, dried tree leaves.

Apart from our new friends' skill, what amazes us is the way they join forces to get a job done efficiently. When it's time to plant the rice, fell trees or go fishing, or when one or other of their houses needs renovating, or all sorts of other jobs need to be done, the Karen help each other. The fundamental importance of the community aspect of life is one of the age-old pillars of Karen tradition. But now that they've received the faith from the missionaries, the Karen way of life has taken on a new meaning: being together now means living out the Christian life.

In Mae To we divide most of our time between being with Kanpon and Kuang's family and enjoying the company of Boti and Sarawut, two Karen lads of our age, catechists who come from a different state. Father Nicholas has given them a vital role: going from village to village to pray and sharing some teachings with the families.

Like Kanpon, Boti and Sarawut only know a few words of English. For the first time since our departure seven months ago, we have no way of communicating with people. In China we had Aliocha to translate for us; in the Middle East we often found people who spoke English, Italian or French. In India nearly everyone could make themselves more or less understood in English. But not here. We have not one word in common. And the few words of Karen we've managed to learn aren't enough. We realize something bizarre. We quite naturally set up a crazy way of communicating: we speak to them in French and they reply in Karen. When we notice it, we realize it's been happening for several days, and none of us thought it odd. As I write these words, I think back to this strange dialogue, which now seems quite absurd. But at the time, that was the only thing we could do – and therefore the right thing.

Our communication problems often lead to comical misunderstandings in which we are completely at cross purposes with our Karen friends. One evening, very flattered, we prepare to meet Kanpon's mother, when we realize that 'Mama' is a local brand of noodles.

We're the noodles! We don't always get the meaning of the words being spoken but our conversations nevertheless enable us to establish contact, to have warm, friendly interactions.

Our two friends beckon for us to follow them. We sit behind them on their scooters and ride to a neighbouring village to observe them in their role as catechists. We want to produce a 15-minute film about the church in the village we're visiting. I'm taking some footage from the scooter as we go along. By lengthening the pole and turning the camera around, I can take a selfie of Boti and me on the scooter. Speaking into the camera, I explain what's going on:

'At the moment we're in Mae To, and we're heading for the little village of Baki, with our friends Boti and . . .'

'Yes?'

Boti hears his name. He thinks I'm talking to him. Naturally, he replies.

'No, no, I'm not speaking to you.'

I begin again:

'With Boti and . . .'

'Yes?'

'No, no, Boti, I'm talking to the camera.'

'Yes?'

I put the camera away.

On the steep, rough, dirt roads between one village and the next, our friends fulfil their mission on their motor scooters. In spite of their young age, they are catechists. And we soon learn that in Karen land this word has an entirely different dimension from the way we use it. As the moonless night falls on the silent, densely forested hills, Sarawut puts out the call. He does the rounds of the seven Christian families of the little village of Baki to invite them to come and pray together. He relies on what he has learnt about the faith from his own family – whereas Boti has taken a six-month accelerated training course.

The head Christian invites us to stay at his house for the night. Every village has a head Christian. He's usually an elderly man, known for his faithfulness and good standing. Chosen by the community with the agreement of the *pado*,[11] he helps the community to pray and keep

---

[11] 'Father' in Karen.

their faith strong. He has a constant presence in the village, unlike the periodic visits of the mobile catechists.

The inside of the head Christian's house is plain. It's made completely of wood. The roof is made of overlapping lengths of split bamboo. There's a fireplace for cooking the rice and grilling field rats. A bottle of rice wine stands in full view on the ground. We can see some machete handles poking up from the box they're stored in, and some pieces of washing hanging lazily from a piece of string. And in the middle of all this, a little hanging altar, with a rosary and two candles, which reminds us of the altars in the Lepcha houses in the north of India.

In response to Sarawut's invitation, the seven Christian families join us one by one. Sarawut sits at the front. For about 15 minutes he leads the group in prayer. Nobody knows the prayers or songs very well. Several mechanically repeat the words they remember from the catechists' previous visit several weeks earlier. By way of conclusion, Sarawut stands and splashes the house and everyone in it with holy water.

After making the sign of the cross, they thank each other – '*tableu!*' – and uncork a bottle of rice wine. The Karen hold religiously to the belief that good fellowship must be accompanied by a tipple. The master of the drinks – not necessarily the master of the house – serves every guest one tiny glassful. The alcohol is clearly homemade. After its first maceration or soaking, it makes a brownish foam, which smells like a cowshed, and makes quite a sweet beer. This is then boiled in a still, also homemade, which consists of a round pot with a second pot placed upside down over it, and a piece of bamboo between the two to catch the condensation and draw it off for distillation. Depending on who is making it, more or less alcohol is extracted. But one thing is sure – everyone must make it their business to have a certain amount at the ready: when a friend calls in, regardless of the time, and even if it's unexpected, alcohol must be served. Sitting round in a circle, they drink and the men roll their own enormous cigarettes, with a mixture of tobacco and molasses.

So it's true that the Karen get drunk during a wake. And some make the sign of the cross upside down. It's also true that the Gregorian chants and the marble statues in St Peter's in Rome are part of a world that's more familiar to me than what we find here. But this evening, sitting between Boti and one of the villagers, I listen to their loud discussions and I realize that, yes, I am among real believers. The Karen remain true to the faith that was passed on to them several years ago: they're faithful and committed to the essential truths of the gospel. I close my eyes. I think that, right at this moment, I have a very clear sense of the reality of the universal Church.

I think of Kanpon, for example. He's a 'second-generation' catechist – which means that he was already a catechist when he was 25 and he's still one at 42 years old. In his house there's never a meal that's not preceded by a blessing, never a day that goes by without finishing with a family prayer. Also, every Sunday, in *pado*'s absence, Kanpon leads the celebration of the Word in the village church with the head Christian. It's touching to see these men rolling up their sleeves and getting stuck in, to keep the fledgling faith of their brothers alive – a brand new faith, rough-hewn perhaps, but well and truly alive.

I also think about the rhythm of life here in Mae To. Cut off as they are from the outside world, it's only Father Nicholas' occasional visits that assure these families a link with the wider Church and that world. In France the rhythm of life still runs according to the liturgical calendar. But here in Thailand it would be understandable if the Karen took no notice of it at all. However, when we mention that Lent is approaching, Kuang rushes to the calendar nailed to the wall in the front entrance of the house. She points out the date of Ash Wednesday. The villagers don't receive the sign of the cross on their foreheads with ashes on that day, as is the tradition in France. But on the following Sunday, during regular Mass, the head Christian makes a black cross on each forehead. He uses ground charcoal rather than ash. In this timeless place, Lent begins only several days after it starts in Rome.

We spend the night in the village of Baki. The following day we continue on our rounds, stopping at the tiny village of Pandouepu. All the families here are Catholics. We visit each house. A young widow who is chopping wood invites us into her house. She has two enormous grubs, at least ten centimetres long, cooking over the fire. She offers them to us.

'No, really, you mustn't!'

But Boti explains that it's a generous present, because the larvae are rare and a real delicacy to the Karen. We give in and agree to the tasting session. The flavour of grilled corn, to me, and an earthy flavour to

Gabriel. Unpalatable to us both. No doubt Boti thinks that our silence signals a wonderful gustatory experience. Another evening, thinking he's giving us a real treat, he goes off to the beehive, with bare hands and arms, to get some bee larvae, so that Kuang can make them into a delicious soup for us.

We eat our evening meal with another Catholic family. As is the Karen custom, they spit through the gaps between floor slats and throw all their food waste down between the slats as well. They liven up the meal with thunderous belches coming from deep inside their guts and bring up foul, dirty brown gobs of spit. A young man arrives home, totally drunk. Another comes home from hunting with three rats in his rucksack. His grandmother empties the bag on the spot and, without chopping them up, she skewers them and puts them over the fire to cook.

In this delightful ambiance, Sarawut and Boti sit down in the corner set aside for prayer. Inwardly, I salute their courage and tenacity. In their place I think I would have chosen to go off to bed. Before long we're joined by all three Catholic families of the village. The young woman with the larvae is here. They all pray. Some don't know how to make the sign of the cross because, although they embraced Catholicism six years ago, they don't often have the opportunity to go to Mass.

It's very rare for individual Karen believers to be baptized. Often whole families are baptized together so that the family unit is not divided. The missionaries didn't come here to deliberately upset everything: it's vital that stability and good relationships are maintained. The Catholic community is attractive first and foremost because it constitutes a new clan, a mutual support network, a new way of settling conflicts and praying. Also, Christians aren't obliged to make offerings and costly sacrifices to demons and spirits; they're free from all that. And so on the whole, conversions are more about a group rather than an individual awareness of a relationship with God.

It's often later on that the converts experience the joy of their newfound faith, in a more personal and profound way. Thanks to Boti, Sarawut and Kanpon, we witness this first hand; the Christians who pray do so because they have a personal relationship with the One to whom they pray. The Church usually requires those who want to become part of the Catholic community to spend one to two years as a catechumen[12] before being baptized, in order to give them time to explore the faith they want to embrace: two years to confirm that they really want to take this step, and to receive some training. In exceptional circumstances this rule is relaxed somewhat, such as, for example, at the nuns' school in Mae Ramat, where the children have grown up in such a godly atmosphere. It's not uncommon for a child to ask to be baptized, and if their parents are in agreement, they can receive the sacrament because it's felt that they've already experienced the relational and hence the personal dimension of prayer.

But even the committed Christians, who have undertaken catechism training, retain some of their former animist beliefs. In the school in Mae Ramat, where Father Nicholas is chaplain, the children have just witnessed a tragedy – the cook's young son drowned in the pond. According to Karen tradition, his loved ones must watch over the body and pray for three days in his home. Nothing more Christian than that. But when the time comes for him to be buried, the animist rites get mixed up with Christian practices. Some women bring food and drink to the graveside – according to their animist traditions, the deceased needs nourishment during his journey into the hereafter.

Boti strums his guitar and starts singing, and everyone joins in. As he did yesterday, Sarawut splashes holy water over the little gathering and the walls of the house. The prayer time is no sooner over than the television is turned on. In this family, who are quite obviously poor, and have only just got electricity, the television takes centre stage. A film imaginatively entitled *GI Joe* is showing. It's a long time since Gabriel and I saw an American blockbuster, packed with special effects, muscular, square-jawed heroes and beautiful women with curves in all the right places. Sarawut asks me if it's a French film. I don't hold it against him; no doubt he's never seen any of our typical, French, not-so-good-looking heroes.

Grandmother, bent over from a lifetime of work in the paddy fields, spits and shuffles over to her grandson, with the rat kebab in her hand. I imagine she's saying the Karen version of what parents all over the

[12] One being instructed by a catechist in the principles of the Catholic faith with a view to baptism.

world say to their children: 'Just try it before you say you don't like it.' But knowing her, I doubt she'll say 'one mouthful for Daddy, one paw for Mummy . . .'

I enjoy living here. I feel really good. So does Gabriel. We have time to spend with each person, play with the children, read and enjoy being surrounded by nature, going fishing in the river or taking walks in the beautiful jungle with our new friends. Everything is strangely simple. We take the opportunity to make a first spiritual assessment of the journey so far: we each go off by ourselves for a day, taking a can of fish in tomato sauce for lunch, a notebook to write in, a Bible and a pencil. A 'day in the desert', as monks call it. We'll meet back at Kuang's house for dinner.

I walk for an hour and a half and settle myself on the bank of a little stream with crystal clear water. I'm hidden among the foliage and tall grasses. I heave a deep sigh of pleasure and dip my feet into the water. From time to time a fish glides by. When I get out my little Bible, I realize how much it has aged. The journey has taken its toll on it over the last few months. I take out a leaf of carefully folded paper on which several questions are written to guide me on this retreat day. A priest friend of mine, with whom I've been meeting regularly in France over the last few years, suggested I use these questions. He's helping me to grow in my faith, to put a little more of God into my daily life. He's my 'spiritual father', or as it used to be called, my 'spiritual director'. Before we left, he prepared a reading plan. And I email him when I can and share any questions I have, anything I don't understand or things I've found wonderful or amazing. He always replies.

I'm stunned by the natural beauty all around me. No sound of human making disturbs the song of the water, the birds and the wind. I dive into the Gospel of John. I think about Gabriel and our friendship, which we must continue to develop, of how far we've come geographically and how far we've come inwardly. Spiritually. The simple fact of being happy to stay in one place speaks volumes. I've come a long way since Tal Arboush.

A week before leaving the Karen we welcome a new face. In France, during the year of preparation for this journey, a small group of people volunteered to give us a hand – friends and friends of friends. Some took charge of the Video Discovery Kits about our trip for chaplains to use in schools, others organized crazy events to raise funds for the project, such as weekends away and get-togethers. Still others helped us with the multimedia project. Laurence is one of the latter. She's studying journalism and is joining us for a few days of filming, instead of Pierre. We actually don't know her very well at all, and so we're glad she's spending a few days with us. Especially since she brings fresh news of Pierre, some sausage and chocolate. She's just endured a 24-hour marathon, travelling Paris to Mae To, via Mae Ramat, some of it in a beaten-up old bus and on the back seat of a motor scooter. Yesterday she left Orly airport, where it was 10 °C.

'Hey, it's really hot here!'

Laurence is staying with Kuang and Kanpon. She and Kuang get on like long-lost friends, and she has become the new fashion icon of the Karen women of Mae To.

They'd give anything to have pale skin like hers – not like us, because we haven't come from the grey of a Paris winter. Westerners like to fry themselves in UV rays, whereas the Karen put talcum powder all over their faces to make their skin look whiter. It's all a question of fashion. Here the sun is the sworn enemy of the beauty-conscious woman. In the kingdom of the Karen, white women are queens. And Laurence is the empress.

At four in the morning we're woken by horrible, barbaric screams – not of human origin. They're slitting the pigs' throats. Yesterday we met Meena, a young Karen woman originally from Mae To, who now lives in Chiang Mai; she speaks understandable English. She has fine features and a gracious smile. She tells us that she has come back to get married. We imagine this is to happen at some unspecified time in the future. But no – the wedding is today. And the preparations start with the pigs. We'll be eating pork, minced, roasted or raw, all day. A treat, as long as the coriander and spices don't totally obliterate the flavour of the meat. So here we are, breakfasting on pork in the bride's home. It's early in the day but the whole village is already drunk.

The village women work hard. Despite her heavy load of wood, beauty-conscious Kuang wears winter clothing, hoping to keep her prized pearly white skin

About mid-afternoon a number of pickup trucks roll up and drop off numerous families from all over the region. They slowly fill the church, which was scrubbed clean yesterday by the bride herself and decorated with sumptuous bouquets. Meena wears a white Karen blouse, a skirt made of a single piece of pink fabric fastened at the waist. Talc whitens her skin. Baptiste, her fiancé, wears a maroon Karen shirt. Two processions move towards the church, singing as they go, men on one side, women on the other. Several metres before they reach the church the two groups join and the future spouses are handed over to each other by the crowd. The procession starts moving again. Meena and Baptiste enter the church side by side, each followed by a witness; they stand before the altar, where the priest welcomes them.

The Karen are traditionally monogamous. We witnessed this with the young Burmese couple in the refugee camp at Mae La who were rejected by the families because she had become pregnant. They have very strict laws to avoid vagrancy and any kind of messing around between

Baptiste and Meena's wedding in the church at Mae To

neighbouring villages – it amounts to complete gender separation. In Karen land, a girl doesn't ride on a boy's bike if she isn't his wife, and any amorous relationship is formalized immediately by marriage in the right and proper way. A few years ago, couples committing adultery were taken into the forest and put to death by the men of the village.

After the exchange of vows, the Thai priest, who doesn't normally officiate here, puts his hands around the newlyweds' clasped hands, thus adapting an animist ritual to signify the permanence of their union. After Communion, Meena discreetly leaves the church, followed by her bridesmaid. Back in her house she changes into the two-piece outfit worn by married women. In the church the ceremony concludes with a song. Then the whole assembly takes the young man to his wife. They pray a blessing over them in their new home and everyone congratulates them. Karen society being matriarchal, Baptiste must live with his mother-in-law for several months, to prove he's a good husband before having the right to manage the family finances.

When I go to bed, my mind slightly befuddled from all the alcohol in my system, I think back to the advice given to the Apostolic Vicars who were sent to the kingdoms of Tonkin and Cochin China: 'Give them . . . our faith, this faith which doesn't repulse or harm the rites and customs of any people . . .' We've just witnessed a great example of enculturation: Catholic marriage has embraced Karen tradition. The resulting combination is magnificent.

We pack our bags, pump up our tyres and check our bikes one last time. In a few minutes we'll be back on the road. There's a big lump in my throat. The whole village has assembled to say farewell to us, despite being still tired from three days of wedding celebrations. We don't speak the same language and we still don't understand each other very well, but nevertheless they've all come. Something has happened over these last three weeks. The children don't understand that we'll probably never return, and they run around our bicycles shouting 'See you soon'. Kuang wraps her arms around us and gazes at each of us, with her bloodshot eyes:

'Kuang sad.'

'Charles sad.'

I still have one person to say farewell to – Kanpon. I've kept the best until last. Our film star, his hair in a mess, screws up his eyes, grimaces and says goodbye abruptly, with all the self-control he can muster. With a wild lurch he wraps his arms around us, saying nothing but our names. Just for an instant our eyes meet. And then he retreats, elbowing his way through the crowd, his eyes fixed on the ground. I can hardly contain my feelings. These people are simple in every way, and rough, even when they're praying, but they've stripped us bare. A few days ago, taking advantage of Father Nicholas' visit, we gave them the Tibetan painting of the Virgin Mary that Pierre gave us in Tibet. He took it down from the wall in his living room to pass it on to the next community. The celebration takes place in the village church, in the light of a mass of little candles and in the presence of at least 50 villagers. They give us a beautiful shawl of homespun wool, which we will hand on to the priest in the next village community.

It's in one of my bags. God willing, we won't get it out until we're in the Amazon.

# 12

## The Amazon

### In which Tintin's adventure *The Broken Ear* is better read than experienced

We can make out the curves of the river far below, with its millions of cubic metres of water flowing towards the sea. Until now the Amazon has been a distant goal, an idyllic image. But what we see now out of the window of the plane is very real and far bigger than we ever imagined. Will the legend become a horrible reality? Its vastness is quite disconcerting – it looks more like an ocean than a river. Numerous container ships ply the waters around Manaus, capital city of the state of Amazonas in the north-west of Brazil. And as we make our fifth landing since we left Bangkok 48 hours ago – having flown via Kuala Lumpur, Taipei, Los Angeles and Panama – I feel a slight twinge of anxiety. This was all my idea and, even though Gabriel was quick to come on board when I suggested it, I feel undeniably responsible. What if things go wrong?

'The Amazon, here we come!'

But Gabriel is upbeat and I put my dark thoughts behind me. Particularly when, as if to encourage us, Providence arranges our collection from the airport. It's already late in the day and our immediate challenge is to find somewhere to spend the night. We collect our bags, relishing the fact that for once we don't have to lug our bikes around in their boxes and reassemble them, since my family, who came to visit us in Bangkok, have taken them home. We'll be cycling again when we reach Dakar, but until we get there, we'll be on foot.

'Have you got any ideas?'

'No.'

'Shall we try hitching a ride?'

'Let's.'

There aren't many people in the airport this afternoon, or outside it either. In fact it's quite straightforward – there's only one vehicle, parked just outside the sliding door at the exit of the terminus. The air is hot and humid, even more so than in Thailand. We hail the driver of the 4x4, who is about to drive off. He smiles, takes us on board and drops us 20 kilometres down the road, in front of the diocesan house. Simple as that.

The bishop invites us in.

It's a stately old house, solidly built but so full of nooks and crannies that maintaining it must be a nightmare. It's the kind of place you'd remember if you played there as a child. Monsignor is in a meeting with two Italian priests and invites us to make use of the kitchen. Soon we're enjoying a big bowlful of red beans with a few chunks of meat.

'Come on, we'll take you into town!' one of the two priests calls out in Italian.

The bishop chimes in, in Portuguese, 'Couldn't be better. That's perfect timing. Really! Providential!'

We thank the bishop and follow the two priests. One is tall and quiet, the other short and talkative. We jump into the sedan waiting in front of the diocesan house. The driver is a young, blonde woman. Our two priests ask her to make a detour.

'We're taking you to a new community, Aliança de Misericórdia.[1] We started it ten years ago, in São Paulo, with a nun friend, who has since died.'

They explain that the community's vocation is to be present with the poorest of the poor and young delinquents in the city's worst neighbourhoods. And to use every means possible to reach them with the gospel.

'Our missionaries are all over the place! At all times of night and day! On the tram, the bus, they organize open evenings in their homes. And of course, the big thing these days is the *cristoteca*!'

'Could you say that again please?'

'A *cris-to-te-ca*. It's a classic discotheque, except that the evening starts with Mass, they don't serve alcohol and they play only Christian music!'

---

[1] <www.miseracordia.com.br>.

They're crazy, these Amazonians.

But the chatty little guy assures us the concept has really taken off and, every Friday evening, after a short time of worship, a group of Christian musicians get the crowd really pumped and they dance on through the night to psalms and praise music . . . And we're not talking about just a few enthusiasts; these *cristotecas* regularly attract over 2,000 people.

The tall, quiet one adds: 'We live 100 per cent on God's provision. God gives us what we need every day. We own nothing. Not even a car. So that's why Linda came to pick us up tonight!'

In Brazil the charismatic movement and these newly established communities like Aliança de Misericórdia are a response to a renewal in the Protestant church, which is attracting more and more people, often at the expense of Catholic churches. The charismatic renewal appeared in the 1960s in the USA. It advocates the use of the 'gifts of the Spirit' mentioned in the New Testament at the time of Pentecost. Believers experience a 'baptism in the Spirit' and promote the use of the 'spiritual gifts', such as healing and prophecy. This movement has influenced some Catholics, to the extent that it's not uncommon nowadays for a bishop to celebrate Mass with 'speaking in tongues', during which people pray in a foreign language that is totally unknown to them, pronouncing a succession of syllables that are incomprehensible but have the elements of a real language. Sometimes the liturgy includes times of praise during which there may be dancing and raised hands mixed with the spoken prayers.

Linda parks in front of a one-storey house, beside a small, deserted square. They explain that this is one of the poor parts of town and the house has been lent to the community.

'Ten missionaries live here! Some are seminary students, others are lay people.'

The missionaries, five men and five women between the ages of 23 and 35, seem more like students sharing an apartment than a religious community. They welcome us in and put down two mattresses in the boys' dormitory for us. They jabber away at us in Portuguese, and we mix a cocktail of Spanish and Italian in reply, managing to make ourselves understood, more or less. Julio, a sinister-looking, recently converted, former inmate, who has just started seminary, bombards us with questions. But we're incapable of explaining any-thing, we're so exhausted.

As I lie down to sleep, the same sense of unease returns: I feel like I'm standing at the top of a cliff, about to jump. And I no longer have any choice because the countdown has begun. If we want to be back in France by 5 July and have time to complete our last sector in West Africa, we need to set sail in five days. Set sail. I remind myself why we're here: to buy a wooden canoe or pirogue,[2] add a float and a sail, and then sail down the Amazon to a village that, as yet, we have no idea how to find – our fifth isolated village.

Yesterday we were on a plane. The day before that we were in Bang-kok with almost all of my family. My younger brother couldn't be with us but my parents and my two other brothers and sisters joined us for seven wonderful days. The second farewell was worse than the first, because this time my family's concerns made me seriously doubt the wisdom of our plans. In an effort to reassure them, I argued that we were confident and the plans for the pirogue were flawless, even though we didn't really have much idea what we were going to do. And in all the commotion of leaving, I managed to forget our tent. I left it in a corner of our hotel room. From now on, if someone doesn't offer us a bed, we'll be sleeping under the stars.

*Inshallah.* I fall asleep, too tired to even worry about it. Gabriel is already snoring.

Manaus is an explosion of colours, smells and sounds. On the banks of the legendary Amazon River, which reaches up to 50 kilometres wide in parts, we explore one of Brazil's many faces. The streets are grey and grimy but charming nevertheless. Little shops stand crammed in cheek by jowl. Brown-skinned women throw teasing glances at anyone willing to play. It's hot and the humidity is 90 per cent. Local music blasts from loudspeakers as the crowds wander by.

Over the past six days we've been frantically preparing for our expe-dition. Our first step is a visit to an agency that organizes excursions and survival courses in the Amazonian jungle. Just off a busy main

[2] A light, narrow, flat-bottomed boat, usually propelled by paddle, common on the Amazon River.

road, down a side alley, we find the little shop with its faded façade. The boss comes from Ecuador, the source of the Amazon, and he speaks English. We explain our plan and put to him a few straightforward questions, in a very calm and rational manner, which he kindly answers. Piranhas? That would be a stroke of bad luck given that the waters are high and you would have to fall into the middle of a school to be attacked. Crocodiles? Hey, come on, there *aren't* any crocodiles in the Amazon. Only alligators, and they never attack people. But are there mosquitoes? Yes, hordes of *carapanas*. The main risks, in his view, are related to water currents, storms and the risks of boating in general. When we are about to leave, he mentions that two Swiss men drowned during a similar expedition, after a seven-week voyage, at the entrance of the port we plan to leave from. Great.

'It's 80 metres deep, 18 kilometres wide. No one messes with the Amazon. Are your mothers worried?'

We thank him and decide to exercise our selective memory: we manage to retain the fact that we need some charts. After asking some other shoppers their opinion, we make our way to the Instituto Brasileiro de Geografia e Estatística (IBGE) but, at the address we've been given, the doors are closed. They've moved.

Time is getting on and we must leave for the little town of Manacapuru. Around here everything, or almost everything, is done on the water. People here take the boat like we'd take a bus in Paris. We board a boat-bus that drops us on the floating port of Manacapuru where, apparently, they specialize in building pirogues. If you're in the Amazon and you need a pirogue, this is the place to come. The first vendor we meet is called Juca. He's about 60, with big brown eyes and age spots peppering his tanned skin. He's a kind man and as self-assured as an old sage. There are dozens of pirogues lined up behind his wooden shack. They're beautiful and certainly well built, but they look too low to handle a long sail in rough water and high winds. They're more suitable for the locals, who fit them out with an outboard motor and use them for short fishing trips in fine weather.

At the end of the pontoon we find the boat-building yard. The scene is surreal. Big-bellied, barechested men, obviously inebriated, are busy doing various jobs. Two are caulking an old boat with flaking paint, while a third is cutting the lashings from an old net and soaking them in some sort of molasses before handing them to his two mates. Two other workers, whose clothes stink of sweat and urine, are lying under a shady tree, in a vacant stupor. The whole place is more like a rubbish dump than a workshop. Around us lie piles of the skeletons of old pirogues, more or less stripped bare. We extract some information out of the least lively of the lot – the boss. To have a pirogue made to order takes about a week. Too long for us. While I wait at the carpenters' workshop for a potential vendor, Gabriel goes back to Juca's place. Twenty minutes later he returns with a smile on his face. Juca can raise the sides of one of his pirogues and have it ready two days from now, for half the price this other lot are offering. It's a deal.

Over the next few days we run from one end of town to the other to pull together the bare minimum of equipment to fit out the boat. Near Manaus' commercial port there are several streets dedicated exclusively to ship chandlery and hardware. The shop fronts, once brightly painted, are now faded by sun and wind. Large, gaudy lettering decorates the walls. Inside goods hang from the ceiling in great bunches, which obliges clients to manoeuvre carefully to avoiding knocking the lot to the ground. In these gigantic jumble sales we ferret out, with great patience and our best negotiating skills, almost everything we need: a hammer, some large nails, a good, solid machete, some fine but strong rope for the halyards and stays, some thicker rope that will do for a mooring and a tow rope just in case, some clamps (which we may need for caulking), a plastic bottle (which when cut in two will make a magnificent bailer), two hammocks, a large cobalt blue tarpaulin (which we hope to make into a sail), some strapping, two cheap little lamps (which will serve as a masthead light) and a few days' food.

To speed up the process, Gabriel and I separate. Yesterday, while we were making our first purchases, Gabriel met a boat vendor who offered to help us make a sail. So he goes off to see him with the big piece of canvas, the straps, and his best behaviour. Delighted to assist with the construction of this important vessel, the man puts Gabriel on to his friend's little boat and returns to his shop. The friend takes Gabriel to a little island opposite Manaus, and accompanies him to a house which, Gabriel soon learns, belongs to the kindly boat vendor. In a large room on the ground floor women are busy sewing army uniforms. When they see him, they drop what they're doing and, with Gabriel's guidance and many detailed diagrams, they get to work. Our sail appears two or three hours later. It's a great little triangle. The edges are reinforced with webbing and a little ring sits at each point of the triangle – they will serve as points of attachment. Simple as that.

Meanwhile, I set off again in search of the correct navigation charts. I race from bookshop to bookshop without finding anything. I fall back on our initial line of attack, the IBGE, having been given the new address by a local bookseller. It's a long way and I have to take the bus.

A young girl with olive skin and piercing eyes is also waiting for the bus. When I ask her if I'm waiting in the right place, she bursts out laughing and doesn't reply. On the bus, she writes me little notes on scraps of paper because she's convinced I can't understand her when she speaks. After some preliminary small talk, she hands me one last message that leaves me dumb, with a dazed smile: 'Where's your house? Near your stop? Can I come with you?' A funny place this, where the men are all podgy and sweaty and the women are all stunning.

When the bus stops, I tear myself away from my *belle* and continue on my expedition. I have to walk for a good ten minutes more through some indescribably foul back alleys. In the depths of the Manaus ghetto I finally find the IBGE. A man of about 50, buried amid hundreds of files and rolls of paper, greets me amiably. He gets out two charts: Manaus-Santarém and Santarém-Belém. They are beautifully made but far from detailed enough, giving only a general view of our route. It's the best he can do; the next level up would require 20 or 30 charts to cover the whole area. Too bulky and too expensive. In the end we'll make do with satellite images from Google Maps.

I decide to stop by the harbourmaster's office to try to find information on currents, tides, weather forecasts for the next few days, danger zones, pirates . . . Yes, pirates. I ask a passer-by the way when I get off the bus and he offers to accompany me. We chat like old friends. Then, after several streets, when we're almost there, he stops dead in his tracks.

'I can't go any further. It's too dodgy around here. The place you want is over there, first on the right.'

Great.

I thank him and go on alone. Two minutes later, I hear hurried steps behind me. I turn round. It's my kind friend.

'Hey, I changed my mind. You'll never find it by yourself.'

Some sinister-looking guys who look like hitmen are leaning against the wall of a dilapidated porch; mothers so pregnant they're almost as wide as they are high bawl at little children; rubbish and empty beer bottles are strewn across the street. I finally enter the harbourmaster's office.

A soldier with an impressive physique indicates that it's closed.

'Come back tomorrow.'

Blast.

After four days spent running round the town, each of us on our own errands, we finally consider ourselves ready to go to find our pirogue in Manacapuru. We find Juca, who has kept his word: the pirogue is ready.

We spend another two days getting ready, during which time we camp on the pontoon, right beside Juca's house. For €5, a scrap-metal dealer agrees to fashion eight metal parts into fixtures that will attach the floats to the hull. We also go in search of lengths of bamboo, which we see everywhere when we're not looking for it but which becomes quite scarce just when we need it. Finally Juca's neighbour's son takes us into the garden of a family he knows, where there is some thick bamboo. And the amazing thing is that they let us cut down half the clump. We bring back four long, straight, supple poles on our shoulders. One will be the mast, while the others will be made into an outrigger, which we'll attach to the hull. This will make the pirogue more stable when it's rough.

We took this idea from two Frenchmen who are crazy about the Amazon. They attempted a similar expedition several years ago. When I was looking for information on a journey in a pirogue on the Amazon 'river sea', I came across their story.[3] Interestingly, theirs was the only story I found, which reassured me that navigating the Amazon in a pirogue isn't about to be as trendy as touring Vietnam on a motor scooter.

---

[3] Marc Gayot, *L'Amazonie malgré nous: le Rio Negro et l'Amazone, en pirogue, à la rame et à la voile*, Chevagny-sur-Guye: Orphie, 2008.

On the afternoon of the second day, when we can wait no longer, we adjust our straw hats and cast off our moorings. Our turnaround manoeuvre is ridiculous and we narrowly avoid squashing our float beneath the pontoon. The villagers watch us go, waving shyly.

Over the last few hours the news of our departure has got around and some curious types have come to see the Europeans who take themselves for locals. But they just take us for *locos* (fools). As we slip away from the pontoon I'm already missing Juca's neighbour, who sells her homemade cakes and biscuits. The aromas from her kitchen have been like balm to me these past two days, as I lay on the pontoon with the sound of the water lapping below. One old man stays on the pontoon a little longer than the others. He's the one who cut Gabriel's hair an hour earlier, to remedy the style I had created against my better judgement: a Mohawk. He's also the one who gave us the final warning.

'Watch out for the *ondas*. They're dangerous.'

The *ondas*, the waves. Huh, we'll see about that.

At first it seems that we have no control over anything. We drift gaily about on the strong current of the Solimões.[4] We put in a few token strokes of the paddle from time to time to avoid being carried out into the middle of the river, but otherwise the current does it all. It's a conveyor belt and we feel like exactly what we are – a little cockleshell. The sky is blue, the temperature is mild, and with evening approaching, the sunshine is becoming gentler. We're on the alert in case we discover a leak, break a paddle or bump into an anaconda – in short, waiting for the sky to fall on our heads, as everyone has been predicting endlessly over the last five days. But no. We drift along, our only discomfort being the worry of not knowing what we're getting ourselves into. For the moment we don't have any idea of distances and no charts of a large enough scale to help us. We get acquainted with our pirogue, trying to get to know her, make her a trusted ally with whom we feel safe. We're timid, wary, on the lookout for the slightest sign from the universe, a bird flying across our bows or the sudden splash of a fish breaking the water, which might indicate that we're disturbing the natural order of the river.

[4] The Solimões River joins the Negro River near Manaus to form the Amazon River.

As darkness gradually veils the riverbanks, we spot a pontoon jetty approaching, several hundred metres away on the north bank. It's the first sign of human life we've seen and we decide to stop there for the night. We have to work hard to manoeuvre our craft close to it. We still make too many air strokes; we need more practice. We've barely stepped ashore when two men burst out from nowhere, shouting at us.

'Hey, you guys are crazy! Good thing you've stopped. There's a storm coming!'

There isn't a cloud to be seen. They're the fools, not us. We thank them for the warning and hang our hammocks beneath an awning, with the satisfaction of a job well done. We're not a little proud of having remained afloat so far.

'Hey, it's not too bad, is it? An afternoon on the Amazon?'

'Yeah, the Amazon's not so bad. They were just trying to scare us.'

Barely 15 minutes after our two prophets of doom leave us, a loud boom rends the night and flashes of lightning streak the sky. The buzz of insects abruptly ceases and torrents of rain come lashing down on the river. Within seconds our little boat, tied to the pontoon, is full of water. A violent wind whips the swell. It's an apocalyptic vision. We shudder to think what will happen if we're on the water next time this happens. In the meantime, we take a shower in the diluvian rains and curl up in our hammocks. We're not feeling so clever now.

If people ask about our trip, there's one part of the journey I never mention – the two weeks on the river after the storm. Even for a large sum of money. It was worse than sunstroke in the Syrian Desert, worse than our steepest climb or our coldest night.

We very quickly realize how horribly evil the Amazon serpent really is: it's a 2,000-kilometre, barbed triffid whose spines are the sun, the wind, the rain, the waves and the mosquitoes. There's absolutely nothing to make sailing it enjoyable.

As we set out on our second day, under a blue sky, we hear a dull roar in the distance. With every second it grows closer and louder. It's a thunderous sound, but muffled – the roar of a muted ogre. We realize that it's not coming from the sky but echoing up from the depths of the waters. And it's there that we first notice the turbulence. At first it's well behind us, then it approaches and overtakes us. The surge of the waves and whirlpools, some enormous, others small, have stirred up the river. Just when we think we're in the clear, the boat starts spinning. We're caught in a vortex that sucks our float down towards the bottom and spins the hull around like a compass. We paddle like madmen and it suddenly spits us out. This whirlpool was mild. I know we're both thinking the same thing: what will happen if we're sucked into a bigger one next time? Within its waters, 80 metres deep, the Amazon has an underwater life we can barely comprehend, much less imagine.

'So that's what they mean by their *ondas* . . .'

The sky is still an insolent blue. We get ourselves back into position to continue our slow drift. I'm relaxing, with my straw hat for shade, feet up and a book propped on my chest while Gabriel steers, roughly. Our stupor is interrupted only when a pod of dolphins keeps us company. I start and almost drop my book into the water as one surfaces for breath centimetres from my face. At least 10 or 12 of these characters circle us, performing acrobatics all around; just showing off.

We pass from the Solimões into the Rio Negro, inching our way painstakingly past Manaus. The surface of the water has a pearlescent sheen, but the water is black . . . the Rio Negro! We're sailing on a sea of Guinness! Before a backdrop of monstrous silos and dirty grey warehouses, container ships as tall as a five-storey building and rusty oil tankers are loading and unloading at the Port of Manaus. In the failing light, with our headlamps flashing on our foreheads, we cross the shipping lane, weaving timidly between these monsters, knowing it's up to us to avoid a collision, because they're totally incapable of stopping. Their angry sirens remind us that they're indifferent to the risk we're running: they could reduce us to woodchips. We paddle on and on, bone tired, almost all our strength gone. In this port zone, we can't find anywhere to stop for the night. We even try our chances with a Brazilian navy ship; it pushes us off summarily and follows us with a yellow beam from its searchlight for several long minutes. About two in the morning we wash up, bodies and boat, on a clay beach which stinks of fuel oil. We sleep like logs under our mosquito nets.

Our third day on the river is no more enjoyable. We leave our beach, which proved to be infested with mosquitoes, without much enthusiasm. But the wind won't let us escape and invariably pushes us back on to the riverbank. We must start over at least six times before managing to leave the cove behind us. And when we finally make it out into the stream, there's no current. Absolutely none. Zilch. Fed up, we paddle with all our might but it's like trying to drive a tank with a lawnmower engine. We feel furious and then we just feel plain discouraged. The sail eventually enables us to make way. We cross a string of floating islands – the remains of landslides – and reach a little commercial port within the Manaus industrial area. As we approach, several men signal for us to stop. Hardly have we thrown our mooring line than 10 or 12 big, hulking men grab our pirogue and haul it on to a two-level slipway, several metres high. Beside us, they're unloading a container ship.

'Hey, lucky you stopped. A storm's coming!'

'But the sky is . . .'

This time, I stop mid-sentence. The sky is blue. Just like two days ago. Which doesn't mean it's not going to pour down with torrential rain. Once again I narrowly avoid looking like a complete rookie, and quickly shut up. And rightly so, because the breeze soon freshens and the sky darkens. In less than 15 minutes an extraordinarily violent storm blows up. White horses cover the river, the water level rises almost to eye level. And our pirogue is filled with rain. Again. In the shelter of an old shed, wet and shivering, we watch the elements rage. We've just, providentially, escaped our second storm. For the second time in three days, we stop for reasons completely unrelated to the weather and find ourselves dragged out of the water, *in extremis*. I can't help feeling our lucky star is watching over us, again.

When *la tempesta* calms down and we finally set off again, we're caught in the same drama as this morning: impossible to get away from the shore. In our little boat, tensions rise as tiredness overcomes us. I wonder how we could ever have hoped to reach Parintins. How arrogant! Here we are, two little upstarts, swept against the jetty yet again, and we can't do a thing about it. A crowd gathers to watch the comedy; they're quick to laugh at our incompetence.

When we come in to land that evening, Gabriel trips and winds up spreadeagled in the mud as he tries to pull the pirogue out of the water. It's the last straw. We've reached rock bottom.

'Look, we've put up with this crap for long enough. Let's head home now, eh?'

I'm incapable of replying.

Three days. That's how long it's taken us to fall to our lowest ebb, exhausted of every ounce of energy and optimism.

On the third evening we feel drained and weak, but on the morning of the fourth day we come back to life, not really knowing how or why. When everything was going wrong, suddenly things start to improve. After three days of struggling and putting up with everything the Amazon had to throw at us, our confidence grows and we become, slightly more, masters of our own ship.

And the extraordinary thing is that, at the moment, we're making progress. A little breeze ripples the surface and fills our sail. We play with the breeze and try to point as high as we can into the wind. Like a painted backdrop, the landscape rolls by. On board we're getting more organized. I screw a cleat to the foot of the mast to which we secure the halyard. Gabriel rigs up a makeshift block and tackle to help the helmsman haul in the sail with one hand. We find a permanent place to stow the food bags.

Our pirogue is six and a half metres long, giving us a living area of about nine square metres. There are four transverse benches, but we only use two, one at each end of the boat. We each sit on a fluoro orange life jacket, our backs against the hull and our legs stretched out, resting on the blade of one of the oars. Most of the time we spend reading or writing. We talk as well. Everything is extremely slow. Sometimes, in a mad burst of activity, one of us will get up, get out the fishing line, and try to catch some fish; they look repulsive, very like the fish-shaped rubbish bins in French ports. We gut them, drop them in a bucket of water and cook them for dinner.

The heat is oppressive and we didn't think to bring an awning to protect us from the sun. It burns the backs of our hands and the soles of our feet, makes the wooden parts of the boat untouchable and fries the skin on our faces. If we didn't treat ourselves to a swim several times a day, it would be unbearable. Before we dive in we always feel slightly queasy, wondering whether, by some incredibly bad luck, we might dive into the middle of a school of piranhas, or whether the brown water might conceal some rogue alligator.

Two or three times a day we have to bail out the water that seeps in imperceptibly through tiny holes. It works silently, slowly and conscientiously filling the bilge. It weighs us down and slows us down as well. One of the high points of the day is preparing our meals; we make sure this takes as long as possible. With our minuscule budget, there's no variety; the menu is always the same – canned sardines or mackerel and *farinha* (manioc flour). To make it palatable and digestible, we pep it up with lemon zest or smother it with sauce from a can. For breakfast and dessert we have guava paste from a big, red plastic pack, which we spread on crackers or mix with *farinha*. And for drinks we have the water all around us – a permanently open 'bar' of murky water. We take it from the middle of the river, where it's deepest and the water seems most fresh, and therefore the least dirty, and store it in bottles, throwing in purifying tablets, which give it the inimitable flavour of bleach. But not even the locals drink the river water, which contains copious amounts of excrement, both human and animal. I don't realize it at the time, but I'm incubating a nasty bug which won't show itself until later, when the Amazon is well behind us.

With experience comes knowledge. We now know, for example, that tens of millions of mosquitoes prepare their proboscises for action every evening at precisely twenty past six. And so, in spite of the heat, we wrap ourselves up in our oilskins, tie our Syrian scarves round our heads and tuck our trousers into our socks.

It rains every night, or almost. Sometimes just a few drops, sometimes a deluge. With no tent, since we left it behind in Bangkok, we sleep little and fitfully in our damp duvets. It's a Catch 22: either we use the stakes to make the sail into a tent that protects us from the rain and do without mosquito nets, or else we opt for our set-up with the mosquito nets and put up with the weather. Every time the rain wakes us in the middle of the night, we ask ourselves if we've made the right choice, but the second option invariably wins out, because of the horror of the mosquitoes and also because laziness always reigns at three in the morning. But when the squalls are too strong, we have no choice but to break camp and set sail in the middle of the night.

Some evenings we choose to spend the night drifting, taking turns keeping watch. Darkness sets in, potent and overbearing. It's even more infinite than the water and trees surrounding us. Ferries disturb the silence and interrupt the crickets' song. Freighters travel up and down the Amazon; on the decks the passengers lounge in colourful hammocks. Here and there we see a huge barge pushed by a tiny riverboat with powerful engines, out of all proportion to its size.

It's difficult to assess distances in the dark. Distant flashes of lightning, mute and therefore innocuous, light up the sky. We signal our position to other boats with two blinking flashlights, which we haul to the top of the mast. Gabriel lies down to sleep on two planks placed between the benches, while I take the first watch. As I stare out into the empty night, I think out loud so that Gabriel can benefit from my profound thoughts. I figure that the river is carrying us away and messing us around, that we're masters of nothing; it's taking us wherever it pleases. We should let ourselves be guided by this powerful current that's taking us forward far faster than we could have dreamed if we were depending only on our own means. In a way, it's the same with my faith. I didn't choose it. I'm a Christian precisely because I don't have the choice. It forces itself on me while it hardly touches my colleague at work and I don't understand why. Nor do I understand what this faith involves. I don't know where it might take me if only I'm willing to let myself be carried. I do what I can, trusting in something that's much greater than I am.

To keep myself awake, I paddle. Half-heartedly. But I paddle. And I scan the horizon praying I won't see a mass of clouds piling up, one on top of the other . . .

On Sunday, 21 March, exactly a week since we left Manacapuru, we step ashore at Itacoatiara having completed the first half of our journey. The town sits on the north bank of one of the numerous narrowings in the river. The current here is extremely strong. We need to stock up with food and warn the Bishop of Parintins that we'll be arriving late. We met him by chance as he was passing through Manaus, the day before

**Our trusty vessel, tied up at nightfall. We sleep dry in Itacoatiara**

our departure. He's expecting us, 200–300 kilometres downstream, and will direct us to a village in his diocese. Our fifth isolated village.

Itacoatiara is a fishing village. The streets are empty. The houses are squat and painted in pale colours. We treat ourselves to the luxury of lunch at a little restaurant. It's about 15 metres square, a squalid hole, but the boss lady is plump, which reassures us that she, at least, enjoys her cuisine.

'Are you English? No? French? Oh, even worse!'

We stay for a good three hours, happy to see other living beings and tell exaggerated tales of our nautical misadventures. The coating on my sunglasses has progressively disintegrated since last July, and my eyes are sunburnt. Now one of my lids is permanently closed. I cover it with my headscarf, which makes me look like a resistance fighter at best, but more likely a clown; in any case it seems to amuse the sweet, little old lady.

'Are you going to Mass?'

'Yes.'

'Oh! Very good! Pray for me.'

'You're not coming?'

'What do you expect? I've got far too much work to do.'

After attempting a siesta to catch up on the hours of sleep stolen from us by a stormy night, we go off to attend Mass. Opposite the church stands an imposing seminary building. Between the two is a square that's said to be the liveliest in all of Itacoatiara. Young people play basketball, girls in short dresses flaunt their figures, couples eat sandwiches at street cafés. In the middle of this Amazonian *dolce vita*, six young men, smartly dressed, make their way through the crowd. They're seminary students. The contrast is striking. During Mass they stand on either side of the priest, in their immaculate white robes. In spite of their youth, they're learning to give themselves totally to God.

It's Saturday, 27 March, the last day of our journey, and today our already shaken boat is almost completely ruined.

At three o'clock, heavy rain bombards the boat and bullies us out of our sleeping bags. The wind whips up the water, making the boat pitch and roll. We sail close to the embankment to avoid being carried away by the wind and the current. But the obscure dawn half-light is treacherous and, a fraction of a second too late, we notice an uprooted tree floating ahead of us.

Unable to avoid it, the pirogue buckles, creaks and careers awkwardly up on to the log. We're stuck. I feel a rush of adrenaline. The wind is freshening. We're heading straight into the waves, which smash on to the log, dumping bucketloads of water into our boat as they pass. We don't even think about bailing; that would be like emptying a bath with a soup spoon while the tap is still running. We use the weight of our bodies to rock the boat off the log, so that it will slide back into the water. In vain. We watch horrified as the wind picks up even more. And then, with one last desperate burst of energy, Gabriel jumps out of the boat on to the log, and stands up on it. Then with the full weight of his body he pushes with his arms on the log and his legs on the boat to break the two apart. We slide a few centimetres. And then we splash back into water, completely free.

But almost immediately the wind slams us against other floating logs, which are swept along by the storm. We're struggling to keep ourselves from being crushed against the embankment, which is coming closer and closer every minute. We're exhausted. How long has this been going on? Ten minutes? Twenty? Thirty? We're powerless, fighting a losing battle against the elements, which are oblivious to our plight. The rain is torrential. It's a nightmare. I close my eyes.

And then the wind dies down.

I realize, as the water flattens and we finally move further from the bank, that we hadn't raised our voices. We paddled as one man. That's all. We take advantage of the lull in the wind to get ourselves well clear of the bank, positioning ourselves in the middle of the river.

'I'm going to have a swim!'

Gabriel turns round in surprise. I'm already in the water, still fully dressed. I was soaked to the skin anyway. I couldn't control the urge. I feel I can thumb my nose at this wretched river. A sudden thrill, and a deep sigh of satisfaction. The water is warm. Soothing.

Thanks to a bend in the river, we catch a glimpse of some buildings in the distance, which probably means we've almost reached Parintins. But as I climb on board, there's another roar of thunder. It starts raining even more heavily than before. The storm is coming from behind us and bringing with it some wind – from the west! A miracle! For once, it is coming from behind us! We hoist the sail, which fills immediately, and knuckle down to work together. Gabriel steers while I haul in the sheet, with two hands because the wind is so strong. We can't believe it! We take off downwind, ploughing through the water, leaving an impressive wake of white spray behind us. We race along at a great clip, intoxicated by the speed. We double-cross one storm, then a second. They erupt behind us and we carry on regardless.

Soon, however, the black cloud catches up with us and darkens the water around us. Within seconds there'll be thunder and lightning. Releasing the halyard and sheet, we rush to lay the mast down inside the boat. In the middle of this vast plain of water, our mast is as attractive to lightning as a metal pole in the middle of a field. The storm breaks above us, but no matter.

Then, after paddling for an hour, we reach Parintins. In the rainy haze we can make out a church tower on the skyline. We pass between two enormous coloured beacons that mark the entrance to the channel, and paddle a few last strokes before reaching the main port, where we tie the pirogue at the stone steps that function as a jetty. Our clothes are drenched but at least it has stopped raining. When

Monsignor Giuliano comes to meet us, the sun finally bursts through the clouds. It's eleven o'clock in the morning. The bishop has alerted the diocesan television to our arrival, and two journalists pummel us with questions in Portuguese, to which we reply as best we can. We follow our host like robots to his home. After a piping hot shower, we celebrate our introduction to the local church with a long siesta.

To get acquainted with the church, there's nothing like hanging around with the local bishop. It's also the best way of getting VIP treatment. Like the majority of the clergy in this diocese, our bishop is Italian, a PIME[5] missionary. He loves speaking in a loud voice, telling jokes, slapping us on the back and eating well. He obviously likes to perpetuate the Italian stereotype, and it's nothing to do with us – apparently he's always like that. When we get up on Sunday morning we find him in the little bishop's chapel, in prayer. Then he's off to prepare a festive breakfast, followed by a lunch of pasta and an exotic fruit crumble slathered with whisky; an episcopal dose for Palm Sunday.

We join one of the five processions that will converge on the cathedral in the middle of the town this evening. Originally planned to kick off at five in the afternoon, it's starting late.

'In the Amazon, times are only a general indication!'

Dom Guiliano is laughing his head off as he slips on his robe. A warm-hearted man, he shows his enthusiasm by bobbing his head around from side to side sporadically as he talks. He's continually smiling his broad, bishop's smile.

Dozens of little choir girls and boys lead the way, carrying palm branches. The priests and the bishop follow. Then come hundreds of people who are there for what is to them a cultural event as much as a statement of faith. Around here everyone, or almost everyone, is baptized, to the extent that the official sponsor of the diocesan jubilee is none other than the Amazonas state government, and on the first page of the diocesan magazine there's an interview with the governor, who says he's proud to see this religious event being held in his state.

---

[5] Pontificio Istituto Missioni Estere (Pontifical Institute for Foreign Missions) is a society of secular priests and lay people who dedicate their lives to missionary activities in several parts of the world, notably in Asia. It was founded in Italy in the mid nineteenth century.

An exuberant choir sets the rhythm; they're perched on the top deck of an electric-blue open-top bus. A platinum blonde dishes out the decibels to the passers-by. The last rays of the sun light up the scene as we amble along the riverbank, with palm trees waving gently above us. Soon we join the processions from the four other churches. Several hundred believers converge on the cathedral of Nossa Senhora do Carmo. People are joyful, the ceremony vibrant. The bishop, who several hours earlier was treating us to the delights of the *caiperinha*,[6] is now as serious as a pope. Beside him two young girls assist. One of them wears big, round, shiny earrings. Even in the presence of the bishop, it's a beauty contest.

Back at the diocesan house, sitting in the garden, we put some questions to the bishop while he struggles to crack open a coconut with a machete. He explains that the Church here is quite different from what we're used to in Europe. It's a confident Church – full of warmth and humanity, and a grassroots faith – an integral part of everyday life, to which this evening's celebrations bear witness.

'And yet although Brazil is the largest Catholic country in the world, it is still a mission field. Here in my diocese, people have no trouble accepting the message of the gospel. But they forget it just as easily! The challenge for us is to allow each person to internalize the Catholic faith through his reason, and not solely through his heart, his emotions. It's only when they see that the gospel makes sense that their faith will become deep-rooted, strong. We're trying to make this change happen through the catechism, evangelism and prayer.'

He's cracked it! The coconut is open. The little man relaxes into his plastic chair.

'But the work of spreading the gospel in Brazil is done primarily through the media!'

In fact the Catholic Church alone has five national television channels and as many radio channels and newspapers. And that's not counting the local media such as the Parintins Diocesan Television, whose programming is supervised by the bishop himself.

'To understand the success of televangelism you have to go back to 1978, when Father Jonas, with the support of his community,

[6] Brazilian alcohol.

launched a television channel in São Paulo. They show Mass replays, sermons, the Rosary, Christian films. It met with rapid, unequivocal success. Canção Nova soon became the third most popular television channel in the country.'

We spend three days in Parintins, enough time for us to recharge our batteries and for Monsignor to decide which village to send us to. In the sixteenth century, when the Amazon was evangelized, several orders from the Old World shared out the area like pieces of a pie, dividing it into spheres of influence. At the beginning of the twentieth century, the first bishop of Parintins, Dom Archangelo, bought land beside the Amazon for families to live on; their main resources were fishing and farming. Each family participated in the construction of the church as they were able. Some gave a bag of cement, others a bit more. The bishop at the time wanted these little villages to become active and autonomous Christian communities, supported by regular visits from the missionaries. Rather than exhausting himself travelling all over the countryside visiting isolated families and tiny little hamlets, he brought them together and made evangelizing them infinitely more straightforward.

Mocambo was one of those villages.

'*Voilà!* The pirogue is sold!'

Gabriel returns victorious. The man at whose shed we left it last night has found someone who'll take it for $200 Brazilian. It's not much, but we don't have any choice. We're just in time to catch the boat to Mocambo. On the quay, Magalie gives us endless advice in a very motherly way. Magalie is in her forties; she was sent to Parintins by her diocese to share the gospel with disadvantaged women and children, particularly among the Indians. But most importantly, Magalie speaks perfect French, and so we were introduced to her straight away.

The decks of the old tub are crowded with hammocks strung at different heights to maximize the space. Mocambo is several kilometres upstream. We admire the birds flying above the forest, the sidestreams that snake in and out of the greenery. When we contemplate it from here, the forest seems majestic. As the sun goes down I watch a replay of a film of the first missionaries to Mocambo. The most iconic is Augusto – *Padre* Augusto. Arriving in the 1950s from his native Italy, he was loved and respected by the villagers. He was powerfully built and had a complicated mind; he was always afraid that he wasn't doing enough. He was also daring, an explorer and adventurer who could swim and row faster than any of the locals, a man capable of getting out of the worst situations, and an experienced hunter. When he was in Mocambo he never really settled down. He had no home. He went from house to house begging hospitality from the villagers, which they were very glad to supply. His ideal was 'to live like the early Christians'. A real giant, this Augusto.

After five hours of battling upstream against the current, we reach our destination.

## Fifth isolated community: Mocambo

In the oppressive humidity that always precedes a big storm, Priscilla rocks a little pink hammock to the rhythm of the music. In the hammock lies her baby. Priscilla is about 30 years old, quite strong, with reddish hair, tanned skin and a slightly flat nose. She's our hostess, with her husband Léomar, who is in charge of the Mocambo Catholic community. They live in the presbytery and they've given us two rooms for the duration of our stay. The CD player fills the courtyard with the Latino songs that Priscilla obviously adores. 'All for Jesus. Nothing without the Virgin Mary', the song by Deacon Nelsinho Correa. The record sold over 20,000 copies. This music is 'pop praise', which is having difficulty breaking into the European market but here is loved by everyone. There's a long list of singers: Father Fábio de Melo (Golden disc in 2010) who, on the cover of his bestseller, looks like a Hollywood star; Monsignor Jonas, who has released several albums which are selling well; Diante de Trono, the Christian worship band capable of attracting two million people to their concerts. Priscilla and her daughter Carla-Jessica, a child from a former marriage, idolize these singers. Since we arrived a week ago, we've had the opportunity to sing some of these songs with them. And on the best evenings, Carla-Jessica gives us a few dance steps, which puts her into an absolute trance.

Carla-Jessica has just come home from school. She's 12 going on 17. It seems to be the case for all Amazonian women. They look older than they are and can do things earlier than everyone else. Who knows if it's a cause or an effect? For example, Priscilla and Léomar's neighbour, who answers to the name of Aquila, is a pretty young lady of 21, whose first son is 7 years old. They're not slow, here in Mocambo. The women can be grandmothers at the age of 30, when a French woman is vaguely thinking about having her first child. Here a girl isn't a woman until she's a mother, so that becomes a short-term goal for most young girls.

After the ordeal of the journey in the pirogue, it's wonderful to spend whole days here doing nothing. The change of rhythm each time we stop in one of our isolated villages is a shock, but I must say this time it's particularly welcome.

Our hosts really put themselves out to make us comfortable. They introduce us to new kinds of fruit with catchy names. We taste *acerola*, little acid fruit the size of a large cherry and full of vitamin C, *maracudja*, which we call a passion fruit, *azeitona*, *cuja*, *marimari*, *ingacipo*, *cupu* . . . The widespread obesity among these people bears witness to a high level of culinary activity, which is just how we like it. Our new friends have an almost religious adoration of carbs of all kinds, and love to mix them together: they love floury cakes and biscuits with sweetened condensed milk toppings, pizzas and guarana-based soft drinks. We can feel ourselves getting fatter.

When we arrived on the boat, a welcoming committee was waiting for us with huge smiles on their faces. Among them was Léomar, who drove us to the presbytery. He's short with thick, wiry hair, an angular face and dark eyes set deep in his cranium. We quickly realize that Dom Guiliano, being a typical Mediterranean, has overplayed the village's isolation and small size. He guaranteed us 250 families 'at the absolute maximum', but we discover a town that the locals tell us numbers 5,000 people, four groceries and tar-sealed roads (only since last year, but even so). Electricity is everywhere. Mocambo was doubtless an isolated village ten years ago, but today it's growing in leaps and bounds.

We chose the Amazon for our fifth stop, imagining we might meet *Indios* Christians, men in loincloths toting bows and arrows, and missionaries in flip-flops. Back in Manaus we were beside ourselves with joy when Dom Guiliano, whom we met by chance as he was passing through, assured us that this wouldn't be a problem and that, as it happened, a priest would be leaving for a tour of the villages just when we were due to arrive in Parintins. From Itacoatiara we had telephoned to warn him that we would be late and to ask the priest to wait for us for two more days in Parintins if he could. Despite my very poor Italian, I thought everything was quite clear. And so we were a bit surprised when we learnt, on arriving in Parintins, that the priest had left for the villages several days earlier on an adventure that made us drool with envy. Then Dom Guiliano promised us something better – as if, in the great catalogue of attractions in the Catholic diocese, there could be an even more exciting prospect. It was Mocambo. According to him, this is a village isolated from everything, very preserved: an example of an autonomous community after successful evangelization. When we got off the boat and discovered this little town, we cringed at first, and then we came to terms with it. If Providence had brought us here, there must be a good reason for it. Up to us to adjust our ideas, even if it means not getting what we wanted.

Mocambo boasts three schools and a little open-air stadium. The island is so small that you can ride from one end to the other on a motor scooter in three minutes. Electricity cables, installed only a few months ago, criss-cross the sky. The asphalt on all the new roads contrasts with the dilapidated state of the tiny houses, clad in brick and wood. A hideous army of satellite dishes has invaded the rooftops. Opposite the presbytery there is an 'after-school centre' run by the parish, which caters for 200 children and teenagers. When we visit, some are making little dolls, others wooden aeroplanes. Each activity starts with a prayer led by one of the six adult supervisors. The children speak to us in Brazilian Portuguese as if we understood everything, and we find ourselves sitting in a circle with 20 kids, playing strange games.

Outside a man is selling fish. He has a toothless smile and his shirt bears the emblem of some obscure basketball team. He has all kinds of seafood on his stall, whereas we only managed to catch rubbish-bin fish from our pirogue. He has *marapas, piranhas* (we learn that the red ones have the best flavour), *tambakui, piracucu, bodo, apapa, surubin, pirara, jaraqui, pacu* . . . of every size and colour. Some are long and speckled, others are thick and covered with scales; some have a long moustache and others long, protruding teeth.

Nature gives of its abundance: fruit, fish, game. You can shake a tree and masses of fruit will fall to the ground, or you can nonchalantly throw out a net and pull it in bursting with fish. We get the feeling that life's not too difficult here in the Amazon.

It's Holy Week. For a Christian this is the most important week of the year: the week during which, 2,000 years ago, men put the Messiah to death; the week that justifies our faith because it culminates in the resurrection; the week that is both an ending and a beginning. At this very moment, all over the world, for Christians there's a gradual crescendo building up to Easter Sunday, when they can finally release their excitement in an explosion of joy and thanksgiving. For the first time in 40 days they will sing 'Hallelujah!'

In Mocambo, as in numerous places all over the planet, there is no priest. A year ago their last priest died of a heart attack when he was crossing the river, and the new priest, based in Manaus, finds the village too isolated and impractical to visit. So even for Holy Week, the villagers will be on their own. Over the last year the community has organized everything without a priest. Léomar is in charge of coordinating parish life. He is supported by four 'ministers of the Word', who are responsible for reading the Gospel on Sundays and, if necessary, preaching, and two 'ministers of the Eucharist', who step in after the liturgy of the Word to distribute the elements to the congregation. They are nominated by the bishop and take the ferry to Parintins regularly to get the consecrated bread.

'Come on, we're going to pray!'

Léomar leads us to the church, which is adjacent to the presbytery where we're living. It's a humble building, constructed with masonry blocks and concrete. Inside, the grey paint is flaking; the lighting is dim. It's drab and uninviting. Brazil is the largest Catholic country in the world, situated in the most Catholic continent in the world. If, like the rest of Brazil, 80 per cent of the population is Catholic, then

4,000 of the 5,000 inhabitants of Mocambo should flock here this Ash Wednesday. We wonder, 'How will they all fit into this little chapel?'

But when the ceremony is in full swing, there are only about 15 of us; many are children. A woman wearing a white robe edged with a green border leads the liturgy. She is one of the two ministers of the Eucharist. Whereas the Tibetans, the Indians and the Karens never venture behind the altar, this woman has no qualms about taking the place of a priest. And as she stands there, she starts singing a worship song and the choir responds with resounding Hallelujahs, which is not really appropriate during Lent.[7]

Thursday's celebration is much the same, and the high priestess takes the service again. This time there are about 20 people present.

On Good Friday, the day of Christ's passion, the villagers are busy all day in the stadium. Dozens of young people are preparing the stage for the play they are to perform tonight. At eight o'clock the stadium is completely full. There must be 400–500 people in the audience. The choir will accompany the actors as they re-enact the Way of the Cross. The villagers roar with laughter at every crack of the whip on Jesus' back and every tear shed by the improbable Mary, who lays it on thick and shakes her fist at death. The choir thoroughly lambaste the Gospel of the Passion. It's a great show, even if it's not high art. Jesus is stripped of his clothing and hung on a cross. His executioner mimes the crucifixion and Jesus cries out. And when he is lifted up on the cross, green and red lights flash on and off. The crowd quietens down, and the choir sing on, louder than ever. The children are ecstatic.

I can't make myself pray. Not even for a second. I can't understand them at all. I don't know what's happened to their inner life, to silence and contemplation.

The celebration continues in the church. On the way there we lose half the crowd. Gabriel and I can't help distancing ourselves from them; we'd rather be observers than participants. Whatever it was that made us feel at home in the other communities, it's not here. We had thought that the language and the recent presence of European missionaries might help us feel closer to the people. But we're lacking any frame of reference. We're completely at a loss. Strangers.

---

[7] During Lent (the 40 days before Easter), Catholics do not say or sing 'Hallelujah' (Praise God).

**Re-enactment of the Way of the Cross**

The people of Mocambo are friendly, enthusiastic and kind. Better still, they contribute their time and means to foster the life of the community. But the religion they practise is moving away, little by little, from the Catholic faith, to gradually become something else. Something emptied of its mystery, its sacredness and, in the end, its *raison d'être*, God himself. Something that could soon be nothing more than an enjoyable humanist get-together or a football match 'High Mass'.

In Mocambo we don't seem to sense God. All we see are lifeless, pointless rituals.

'It's the direct result of liberation theology!'

Magalie joins us the next day to celebrate Easter with us. We're particularly happy to be able to discuss these things with her in French.

'You know, the last priest in Mocambo was a good man, a man of prayer, but he fell away from the Catholic faith. But later on, towards the end of his life, he became more evangelical.

The rapid growth of a new brand of Protestantism is the most significant religious phenomenon to hit South America since it was first evangelized. In 1990, 20 per cent of the population said they were Protestant, compared to 63 per cent who claimed to be

Catholic, but at the same time, 20 million Protestants attended Sunday worship compared to 12 million Catholics![8] Between 1960 and 1985, the number of evangelicals quadrupled thanks in part to the media, which Protestant churches use very effectively. In the USA they have the evangelist Billy Graham, for example, and Brazil has its own televangelist stars, who feature regularly on television and radio. It's a new religious model, very different from that of the Catholic Church or even the historic Protestant Churches. This new brand of Protestantism comprises a range of Christian initiatives that have a number of characteristics in common but remain as separate organizations. They're less institutional and more charismatic than the Catholic Church. Interestingly, they're growing particularly fast in areas where there aren't enough priests, which leaves communities to organize themselves, as in Mocambo. This kind of situation tends to produce Catholics who view the sacraments as a relatively minor part of their faith and who are used to getting by without priests. In Brazil, and in the Amazon in particular, this type of approach could be called a sort of 'Catholicism without a priest at Mass';[9] it's really a 'counterfeit Catholicism'.[10]

It's Easter Sunday! Today the church of Mocambo is full. Renato, the other minister of the Eucharist, celebrates Mass. He exudes a sense of calm and encourages a more contemplative atmosphere, which spreads through the congregation. This time I find the ceremony moving. The songs are beautiful. I still have some difficulty praying but at least I feel I'm participating more in what's happening around me.

It's Easter! We kiss and hug each other. The kiss of peace takes place with a great hullaballoo, during which everyone feels they must embrace half the congregation. Lots of noise, lots of joy. Here, Easter has a nickname: the 'Hallelujah Carnival'!

After the ceremony the young people meet in a large room with plastic flooring and a plywood stage. This is where all the parish

[8] Andrea Riccardi, *Jean-Paul II: La biographie*, Paris: Parole et silence, 2011, p. 282.

[9] P. Chaunu, *Histoire de L'Amerique latine*, Paris: Presses universitaires de France, 1977, p. 111.

[10] Jean-Pierre Bastian, *Le Protestantisme en Amérique latine. Une approche socio-historique*, Paris: Labor et fides, 1994.

activities take place. Léomar and Priscilla step up on to the stage. Behind them a band is tuning up. I have a feeling we're going to get an earful. The room fills rapidly with teenagers from 12 to 17 years old; the vast majority are girls. Several old women stand at the back 'to keep an eye on the young ones', while others peer in between the bars on the windows, inquisitive and excited. The young people push back the tables and line up in several rows. The young girls stand in the front row to set the rhythm. Gabriel and I are worried. We try to lie low. And Léomar confirms our worst fears.

'Charles! Gabriel! Come into the middle!'

*Ay carumba!* Help! No! Not the middle! We don't move, making out we haven't heard.

'Come on! Come out into the middle! Are you shy?'

Shy. That's it. Exactly. We're shy. And we'd really rather just watch. But Léomar, from up on the stage, with the firepower his microphone gives him, won't hear of it.

'Helena! Carmen! Show them!'

That rascal! We're cornered. Two 16-year-old girls – who look like 20-year-olds – grab our hands and force us into the front row beside them.

The inevitable happens. The guitars thump out the rhythm, the drums explode and Léomar and Priscilla are transformed into praise pop stars. And the lyrics are all spiritual!

'Come, Holy Spirit! Breathe of God! Breathe on me! Fill me!'

To get the crowd going, Léomar invites us to sweat as much as we can. As if we had any choice.

'I want everyone to be HOT! Are you hot yet?'

I'm dyyyying of the heat.

The teenagers wave their limbs around in all directions. This is a praise and dance party. These events exist in France too – but I don't know if the French wiggle quite like they do here because I've never been to one. The young people go from one dance movement to another, mastering each perfectly. I think Gabriel and I are a pathetic cross between a refrigerator and a broom – we're so awkward when it comes to dancing.

After the time of praise comes a period of more gentle prayer. The music is subdued and the notes more stirring. Léomar's suave voice intersperses the lyrics with short, pressing prayers. Everyone's eyes are closed, including the grandmothers at the back. The dancers sway from side to side, their arms in the air, their hands outstretched towards heaven.

'Let's give thanks to Jesus and to the Virgin Mary who gives us such joy.'

We form a circle to conclude the evening with prayer, led by Léomar.

It's our last day in Mocambo. Yesterday Léomar and his brother-in-law took us to visit some smaller villages. We met several tiny fishing communities, places that seem sublime to our European eyes but poor and television-less in their eyes. In the evenings they took us fishing. Seeing the miraculous size of their catch, we spared a thought for the Lepchas in their underwear who had to beat the heck out of the riverbed with a heavy rock to catch a few measly sardines. Here, all they have to do is stretch a net across a little arm of the river at twilight and pull it in half an hour later to get ten magnificent fish, each about half a metre long.

We find Léomar in the parish centre. Under the awning about 30 young people have gathered. During Easter Mass we gave the community the gift from the Karen people: a hand-woven stole for the priest they don't have. It's the thought that counts. Today it's their turn. In the middle of the circle of children, set on a stool, stands the gift they're giving to the next village, in Senegal. It's a rectangular piece of plywood with a brightly coloured painting of a chalice overflowing on to the world. The children hold out their hands, their palms turned down towards the present and, with eyes closed, they pray for the Senegalese.

That evening, after a French dinner made by Gabriel and me, we do the rounds of the houses to say farewell to everyone. We linger a little with Renato, the minister of the Eucharist. He tells us fishing jokes in his poorly lit kitchen built of wooden planks. Between a net and an old, worn-out television, enthroned on a kind of lectern, lies an open Bible.

'In my house, we turn the page of the Holy Bible every evening to the text for the next day.'

The old man has taken a liking to us. Just as he's leaving he says: 'You can tell your parents you've got a second dad, in Mocambo!'

The next day we board a boat with hammocks that gets us to Manaus in two or three days, where we meet the missionaries from the Alliance de Miséricorde again. They hail us as true heroes. On the prow of our ferry, written in black letters on a white background, are the words *Se Deus é por nós, quem será contra nós?* ('If God is for us, who can be against us?').[11]

[11] Romans 8.31 (NIV).

# 13

## Senegal

### In which time pushes us on

15 APRIL, 9 MONTHS AND 10 DAYS AFTER DEPARTURE
A two-hour stopover in Paris gives us just enough time to dash from Roissy to Orly, find that the Paris traffic hasn't changed, have lunch on the run, pick up our bikes and kiss our families goodbye. And then, after two days of sitting in planes and airports, we land in Dakar in the dead of night. An old Muslim woman wearing a traditional Senegalese *boubou* (kaftan), who sat beside us on the plane, has offered us her husband's apartment for the night.

In the arrivals hall of Léopold-Sédar-Senghor airport we wait for Antoine, an old school friend. He is abandoning his books for a few days to get a bit of exercise. He's impossible to miss, with his beige shirt, complete with epaulettes like the French foreign legionnaires wear in the Sahara, his white face, fresh from a sunless Paris, and his 1.9 metre frame, which towers above the sea of black taxi drivers and families who've come to meet their loved ones. Antoine is too white, too clean and too clean-shaven; he attracts conmen like honey attracts flies. We've barely reached him when we're assailed by a dozen drivers who see us as gullible *toubabs*[1] – a juicy source of income to round off their evening's work.

The next day, all it takes is a quick call and we're invited to stay with Georges, even though he's never met us. 'Papa Georges' teaches history in a Dakar *lycée*. Mutual friends gave us his telephone number before we left France, for when we arrive in Dakar, 'just in case'. He's married to Édouarda, an energetic, smiling little lady, and is also the head of the Emmanuel Community, an organization of lay people and priests who together try to live for Jesus in their community. The cheerful,

---

[1] Europeans.

lilting way Édouarda speaks is incredibly endearing. She's so good-natured and cheerful that every sentence she utters is a hymn to life that brings a smile to her listeners' faces. They have six children; the older ones are living and working in France. Every morning Georges goes to Mass to worship for an hour. Édouarda spends two days showing us around the city. She takes us to the Mauritanian embassy to sort out visas, which we get without any problem. At the Algerian embassy things are a bit more difficult. The consul refuses to issue us with a visa if we go by land. We don't even dare mention cycling.

'Without a flight ticket, there's no point your even coming back here.'

From Dakar we plan to head back to France after a stay in Algeria – the last part of our trip. We haven't worked out where we want to go, or how we'll get there, and we imagine there must be numerous different possibilities. But after some research, we realize that there are, in fact, only two possible routes: through the Algerian *Grand Sud*, which means travelling through the desert and crossing areas where there's a high risk of kidnapping, or going north and taking a ferry from Tangier to Algiers or Oran, the land border between Morocco and Algeria having been closed for years. We're very hopeful about this second option, until we find that there's no sea link between Mauritania and Morocco. Of course, on the internet there's a company that claims to 'provide a connection', but it really should say, 'hope to one day provide a connection'. So far this has failed to materialize, and to get from Morocco to Algeria you have to fly. It's absolutely ridiculous. We resign ourselves to it and return to see the consul with flight tickets from Casablanca. Two days later, we receive our visas. Given how difficult it is generally for the French to get visas for Algeria, particularly if the purpose is to visit the Christian community, we realize how lucky we are.

Édouarda also takes us to buy some new clothes. Our luggage was lost between Brazil and Senegal, and we only have what we had in our hand luggage: the audio-visual equipment, and one toothbrush between us. We visit a second-hand clothes shop. I find a pair of black linen trousers, lightweight and practical, that make me look like an effeminate Greek tourist. I notice that bartering in Senegal is nothing like what happens in the Middle East, where the interaction is a pretext for a cup of tea and a chat. Here it becomes a real showdown, in which the buyer makes an offer and then acts totally indifferent or makes as if he's about to wander off. It's a power game. The toughest wins. Unless he's the poorer of the two.

Over the last few days, red blotches have appeared on my face, irritating the skin on my cheeks and around my eyes. But more seriously, I've been having violent stomach pains and sudden bouts of nausea, forcing me to take to my bed several times a day. So I make a detour to a private clinic to have myself checked out. I take a taxi, leaving the hustle and bustle of the town centre, and wind up in the foreigners' and ambassadors' quarter, where the streets are clean and most of the people on the street are men in uniform. The doctor diagnoses a gut infection, prescribes a bowel treatment and gives me enough tablets to supply an army. I'm not to know that he's sadly mistaken, and I dumbly swallow his cleansing tablets.

Papa Georges suggests that we stay in the village he comes from, Pandiénou-Lehar, about 100 kilometres from Dakar. We haven't any better ideas. So we're heading for Pandiénou.

The silence is magical. Profound, unearthly. After dining with the monks and praying Compline with them, we find ourselves alone, just the three of us, in the darkness of the monastery church. A light shines at the altar, over the eucharistic bread and wine. Out of the corner of my eye I can see Antoine. He's here with us, a non-believer. The last monk gets up and leaves to go to bed, his robe like an angel's or a phantom's, billowing in the night air as his black face disappears into the darkness.

Sometimes God speaks to us in the turmoil of the storm and shakes us in our complacency. But God also reveals his secrets to us in the gentle breeze, which stirs us in the silence. I love these moments that the monasteries give us. People here know how to be quiet, how to restrain themselves. Learning to hear the voice that speaks softly to us when we allow him to. It's an extraordinary experience, mystical; a stillness without which it is impossible to know oneself. As Nietzsche wrote, 'the way to all greatness is through silence'.[2] A commitment to

---

[2] *Le chemin vers tout grandeur passe par le silence.*

silence demands that we renounce idle chatter, static interference and the films we play over and over inside our heads if we don't make a conscious decision to turn them off. The right to solitude is upheld here. We suddenly find we've become gluttons for silence. And when the clamour inside our heads is stilled, we're completely absorbed. Swimming, floating.

And then opening my eyes and contemplating the cross and Jesus' face looking back at me.

The creak of a bench echoes around the church as Gabriel finally stands. We go to bed without a word. Tomorrow is Sunday; we will attend Mass with the monks.

We're at the Abbey of Keur-Moussa, founded by Benedictine monks of the Abbey of Solesmes in France in the early 1960s. There's now only one Frenchman among the 40-odd monks; the Senegalese have taken up the baton, which puts paid to those who claim that the contemplative monastic life is not for Africans! The Keur-Moussa chants are known all over the world – they're a beautiful mix of the Gregorian and African traditions, a magnificent example of cultural integration. Throughout Mass, in the packed church, the monks' voices blend with the sound of the *kora*[3] and the tom-toms in a surprising musical ecumenism. Peace emanates from the choir and resonates in the hearts of the congregation. It's impossible not to be moved by the chants of these black monks in their pure white robes. Some 40 voices rise in harmony before the red African fresco on the wall behind the altar.

After lunch, during which we knock back several carafes of grapefruit juice 'made in Keur-Moussa', we're invited inside the monastery to meet the monks, who are sitting in a circle under a shady tree drinking coffee. We tell them some of our stories of the past few months, our impressions of Senegal and our delight to be with them. They laugh and ply us with questions. We get back on the road in the afternoon and in the evening we reach Pandiénou-Lehar. Our sixth village. But we won't be staying here today. We'll be here just long enough to meet the priests who will welcome us back in a few days' time, and for Gabriel and Antoine to enjoy the hospitality of a kind mama and

[3] A West African harp with up to 24 strings, made from a large calabash cut in half and covered with cow skin, with a long hardwood neck.

her apparently incomparable *thiéboudieune*,[4] while I go and lie down in the presbytery because of a nasty stomach bug. We decide that the three of us will push on to the Mauritanian border. Antoine has come with us to experience a bike trip, and the few kilometres we rode yesterday wasn't long enough. So Gabriel and I will find somewhere to leave our bikes and then return by bus to Pandiénou.

There aren't many roads in Senegal. The one we take links Dakar to Saint-Louis, making one of the six sides of the country's hexagonal shape. The road is lined with the skeletons of cows, goats and mules. Outside each village there are roughly painted signs: 'Sustainable Manufacturing Development Project for the Women of . . .' or '. . . Forest Wildlife Restoration Project' or '. . . Road Reconstruction Project'. But it seems to us that the women stay well and truly in the home, the forests are non-existent and the roads remain well-nigh impassable.

We say '*Ça va?*' to each passer-by to which they invariably reply, as if we've known each other for years, '*Ça va bien, merci. Et toi, ça va sinon?*'[5]

We spend the night in the parish of Louga, at the invitation of the priest. The next day we ride 70 kilometres to Saint-Louis.

Our friend Antoine has a problem – he's got a sore backside. After a few kilometres, he's experiencing the torture well known to riders of traditional upright bicycles: pain in the butt, pain in the back, pain in the wrists, pain in the neck . . .

After riding along a strip of land surrounded by salt marshes that drain into the sea, we reach Saint-Louis. Here too we're put up by the parish and we enjoy the evening exploring the long beaches where numerous brightly coloured fishing boats lie stranded on the sand at low tide. Saint-Louis was once considered the showcase of France in Africa and the capital of Senegal and French West Africa. The imposing architecture on every street bears witness to its colonial past.

The next day a hot headwind springs up at about ten in the morning. There's no escaping it. We manage 10 or 12 kilometres per hour. The landscape becomes arid and featureless. Little shrubs grow here

---

[4] Traditional Senegalese dish of rice with fish.

[5] 'How are you?' . . . 'Good, thanks. How about you?'

and there. Piles of dry animal bones, polished by the wind, lie half covered by sand. We stop soon after midday, when the heat becomes overwhelming. It's the worst we've experienced so far, except in Syria. It's dry and we drink like camels. I stand on the road and stop a passing truck, which replenishes our supply with murky, lukewarm water. We throw a sterilizing tablet into each flask. Antoine says nothing. Under the trees we devour our tomato and sardine sandwiches. A siesta is unthinkable in this heat. And anyway, some kids pester us, trying to sell us their goat. We get back on the road towards half past three; we reckon the first hour will be tough but the temperature will drop after that. The wind blows even harder. Antoine is still suffering.

The dust irritates our throats. From time to time a truck overtakes us; the driver shouts as he passes. Suddenly our nostrils quiver. We sense moisture in the air. In the distance, towards the horizon, the sky looks slightly darker; it's rain, and the relative coolness sweeps across the desert within seconds – the time it takes to inhale a lungful of fresh, cool air.

Ten kilometres from the village of Richard Toll the vegetation changes completely. From here, on either side of the road, there are vegetable crops and mango trees, irrigated with water from the Senegal River. The air freshens as evening falls. We stop at a service station on the outskirts of a village. We're parched; we feel as though we've crossed a desert. Each of us downs three large bottles of cold soda, one after the other, having drunk warm, bleach-tainted water most of the day. A man approaches us and, in very poetic language, offers us women for the night.

'Two thousand CFA francs![6] That's cheap! And with condoms, three thousand francs!'

We pass the Senegalese Sugar Company. It's the only place in the whole country that produces sugar. And with 50,000 workers it's the largest employer in the region. Around here everyone works for *la Compagnie*. But paradoxically, in Richard Toll itself they use sugar imported from Mauritania – it's half the price.

We finally reach the Mauritanian border. Here again we find a church. And it's a Catholic school. It's run by French monks. In fact they're not just any old Frenchmen – they're from Brittany! The

[6] West African CFA is the name of the currency in Senegal. It has a fixed exchange rate with the euro.

brothers of Ploermel. No doubt about it: it was meant to be. We leave our bikes and equipment with them before taking the bus back to Pandiénou.

A seven-hour trip, squashed like sardines into a vehicle that's hardly more robust than a sardine can . . . We cover 300 kilometres like this. Happiness in a can . . .

## Sixth isolated community: Pandiénou-Lehar

Ochre-coloured dirt roads, sand paths, a mill that drives nothing but thin air, a rusty tank overlooking the village and the surrounding scrub, a few earth houses topped with palm leaves, and a large church, packed every Sunday, that was founded in 1985 by a French missionary. Today, pastoral care for the surrounding villages is carried out by two Senegalese priests and three Ursuline nuns.

It's a week since we arrived in Pandiénou, 40 kilometres from the town of Thiès, and Antoine has just left us. We're living in the presbytery with the two priests and we're following the parish priest, Father Bernard, around on most of his visits.

'Hey! I'm going to the elders' meeting. Are you coming?'

Father Bernard is terrific! He wears a brown cassock and sports a thin moustache above his enormous lips. His hair is greying. He rolls his 'r's generously and the pitch of his voice goes right up when he emphasizes a point. He seems so splendid, so extraordinary, that I keep wanting to call him 'Bernard the Magnificent'. He's a born comedian. We ask him if many foreigners come to Pandiénou.

'Ah! You're not the first, but you are certainly the last!'

We pile into his beaten-up old Peugeot 405 and he takes off, kicking up a cloud of sand that spreads all around the presbytery courtyard. We follow a rutted track and stop beside a huge tree that stands alone in the middle of the scrub. Enormous branches stretch out horizontally from the massive, gnarled trunk – the spokes of this natural umbrella. The foliage is a vivid green seldom seen in these dry parts.

The sun is almost at its zenith. Old Martin, one of the village elders, scuffs his plastic sandals along in the dust, leaning on a walking stick that's almost as bowed as he is. A little cloud of dust rises from each footfall, to be carried away by the hot wind that stirs the palm leaves, making them gently sigh. Martin, Barthélémy, Pierre, Jean and the other elders come plodding at snail's pace along the path. They settle themselves down on the tree's exposed roots, which serve as seats. The priest's ochre cassock blends with the dusty ground. He greets each of the elders warmly and sits down himself once they're all seated.

'*Nanga def?*' How are you?

They fall silent and put their hands together respectfully in prayer – a Hail Mary, the Lord's Prayer. The customary talks can now begin. There are 15 elders and about 15 litres of palm wine. They meet like this every week to debate and make important decisions for the village. On the agenda today: should they join the Diocesan Catholic Men's Association? After long discussions they pronounce their judgement: no. They will pay contributions to their own village association. One keeps the accounts in an old graph-paper exercise book. Before long they break open the jerrycans of wine.

Father Bernard singles us out in front of the little gathering.

'You French people, you're always in a hurry. You're always running after time. For us it's the other way round: time pushes us along!'

Gourds chopped in half serve as glasses. Each in turn they drink the precious liquid, which is harvested patiently at sunrise from the base of the palm trunks. On contact with the air, the sap ferments very quickly. Now they get drunk slowly.

Very slowly, because there's no reason to hurry. Because time will push them on.

The next day they put on a great spread. This year the parish festival falls on the same date as the World Day of Prayer for Vocations – an excuse to put on a big party and treat all the neighbouring villages. The Pandiénou church is full. Men and women are in their Sunday best. A chorale of one hundred are giving it their all. Their majestic voices harmonize as they sing to the staccato beat of the Wolof[7] chants and the rhythm of the tom-toms. The young choristers smile broadly.

[7] Wolof is the language of Senegal, the Gambia and Mauritania, and the native language of the Wolof people.

In red letters above the altar are the words 'The Year of Vocations: The Gift of the Eucharist, the Gift of the Priesthood'. Father Bernard preaches with vigour. He points upwards and preaches with all his might.

'God is calling, the Church is calling, the world is calling!'

Hundreds of villagers gather under large tents for a sip of palm wine and a taste of the fish and rice *concassé*. They stand around in little groups dipping into shared dishes, some with their fingers, some with a spoon.

We go from group to group and from tent to tent. People have come from all the surrounding villages for this big celebration.

'It can't be too bad being a priest here. They wait on you hand and foot!'

Gabriel chuckles as they shove another bowlful of rice into his hands. But he's quite right. Here the priest is really someone. He has status and authority, which comes with his ministry.

The priest gives his life to the parishioners and they appreciate him and do their best for him. He has a monopoly on administering the sacraments, while the pastoral work is largely done by lay people. In the little village of Pandiénou there's also a charismatic choir, a Gregorian chant choir, three children's choirs, the Legion of Mary, the Association of Catholic Women and the Association of Catholic Men. Each of these has a president, a secretary, an assistant secretary and a treasurer – which is quite logical and curiously instinctive for these bush parishioners. Every day they meet together, put forward ideas, have long discussions, plan and submit their ideas to the priest, so much so that Father Bernard doesn't have much to do except administer the sacraments. Time pushes them on, certainly, but the machine is well oiled.

In the late afternoon, after Vespers, as the celebration continues, the women are washing the dishes behind the presbytery. Suddenly one starts thumping on an old pot. Another joins in. Soon they're tapping out a terrific beat on metal basins, empty jerrycans and plastic barrels.

Some dance in the middle of the circle, and there's an explosion of joy, a whirling of bodies and a blur of colourful *boubous*. The priests and some of the men join in. Surrounded by pots and pans, the festival

A joyful outburst of singing and dancing

An impromptu jam session on pots and pans interrupts the dishwashing

bursts into a riot of rounded forms and irresistible rhythms.

And in the dust kicked up by the dancers' feet, the hens are pecking.

Since our arrival I've been forced to lie down and sleep more and more often because of a bad headache and dreadful nausea. At first I thought the food didn't agree with me or it was the palm wine.

'That's it! I'm not going to touch another drop!'

But that doesn't seem to make any difference.

One Sunday morning Father Bernard takes us in his beaten-up old car to attend Mass in a neighbouring village. During the ceremony I develop such a bad headache that I can't even open my eyes. I assume it's a migraine. Back in the presbytery I lie down but the pain only worsens. My head is pounding and I have a high temperature. Late in the afternoon Father Bernard takes me to the Diocesan Hospital in Thiès. I'm moaning like a child.

The priest points to a notice stating the fee for admission to the Emergency Department: 12,000 CFA francs.

'What if we don't have it?'

'Oh well, we're not going to the Emergency Department . . .' the priest says bluntly.

I lose all track of time and find myself lying in a single room, with an infusion of antibiotics, while most of the other patients are piled up eight to a room of the same size. I am constantly nauseous and vomit twice. Gabriel and the nurses take care of me. They're very motherly.

The diagnosis is soon announced: typhoid.

'It can't be! I've been vaccinated!'

But the verdict is correct. There are various strains of this delightful organism and I've caught one of them. They say I must have swallowed some faecal matter. In the Amazon for sure.

Father Théo, one of the Pandiénou priests, comes to visit me the next day. He brings oranges and tells me an encouraging story. A year ago a woman was admitted to this hospital for an intestinal infection. A nurse came to give her an injection near her eye. The woman expressed surprise and protested that she had no problem with her eye. The nurse insisted and the patient acquiesced. Later the nurse came back to apologize for giving the injection to the wrong patient and also for giving the wrong drug. A little while later the woman lost her eye.

But for me there's nothing to fear. After one night in Thiès I'm transferred as if by magic to Dakar, thanks to my health insurance. I soon find myself in an air-conditioned room in which everything is white from the floor to the ceiling. I'm served gourmet food as I look out at the sea view. I'm discharged from hospital for three days' convalescence at Club Med, enjoying a deluxe room with all mod cons.

Back in Pandiénou, I find Gabriel, Father Bernard and the rest of them. They haven't been at all concerned about my absence. We spend the afternoon with Father Bernard, who regales us with jokes and other tomfoolery, and we finish the evening in the back of the village grocery, sipping pastis with the priest and his friend Roger, to the strains of Alpha Blondy.[8] Between sips, we put the world to rights.

Before speaking, the priest puts down his glass thoughtfully, lowers his head and screws up his eyes. And then, with an indescribable expression, he delivers a joke, an amusing anecdote, a reflection or some spiritual encouragement. But he doesn't give any warning. One minute we're laughing out loud, the next we're talking about the call to the priesthood. Father Bernard is a comedian and he likes to use it to advantage in his ministry. And Roger is a former novice at Keur-Moussa, with a cavernous voice and a wild look in his eyes, who confesses that he used to sneak off to the monastery roof for a cigarette on the quiet. He became a priest after having been a compulsive runner. They're two of a kind.

They're such a great pair that our evenings in Pandiénou are thoroughly enjoyable. We dine with families who have invited Father Bernard and ask us to come along too. Tomorrow evening we're invited to a special dinner at Marcel's place. Marcel is the abbot. He was from this village originally but now lives in another parish. This evening we're celebrating the anniversary of the priesthood of the two priests, who are old seminary friends. Thirty years ago they were studying together to become priests.

'Do you know, I've "done" the Jura!'

---

[8] An internationally known reggae singer born in Ivory Coast.

Father Bernard 'did' the Jura. Which, to him, means he was sent to the Jura, a region in the east of France, to serve as priest in a parish where there was no priest. He seems moved, still quite amazed by his experience there.

'The greatest surprise for me was the snow! I'd never seen it before. One morning I saw this powder falling from the sky and everything was white.'

Father Marcel confides that he has also 'done' France. It sounds like a tourist ticking off the top attractions. Many Senegalese priests leave their family, and the heat and dust of Senegal, to find themselves dropped into some little parish in the depths of the French country-side. For two or three years they serve the Church of France where there aren't enough priests. It's often quite difficult for them to adapt. Accustomed to taking Mass in the heat, in a full church, they're sud-denly dropped into some remote country parish where there's an age-ing population with dwindling enthusiasm. While our country priests are preoccupied with how they're going to maintain their ancient and, most often, empty buildings, the priest in Pandiénou worries about how he's going to find the money to enlarge his already huge village church.

To make matters worse, their reception by their French parish-ioners often leaves much to be desired. They relate their 'war stories'. There was one brother who was asked by the priest when he arrived, 'What are you doing here?' He was then told that his presence was completely unnecessary. Another reported, with great feeling, how a young priest handed him the keys of the church and promptly went off on holiday, entrusting him with the running of the whole parish. Another was never accepted by the parish and still another didn't know how to cope with all the invitations to dinner he received.

But for these Senegalese priests, 'doing' France is also manna from heaven. To support themselves and their pastoral work, their time in Europe is precious. They tell us that when they leave to return to Africa, their parishioners give them a gift and a large cheque to con-tribute to their work. This explains how the priests are able to own a car; beaten up though it may be, it's indispensable for the numerous visits they must make, whereas most Senegalese people get round on foot or by horse and cart.

'But the problem is that some people get envious. And it creates inequalities between priests. There are those who have been to Europe and those who haven't had the opportunity.' Father Bernard tops up our wine and we finish our braised hare.

'You'll see! Senegal is the perfect example of peaceful Islamic–Christian dialogue.'

That's how a journalist friend described Senegal to us before we left France last July. We even read a certain number of articles that seemed to confirm this. Senegal incarnates a model society in which Muslims and Catholics live together in harmony. And they really do live together rather than just tolerating each other. After what we found in the Middle East, it's astounding to meet mixed families here who live under the same roof. For example, Gérard is about 50 and he sings in the parish choir. But his parents are both Muslims. His father has three wives and his brothers and sisters are all Muslims.

This is partly explained by the fact that the Islam practised in Senegal, in orders like the Mouride Brotherhood, is not fundamentalist. They accept conversion to other religions. Also, visually, it's impossible to distinguish a Christian from a Muslim. Very few women wear the veil.

'It was my Muslim uncle who advised me and encouraged me in my calling!'

Sister Bernadette is one of three Ursuline nuns who live in the village and help the priests with the pastoral work. Her uncle corresponded with her, counselled her and understood what she wanted, even though he himself was a Muslim. It seems incredible to us but hers is not an isolated case. It's not so different from Father Théo, whose family is partly Muslim. His uncle, who accompanies us on a trip to Thiès, doesn't see any problem with his nephew being a Christian. On the contrary, he's almost a little too pragmatic.

'I love Catholics because they are honest and well brought up.'

It's clear to him that Christians and Muslims pray to the same God. When we ask him what the most important thing about his religion is, he takes a moment, knits his eyebrows and replies with a smile:

'Loving your brother, doing good, serving others, being generous.'

On the whole it seems that the tiny Catholic minority coexists happily with the immense Muslim majority. However, as if to prove the rule, there are a few exceptions that cloud the picture. Father Bernard tells us that in the town of Tivaouane, for example, there's no church.

They were planning to build a church there, but a fundamentalist Muslim journalist from Dakar caught wind of it. He made a big fuss about it and whipped up a lot of bad feeling. The bishop and the *marabout*,[9] fearing the spread of violence, stopped the project altogether. The government reimbursed the diocese for the expenses incurred and turned the church into a school. Since then the priests of Pandiénou have still been going to Tivaouane every Sunday to celebrate Mass, but in a family home.

We're due to leave in a few days' time and we've only filmed one cassette. While we're here we're supposed to be making a film about prayer. Before we came to this village in the bush we thought, as many people do, that we would find a vibrant, lively Church, as we imagine the Catholic Church in Africa to be. And it's absolutely true. But beneath the wonderful atmosphere of praise and celebration, we've become aware of their remarkable depth of faith. They seem to know how to express their joy, but it passes first through an airlock of inner silence. After Keur-Moussa, I really never imagined that the theme of our stay in Senegal would be silence.

'These people are sincere believers, and extremely warm.'

Father Théo has said this from day one. And we've remembered the warmth. But the most remarkable characteristic of these believers is their sense of who God is. Whether they're Muslims or Christians, they adore God. They live *with* him. They take him very seriously and they talk to him. They pray to him. They teach us a remarkable lesson.

'Prayer? It changes your life! It frees you!'

I'm walking with Sister Bernadette along the sandy roads of Pandiénou. I can't guess her age; she must be in her late thirties.

'God, who is all-powerful, knows everything about us. And therefore he knows my prayers before I even ask. Then why pray?'

[9] Senegalese Muslim Holy Man.

She smiles at my question.

'Prayer is something we do each day. It's not prefabricated, like reciting a formula. Prayer is an encounter. I don't know in advance what I'm going to say, what I will hear and what's going to happen. The important thing is to take the time to meet God. That's why, when I ask the Lord something, it would be sad if I expected him to answer my prayer immediately. Because then it wouldn't be a person to person relationship; it would just be self-interest.'

As the sun falls below the horizon, the choir practice finishes. Some members remain chatting on the doorstep. One man wears his cap crosswise. His short-sleeved polo shirt reveals his muscular arms. Barthélémy is the choir master.

'Barthélémy, do you love praying?'

'Yes.'

'Why?'

'Why?'

'Yes.'

'Well . . .'

There's a brief silence and he looks at his feet. Then he looks up. He looks stunned.

'*Why*? Is that what you're asking me? You're asking me *why* I pray?'

'Yes.'

'Tsss . . .'

He sighs, feeling slightly exasperated.

'If, one evening, I don't pray, I can't sleep! But after prayer I can easily get to sleep.'

'Really?'

'Yes! Of course! But surely you must know that?'

He's aghast. Gabriel is enjoying himself and keeps on teasing him.

'And what do you get out of praying?'

'A lot, my friend! A lot!'

He takes off his cap and scratches his head, and then, looking Gabriel straight in the eyes, he gives him his magic formula.

'There's a song that goes like this:

"What God has done for me, I can't begin to tell you,

He saved me from sin, so I sing Hallelujah . . .

I sing, I dance, I laugh, I praise! Hallelujah!"'

Barthélémy has a superb singing voice, deep and clear. He nods his head with a certain pride, his eyes moist. The lyrics imprint themselves on my heart. And since then, each time I watch our film, I feel a little lump in my throat, a little bubble of emotion that was born right there with Barthélémy.

This afternoon there's a funeral for a woman from this village. The Mass is beautiful. The family members are composed. Father Théo, who is to take the ceremony, arrives late. The body and the other priests have been waiting for him for half an hour to start the procession. Everyone looks daggers at him.

After the service everyone makes their way to the cemetery and gathers around the casket. When they lay it in the ground, the women howl like wild beasts. Sister Bernadette shakes her head.

'This is the part of a funeral that I don't like. Here in Africa, we shout and scream a lot.'

The next day, before we leave, we enjoy Sunday Mass before passing on the present from the Mocambo community. Father Bernard waves the brightly coloured plaque around above his head and the congregation immediately comes to life. They break into thunderous applause. Then he hands us a cross about 20 centimetres high made entirely from matchsticks.

Together we pray for our next community. It will be our last. In Algeria, *Inshallah*.

# 14

## Mauritania and Morocco: Rosso to Casablanca

### In which we meet a priest with no parishioners

10 May, 9 months and 5 days after departure
To be Mauritanian is to be Muslim.

We know that Mauritania is an Islamic republic and Sharia is the law of the land. Some 99 per cent of the population are Muslims and no other religious groups have ever been officially recognized to this day. And yet . . .

We leave Jean-Yves and Paul, of the brothers of Ploermel, who put us up for the night in Richard Toll. Only ten short kilometres separate us from the Mauritanian border. The official stamps our passports and we join the crowd of hawkers and workers in ragged singlets on the riverbank, waiting for the ferry that will take us to the other side of the Senegal River, which forms a natural border between the two countries. A boat soon appears, but it only takes on board one truck carrying a heavy load.

Rowboats and motorboats also ply the river taking those most in a hurry. But we're not in a rush. We've got all the time in the world. We're still in Senegal and we've adjusted a little to the tempo; these days it's time that pushes us on! We notice that the ferry company is Mauritanian. At the slightest diplomatic dispute the government can decide to close the frontier immediately. On the other side, several young people greet us, eager to 'help' us fill out our paperwork. Then there are the customs officials who try to get some baksheesh. It's not every day that they get two *toubabs* passing through; they must make the most of it. Seeing my exasperation, one of them decides to drop it.

'*Allez!* You look tired. That's fine, go on. It's free.'

The two banks of the Senegal River are quite different: on one side, mangoes and lush crops; on the other side, dust and squalor. The people are poor, even poorer.

There are no sealed roads; sand reigns supreme. After weaving between rubbish bins and mangy dogs, and struggling to steer our bikes through a thick layer of filthy sand, we finally arrive outside the walls of a church compound – the church that the brothers of Ploermel pointed out to us yesterday. A man lets us into a large, rectangular courtyard enclosed by high, yellowing walls. In the middle stands the little church of Rosso. Perhaps it's because it's under renovation, but it immediately reminds me of a phantom church – a place full of memories, the walls of which are imbued with the songs and smells of the past. In one corner of the courtyard we find the presbytery and a few little mud huts for passing guests.

'Welcome! I've been expecting you!'

The little man who greets us is smiling from ear to ear and from the depths of his piercing blue eyes. He's French. Everything around us is dry, and his sea-blue eyes are like an oasis. The brothers of Ploermel called him earlier to let him know we were coming. When they told us about him, we were keen to meet him. He's the priest without parishioners.

'Do you live alone?'

'Oh no! There's a Spanish seminary student and three nuns who live on the church compound!'

'And that's all?'

'That's all.'

The presbytery is composed of a succession of little rooms with low ceilings and no windows, to protect the inhabitants from the sun. Light comes in through little holes cut out of the white walls in a geometric pattern. A shelf carries dozens of works of Christian and Muslim spirituality and texts on Mauritanian and Arabic culture. We want to record an interview with Father Bernard, but the presbytery is too dark for filming. So we set up outside in the shade of a scrawny tree. We sit on a stone seat that's propped up against a rough wall.

In front of us stands the phantom church. Father Bernard points out that it still has a visible cross – the only one in Mauritania. After independence the Muslim Brotherhood wanted it taken down but the village elders argued against them, claiming that it was part of the town's heritage. Built by a priest named Salomon, the church is called the Temple of Salomon.

'I've been in Mauritania for 41 years. Relations with Muslims are generally very good these days.'

Before independence and the departure of the French army, the church at Rosso was full every Sunday. These days, besides the priest, there are only the three nuns, the seminary student and sometimes one or two foreigners who are passing through. A church without a congregation; a priest from a missionary order who doesn't evangelize.

It seems to Gabriel and to me that the Islamic Republic of Mauritania is synonymous with the persecution of the few Christians who live in the country (0.25 per cent are Christians, or approximately 10,100 people, the vast majority of whom are Western expatriates, mostly French, and Mauritanians of African descent). Conversion of a Muslim to Christianity is forbidden and punishable by death. It seems that there must be persecution. How could such a tiny minority, with no public identity, mix happily with the rest of the population? And yet . . .

'When I came here my bishop said to me, "Your mission is to go to be among the people. Be discreet. Never give or accept any gifts. But make contact with the people." At that time, it was an underground church, barely visible. But as the years have gone by, it has become better known, even if it hasn't been officially recognized. People understood that we were not here to "Christianize" them but were here as simple "witnesses", through our charity work and interactions with people, and that we had great respect for their culture and religion. In return, we ask them to respect our religion, and our relationships which, with a few minor exceptions, are excellent in all the parts of Mauritania that I've visited!'

One of the keys to the presence of the Church in this Islamic republic is having a great respect for the Muslim faith. The priest only teaches in the mission compound and doesn't offer baptism.

'When Pope John Paul II was dying, an imam friend told me they were praying for his recovery in the mosques in Rosso. And when the pope died, he came back with these words: "We're praying that God will receive John Paul II to himself." And on all the Christian holy days he wishes me *bonne fête!* At Ramadan the Vatican writes a letter addressed to Muslims. I give it to the imams and some of them read it aloud in the mosque! These are little gestures, but they help to forge bonds of friendship.'

A man wearing a long, fine-linen cloak and a black turban comes to greet him, not in the least concerned about the camera. The two men talk for a few moments.

'His brother has just died. He has asked for some help for his family. As Christians, we try to accept people unconditionally, irrespective of their faith. Obviously we can't meet everyone's needs, but we do our best.'

'Do you take the opportunity to convey something of your faith?'

The priest is startled.

'No. We don't help people so that they will convert. The people I'm in contact with here are, first and foremost, human beings and I welcome them as such, just because they are men and women. The Church is here for everyone. Some Christians here would like us to favour them, but that's not what we do. Jesus of Nazareth lived among the people. Doesn't his life show us how to engage with people, how to act towards the *other* who is different from me?'

The man leaves the presbytery courtyard; a cloud of dust rises from each footstep, obscuring his feet.

'"To God, a thousand years are as a day." These aren't just my words – they're in the Bible. Here we don't work for an immediate result. In a thousand years, we'll see!'

He pauses before starting again, looking Gabriel straight in the eyes.

'We tend to forget, but it's never man who converts someone, it's God himself. Personally, I like to think that if we enable men of different cultures, colours and religions to live together then the kingdom of God is not far from us.'

There's one question I'm dying to ask.

'Do you ever wonder if your presence here is perhaps a bit pointless?'

'No, never. I was in Algeria when I heard the call to become a priest, as I witnessed the faith of Muslim people. I've been very touched by Charles de Foucauld, the French priest who lived among the Tuareg people of Algeria, whose approach was quite simply to be present among people, which means that one's commitment must make no demands. Sometimes the isolation weighs on me. I would love to have a little community of Christians around me. During Easter week, for example, it would be lovely if there were more than just four or five of us. So from time to time I cross the border and go to Senegal to recharge my batteries within a strong Christian community! I certainly don't think everyone is called to be a priest in Mauritania. But I have no regrets about what I'm doing or what I've done. And if I had to choose, I wouldn't want a different life!'

In his sensitive blue eyes, which really are entrancing, we see real strength.

'And also, I'm convinced that the reason for our presence here is something far greater than us: it's to celebrate the Eucharist. When I say the words of the Offertory,[1] "Blessed are you, God of the universe, You who give us this bread, the fruit of the vine and the labour of men", I don't say "of Catholics" or "of Christians"! I say the work "of men", which includes our Muslim brothers. In the Eucharist, I bring before God all that my Muslim brothers do that is good and beautiful, and that's what I offer to God.'

Over the last few minutes he has been repeatedly looking over towards the gate. He's on the lookout for his first students.

'Ah, here they are! Come, come, and I'll give you a tour.'

After working on various charity projects, as the three nuns who live in Rosso do, he opened a library within the mission compound in 2005 for the local children and students. It gives the young people access to textbooks, literature and journals, and he pays two teachers to help them with their research. They also offer English and Spanish classes. Even though the students are all Muslims, they feel at home here. The aim is not to evangelize but to participate in the development of the country by training the youth. The library is the only one of its kind in Rosso.

In the entrance there's a group of students sitting around a table; they're part of an English class taken by Marie, a young French volunteer who has come to help for a year. In the long, narrow main room, secondary-school students browse through books and journals with an air of great concentration. The Spanish seminary student who has been seconded here to assist Father Bernard is helping some of

---

[1] Prayer said as the bread and wine are offered to God during Mass.

them with their homework, while one of the library staff is finding documents about forced marriage for senior students who are working on a class presentation. A bright-eyed young girl wearing a veil is researching polygamy. The old priest passes between the tables and greets the young people, who seem delighted to see him.

That evening, as the heat of the day wanes, the muezzins' strident chants echo through the streets. At the mission in Rosso it's time for prayer too. We join Father Bernard, Simon, the Spanish seminary student and Marie to sing and worship discreetly in the little presbytery.

We leave Rosso early the next morning, making the most of the relative coolness to cover as much ground as we can. The wind is already up. The heat will soon follow. Before long we're surrounded by desert. Not the regular succession of velvety dunes you imagine in the Sahara. Not yet. The infertile land at the edge of the desert is dotted with squat, ugly bushes and tiny hamlets, where the people laugh and wave as we go by. We make only 15 kilometres per hour, despite pedalling furiously. The headwind almost defeats us. At this speed the panorama is unremittingly monotonous; we can't depend on the unfolding backdrop to take our minds off our weary bodies. Sometimes a glassy-eyed camel, a scrawny goat or corrugated iron shack add their touch of fantasy to this ocean of tedium. We gradually desiccate in the heat. We eat our lunch under a tree, near a well where a young man comes to draw water with a patched bicycle inner tube for a container. We borrow it from him to spray each other and rinse our eyes.

The wind freshens. We head due north towards Nouakchott. We knew from the start that we wouldn't have time to cycle right up through Mauritania and Morocco if we wanted to stop for three weeks in Algeria. And now we know for sure that the poetry of the desert is lost on us, we've decided to find a truck in Nouakchott to take us to the Moroccan border. *Inshallah*, we'll see what we find when we get there.

In the meantime we deal with the kilometres, one after another. Night is falling and we've had several doors slammed in our faces. A passing car slows down to our speed. Every time we hear a car coming we feel on edge. On this road too many tourists are kidnapped for us honestly to believe 'It only happens to other people'. So whenever a car slows down and tails us, our hearts start pounding wildly and we don't calm down until it has vanished in the distance. Then one car stops. The driver jabbers at us in broken English. He's a Bedouin, a nomad who, like many of his kind these last few years, have abandoned their ancestors' way of life and settled down to live in a shack in town. However, he has retained some of his forebears' traditions, including extending an unconditional welcome to strangers.

'Yes, because that's what the Qur'an asks of us. This evening, you're my guests!'

We dine on bread, yogurt, chicken with marinated onions, with our hosts looking on.

The next day we set off to cover the last few kilometres before Nouakchott, riding through a lunar landscape where stones and craters alternate with dunes. Yes, finally, classic Saharan sand dunes.

Late the following afternoon, after 10 hours of cycling at 12 kilometres per hour at best, we finally arrive. Nouakchott, gateway to the desert. Capital of Mauritania. Etymologically, the name means 'the place where water appears when a well is dug'. However, the nearest source of water is almost 60 kilometres away. Perhaps it's because I'm so dog tired from the wind and the road, but I hate this town as soon as I catch sight of it.

'I never thought a place could be so bad.'

We can't breathe, but we don't know whether it's because of the clouds of dust, the smell of garbage or a gas leak, which combine to produce a noxious atmosphere that suffocates the whole town. In the 1950s Nouakchott was a little French military fort of about 8,000 inhabitants, built to keep an eye on the trade route. It now numbers over 800,000, and there has been no urban planning to control its rampant growth. 'Unauthorized makeshift housing' has spread out in all directions and now 40 per cent of the population live in *kebbé* zones – a combination of earthen houses, canvas tents and living in the open. Anywhere else it would be called a slum. Gleaming 4x4s with tinted windows weave their way among camels and makeshift tents, and domed mosques stand amid a sea of sand and poverty. It's unreal; too ugly to be true, too horrible to be inhabited.

Nouakchott marks the entrance to the desert and thus lies between two worlds. It's also on the border between two cultural areas, because

Mauritania isn't part of either black Africa (since the Moors who speak Arabic are the majority) or the Arab world in the strict sense, since it is also populated by black-African people like the Wolofs.

Filth. Everywhere. It tans our skin like leather. Enveloped in black robes and turbans, leaving only their black eyes uncovered, the people are withdrawn and morose. In the ambassadors' quarter we find the cathedral. With its 5,500 Catholics, Mauritania has only one diocese, one bishop and one cathedral.

'I can put you up!'

The chubby little priest who greets us is French. Like most of the local clergy he is a *père blanc* or 'white priest', an order of missionaries to Africa who are either from Europe or sub-Saharan Africa. Here the church is 100 per cent foreign.

To keep to schedule we need to reach Algeria in two weeks' time. It's impossible to find a truck driver who will take us to Morocco for free. After some research we make contact with the manager of a grocery store in the industrial area. In Nouakchott there's a tariff on all traffic and it's organized by this little grocer. He obviously controls it with an iron fist. He's the middleman between drivers going back up to Morocco empty and passengers wanting a ride. After long negotiations, he puts us in touch with a Moroccan truck driver who is returning to Morocco this evening. We arrange a rendezvous for later in the day and return to the diocesan house to pack. Just as we're leaving, the priest who runs the guesthouse asks for the modest sum of €80.

'Huh . . .'

We explain the whole ethos of our journey, our golden rule, our vow to be poor for a year, to leave room for Providence in our lives. He won't listen to a word of it. After some discussion, he brings the price down, suggesting we pay the 'friends of the diocese' rate, about €30. To him, we're two rich kids and we should expect to pay like everyone else. Perhaps – I don't know. Anyway, now we won't be able to be so proud about never spending anything on accommodation. It had to be broken, just this once, this absolute rule that was too sweeping, too strict. Perhaps it's an invitation to strip ourselves still more, right down to our pride.

With our tails between our legs, we find our chauffeur and his beaten-up truck. We load our bikes into the back, which is completely empty. He jumps into the driver's seat and we squeeze in beside him. Another passenger is already in the back seat, a friendly young man with a nascent beard, wearing a sky blue *boubou*. He's studying Islam in Mauritania in order to become an imam. Fifteen minutes later, as we approach a roadblock, the driver asks us to sink down into our seats and pull up our hoods, while he hands some baksheesh to the policemen. The first of a long series.

I notice he's prepared some little packages and stacked them on the dashboard. We know what they'll be used for. With a foolish grin he says, resigned, 'It's compulsory!'

It doesn't take long for us to realize we've drawn the short straw; this bloke is a nasty piece of work. He's dishonest, rude, volatile. His behaviour leaves us perplexed: he shouts for no reason, roars with laughter and claps us on the shoulders for no obvious reason. Sometimes he shouts harsh-sounding words that sound like a stream of insults. In the middle of the night he stops for a break on a hill, in the town of Laayoune. Mr Foulmouth suggests we lie in the back, while he sleeps in the cab. According to our 'contract' he was supposed to pay for a hotel for us.

A few hours later we start moving again. He drops off the apprentice imam and stops again – we don't know why. It turns out it's because he's decided we're too much trouble and he's going to dump us. Then two more passengers turn up when it's already squashed with three of us. So he changes his mind and decides to push on to Agadir. But then he stops again at a service station a few kilometres further on and sits down with some other drivers for a cup of tea, leaving the four of us, piled on top of each other, in his overheated truck. This time, we've had enough. We get out in a rage and storm across to the group. Mr Foulmouth pretends he hasn't noticed us. We sit down with the men, who offer us a cup of tea. We put our grievances to them. They have a good laugh, but then look ashamed about their two-faced friend. They put pressure on him, telling him to drop us at a bus stop and pay for the ticket. Sensing the tables are turning on him, Foulmouth completely changes his attitude. He promises to take us to Agadir and even refund some of our money.

'No way, you imbecile.'

'Give you discount! Discount!'

'Too late.'

He follows us to the transport company's office, still trying to excuse himself and promising us a quick trip. But we can no longer trust him. I grab hold of his arm and drag him into the office like a naughty schoolboy, and explain the situation to the clerk. As I'd hoped, our driver turns pale. He risks having to pay a 50,000 *dirham* (€4,600) fine for carrying illegal passengers if he gets reported.

'Give us our money back, you crook.'

'How much?'

He's in a hurry to get out of here.

'700 *dirham*.'

'No, 600. I've only got 600. All the rest went in baksheesh.'

He's lying, for sure. But we settle for 600.

That evening we take a bus, which drops us in Agadir the next morning. The Sahara is behind us.

The man has purple, flushed cheeks and hair plastered down over his broad forehead. He's Dutch and he inspects our bikes with the eye of a connoisseur.

'You see recumbents a lot in my country. When I was younger I cycled round Europe.'

Father Gilbert is the priest of the little church of Agadir. We visit him straight after getting off the bus. He shows us around. Everything is clean and tidy, as if it were a museum. He explains that the church is run by a little community of expatriates from various countries and is supposed to be a showcase of the Catholic Church for visitors and tourists. In the porch, leaflets in different languages are on display.

'It's an international community! A real melting pot – 100 per cent foreign.'

A little Moroccan woman comes forward to kiss the priest's hand. She takes two roses from a brown paper bag and presents them to us.

'Welcome to Morocco!'

Although she's a Muslim, she's been working for the parish for 15 years. She absolutely insists on making us breakfast. And we're delighted to accept. But the priest thinks she has better things to do. We ask if it's possible for us to have a shower. We must stink like dead rats.

'Ah! Yes! Go on! It'll do you good!'

We take turns showering in the marvellous, ceramic-tiled shower, where we wash our filthy bodies. At the door we find two enormous glasses of freshly squeezed orange juice prepared by our benefactress. As we leave the parish, I pick up a leaflet in French entitled 'The Church in Morocco Today'. Thirty million people live in Morocco, all officially Muslims, including about 3,000 Jews. The Church was recognized by King Hassan II in 1983. The Christians are all foreigners: French, Spanish, British, Italians, Polish and students from sub-Saharan Africa. The leaflet also says there are:

> numerous little communities of monks and nuns, some of whom are contemplatives, whose role is to accept and make room for the *other*, *the* one who is different, *and find enrichment in those differences. They're called to be a witness by the way they live in the work place, in the community and in their relationships with their neighbours, working for justice, understanding and tolerance.*

As I read this I think of Father Bernard in Rosso, Mauritania. Here in Morocco, Christians are discreet as well; almost invisible.

King Hassan II was an ardent supporter of the reconciliation of the three monotheistic religions. He also worked to bring Israelis and Palestinians together. In 1986 he welcomed the then Israeli Prime Minister, and at other times Morocco's Chief Rabbi and his Israeli counterpart. In 1985 he also invited John Paul II to meet tens of thousands of young people in the main stadium in Casablanca, the vast majority of whom were Muslims. Echoing Chapter 5 verse 49 of the Qur'an, which sees the division between believers as a divine invitation to outdo each other in good works, the Pope made a heartfelt plea to Moroccan youth:

> We, Muslims and Christians, have often misunderstood each other and, sometimes, in the past, we have worn each other out with arguments and in war. I believe God is calling us today to change our old ways. We must respect each other, and also stimulate each other to do good works.

The young people cheered and acclaimed the Holy Father. This visit was typical of Morocco's openness at that time.

*Do not allow us, as we invoke Your Name,*
*to ever justify the problems men have caused.*
*O God, you alone are the One we adore.*
    John Paul II, address to young Muslims, Casablanca, 1985

As we leave the city in the early afternoon, a story from 2006 comes back to me – a story that contrasts strongly with the respect preached by John Paul II and supported by Hassan II.

I ask Gabriel, 'Do you remember the evangelist condemned for proselytizing in Morocco in 2006? I think it was here in Agadir that he was tried.'

It was in 2006. A German evangelist of Egyptian origin was condemned to six months in prison for trying to convert young people by distributing material about the history of Christianity. In Morocco, turning a Muslim away from his faith is punishable by law with a six-month to three-year prison sentence and a fine of 100–500 *dirham* (€10–50).[2] Before 2006, no one ever talked about Muslims being evangelized. But since then they have set up a surveillance unit to keep an eye on Christian proselytizing, and numerous Catholic nuns as well as Protestant missionaries have been convicted and deported. Also here in Morocco, you never hear about the indigenous converts who meet together clandestinely. In any case, we don't hear about them. When Moroccans make a public confession of their Christian faith, they're signing their own death warrant socially; they become outcasts. Among the priests we meet over the following few days, none give us any information on this subject. They all pretend not to know.

Soon after we leave town a fresh wind springs up, laden with moisture, making us forget the harshness of the desert. Over the following days, in this invigorating atmosphere, we ride along golden hills dotted with scraggy vegetation, short grasses and odd-shaped rocks, sculpted by the wind. On my bike I daydream, imagining myself buying some land, keeping goats and pressing olive oil in the traditional way.

'Why live in town? Imagine living in a paradise like this?'

'Yeah, this is heavenly. Spit-roasted lamb and goats' cheese, as much as you want, whenever you want.'

---

[2] Observatoire de l'aide à l'Église en détresse.

In Essaouira, we stop in front of the church and wait for the priest to finish the tour he's taking for a sunburnt couple from Versailles. The priest looks rather unorthodox: he has a big, bushy beard, wears a work apron and has an enormous pair of glasses sitting up on his head, among his mop of unruly hair.

'Hey, you young'uns, I'd love to show you around but I'm afraid I haven't got time.'

But then – we have no idea why – he changes his mind. We sit down with him in his garden. Father Jean-Claude is 63. He's spent 43 of those years in Morocco, including 20 in Essaouira. A disciple of Charles de Foucauld, he built a chapel in his church that has a large portrait of the saint. He has completely renovated the church, which was in ruins when he came here. He put in the altar, the tabernacle and the cross of inlaid wood. To complete the picture, he has two canaries in a cage to celebrate the creation. Father Jean-Claude is very good with his hands. He has also done up the presbytery, restored the paintings, developed the garden, planted a vegetable garden where he grows numerous fruits and vegetables, and keeps rabbits, hens and geese. He gives the produce to the Moroccans and sells some to tourists. His ministry bears little resemblance to that of a priest in France, especially since the community here numbers only about six to eight people, all expatriate Europeans or sub-Saharan Africans.

'We're a small community of brothers!'

He calls one of his fellow brothers, posted in Oujda on the Algerian border, to find out about crossing the border by land. Our fears are confirmed: the frontier is well and truly closed. Just when we're leaving, the priest takes a jar from the shelf and gives it to us. It's lemon curd he made himself. As we shake his big, calloused hand, I wonder why everyone is so kind to us, so thoughtful, when we're always imposing on others. By way of a farewell, he points a finger towards the sky, and says, 'When we get up there, he'll ask us: "Were you happy on the earth?"'

After riding along beside a huge phosphate processing plant that disgorges its cooling water into the ocean, polluting the water, we enter the town of Safi.

'What kind of bike is that? Is it practical?'

'It's called a recumbent bike.'

How many times have we repeated this sentence or its English equivalent?

'They're brilliant, except on hills. You don't get painful thighs, a sore neck, or a sore backside.'

'I love cycling too.'

The young man is wearing a well-ironed shirt and sunglasses.

'My name is Abdou! Welcome to my home town. Come and join us for lunch in my home.'

Abdou is short for Abdallah, which means 'slave of God'. He's a student in the town's fine university, recently built by the young king. On the way to his home we come across his cousin Ishiom, whose back-to-front cap is perched on top of his mop of black hair, plastered down with a thick layer of solidified gel. He's a stuntman on wheels: a tall, skinny thrill-seeker wearing American-style jeans and T-shirt. He's perched on a freestyle bike with massive rear springs and front shocks. Every weekend he rides at breakneck speed down the nearby hills.

We eat lunch in Abdou's house, treated like royalty by his mother and younger brother. Simply because we're passing by. Ishiom repairs bikes. He shows us his workshop and gives our bikes a thorough going-over. Spokes, ball bearings, bolts. Everything is adjusted, cleaned and oiled. Ishiom is a craftsman. When we offer to pay him, he categorically refuses.

'When I travel, I'll be happy if someone gives me a hand!'

'How can we thank you?'

'There is one thing: I'd love to have a go on one of your bikes.'

He's an acrobat. Within seconds he's riding alone without needing any help from us. He weaves between the cars, disappears around a corner and cycles around the block. I can't believe my eyes. It took me a whole hour to be able to ride a few metres. And a whole weekend to learn to ride straight!

About 130 kilometres further north, we enter the port city of El Jadida, after frying all day in the merciless sun. We cycle round the town until we find a church.

A fat, sweaty man with a greying goatee opens the iron gate.

'I'm Father Ladislas. You've come at a really bad time. I've got a fever.'

However, he welcomes us in, offering us a room each, a bed, a pillow, a shower and a meal. We sit around the table talking for a long time. Especially him. He has an extraordinary accent and an abrupt Slavic manner. He served as a missionary for several years in Taroudant, a traditional Berber village in south-west Morocco. He's also spent time in the Central African Republic and in Ivory Coast. He tells us stories of the old days, between mouthfuls of chicken salami. For example, the time he killed a python two metres long, right in the middle of a catechism class.

Father Ladislas is Polish. He was born several kilometres from Pope John Paul II's home. They were friends and used to spend time together in the Vatican when Ladislas was passing through.

'I keep a low profile here, as all Christians do. I make myself available for the few Catholic foreigners and sub-Saharan students. But above all, I don't overtly share the gospel.'

He tells us about the problem of Western paedophiles who come to buy kids to use for a few days or a few hours. Even some of his parishioners do it. He feels powerless. He tells us that he doesn't know what to do; he's out of his depth.

'Everyone keeps up appearances during the day. But at night-time, it's another world. Islam has a strong presence but it can no longer control everything. Every morning the beach is littered with alcohol bottles, and every morning state employees quickly tidy them away.'

Globalization is taking its toll in Morocco. Islam is having to face challenges that the Church has been up against elsewhere for a long time – secularism, atheism, alcohol, the role of the state.

Ladislas tells us about the joy he finds in being a missionary, and assures us that he's never lost his faith. He always feels God with him.

The next day we're in Casablanca, the end of our too brief tour of Morocco. Everything seems modern, ordered, clean. Downtown it's busy and noisy. We pass the Parc de la Ligue Arabe, Casablanca's largest open space, and turn into Boulevard Mohamed Zerktouni, where we come across an enormous mass of concrete, 20 or 30 metres high, topped with a cross. It's more like a fortress than a church – a hefty, concrete colossus. It's dedicated to Our Lady of Lourdes. Poor thing.

In the courtyard a woman lights a candle in front of a cave that appears to be an imitation of the grotto at Lourdes. As she turns to walk away a draught of air blows out the flame. We make our way towards the reception desk. The elderly Father Michel tells us there's no room for us, that it's 'complicated'. We engage in endless negotiations. Then the young Father Richard arrives; he finds us two rooms, no questions asked, and invites us to dine with him and his fellow priests.

'In France every year, seven to eight times more priests die than are ordained and, in ten years' time, the number of priests has declined by 20 per cent. Now there are 20,000 of us, of which one third are no longer working. In 2014 there will be about 4,500 priests in active ministry.'

'That's not many.'

That's right. I sense we're going to spend the rest of the meal lamenting the future of the Church, the vocations crisis and the inability of young people to commit themselves. But then Father Jean-Marie throws these statistics back at us, with a broad smile. He's a real stirrer. He continues:

'But it's not serious. The Holy Spirit is at work. He will inspire us for what comes next. We'll probably see an enormous change in the role of the priest. Personally I believe that, just like in the early Church, Christian communities will have to organize themselves, with laymen serving as leaders, while priests will travel from town to town, providing a link between the communities, guiding the laymen and administering the sacraments.'

He thinks the priests of tomorrow will be hardy old warriors of faith. Why not? I think back over the multiple responses we've had to the question of the future of the priesthood over the last six months. Having given their life to serve God within the Church, priests inevitably have an opinion on the issue. Some put their money on the strength of the Church in the developing world, especially in Africa, which they say will re-evangelize Europe and spearhead a revival. Others claim that the ratio of believers to vocations is staying about the same and so there isn't actually a crisis. Still others avoid the question altogether, in an effort to hide their uncertainty. And some, like Father Jean-Marie with whom we're dining tonight, love to get into specifics about what the Church of the future might look like. Finally, there are those who look forward to tomorrow with confidence, affirming that there will be challenges but that we'll overcome them. And personally, after all

I've seen, I don't believe in the catastrophe scenario at all. The Church that we've met is resourceful and full of life.

We wander around the streets of Casablanca looking for cardboard boxes in which to pack our bikes. At the intersection of two streets, on a hairpin bend, we discover the oldest bike shop in the country. The owner still remembers the era when he used to fit out French racing cyclists before Morocco became independent. He has a multitude of seats, flasks, cables, brakes, all of which are 20 or 30 years out of date. In this shop, time stopped in 1956. It's like an old postcard. Black and white photos of yesterday's winners decorate the walls. His cellar is full of stock that will never be sold. The old man points us towards a more modern shop where, within a few minutes, we find two cardboard bike boxes.

Tomorrow we'll put our bikes on the plane. And in less than three hours, we'll be in Algiers – the last leg of our journey.

# 15

## Algeria

## In which the Church is almost invisible

Observed by several curious onlookers, we reassemble our bikes outside the large sliding doors of the main concourse of the Algiers airport terminal.

'Oh dammit!'

I find that my derailleur has been damaged during the trip. A bike is never as fragile as when it's immobilized. Now I can't get it past third gear.

'You'd think airports hire staff especially to jump up and down on fragile items.'

The centre of town is 20 kilometres away. We take a modern four-lane highway, which disgorges a constant stream of vehicles into the central city. Drivers honk their horns and almost run us down as we ride on the extremely narrow hard shoulder. Before long we come out on to the waterfront, where long wide avenues are flanked by white colonial-style buildings. The town encircles the Bay of Algiers. People smile and greet us enthusiastically. We immediately feel at ease and set about finding a church. Everyone points us to Notre Dame d'Afrique, Our Lady of Africa. In the face of such unanimity, who are we to argue?

'*Et voilà!* That settles it then. We'll go there.'

We soon realize why there are no other cyclists around. The town is built on a hill and the streets are almost vertical. Which also explains why they're taking so long to build the new underground train system. Zigzagging up and down the tiny lanes, where the air is heavy with the aroma of fragrant tea and grilled capsicums, our thighs take the brunt of the one-in-ten slope, and we grind our way heroically up on to a plateau. We finally flick down our bike stands with the sense of achievement. The church is enormous and quite magnificent. The newly restored façade of Our Lady of Africa looks down at us. From up here, we share her panoramic view over the whole city.

'It's huge.'

'Yeah.'

'And beautiful.'

All the same, we can't wait to get to the guesthouse so we can recover from the ride up here. But where is it hiding? We corner a workman beside what looks like the presbytery undergoing renovation.

'Somewhere to stay the night? Here? Certainly not! Try the diocesan house.'

'Is it far?'

'On the other side of the city.'

Great. As the man points us back in the direction we've just come from, I'm thinking that, at times, not planning things in advance is beginning to get me down. We head back in the opposite direction. Just as night falls on Algiers, we reach Hydra, the quarter where ambassadors and the rich have their villas. Every 300 metres we come across armed police, roadblocks and spiked vehicle barriers stretched out across the tarmac to prevent car-bomb attacks. Slightly below this fortress suburb, behind a high metal gate, we finally reach the refuge we're longing for. A carpet of pine needles covers the path to the front door of the grand old residence. The diocesan house at last.

A spindly little man with a bald head, wearing a moth-eaten jersey, comes to the door. He must be at least 80. He's European.

'Welcome! My name is Yahya.'

Must be his surname.

'That's not my surname. It means "Jean Baptiste" in Arabic. It's my Arabic name, you see. Are you coming in?'

We walk through a large refectory where the chairs are sitting upside down on the tables, and into the kitchen. Yahya reheats the leftovers from dinner for us.

'So you're cycling? I did quite a lot of cycling myself when I was young. That was before I was a truck driver in the desert. So, how's the soup?'

His eyes shine. He fossicks around in the kitchen to find us a hunk of bread. I'm not sure where on earth we've ended up, but I do know one thing: this little chap Yahya is quite a character.

'I don't like people who take themselves too seriously. I love young people. They're more straightforward; they don't pretend to be something they're not. Well, some young people, at least.'

'If you say so.'

'I'm also quite anticlerical.'

'Pardon? Then why do you live here?'

'I'm anticlerical but I love God. I'm a priest.'

Fortunately I'm sitting down.

'The dictionary definition of "anticlerical" is "one who is opposed to the power and influence of priests". And that's me. I think we priests only have two functions: to give blessing and absolution. Everything else is . . .'

I try calling him 'Father Yahya' and narrowly avoid a beating.

'Call me Yahya, like everyone else. I'm one of the group called the Little Brothers of Jesus, followers of Charles de Foucauld.'

Each of the countries we visit presents a complex picture to the outsider. To understand it properly you'd have to study the history, spend a lot of time there, meet the people. But we don't really know the history; and as for time, well, we don't have much . . . That leaves the people we meet. And Providence has brought us Yahya. He is the first link in a chain that will lead us to the home of Charles de Foucauld, who said, 'I want to be good enough so that it can be said of me "If such is the servant, what must the Master be like?"' Over the following days we will meet others who increase our thirst to know this country better.

In the afternoon we return to the airport to welcome two new arrivals: Pierre, who is joining us a second time to do some more filming, and Louis, Gabriel's older brother. We all visit the French embassy to meet with the head of security. The place is an absolute fortress. We have to pass through several double security doors before we reach his office. The walls of the little rectangular room are lined with detailed maps of the country. Red stickers indicate the hotspots. He asks us about our plans. Are we planning to travel around the country? Where are we planning to go? We're not too sure yet.

'Most likely in Kabylia and in the south, towards Tam.'

'Have you seen the stickers on the map?'

We can see nothing *but* stickers. Apart from one or two tourist areas, there are red stickers everywhere. We're advised against going anywhere.

'In Kabylia, for example, there's one kidnapping per day. At least. And since there are no other foreigners, you won't go unnoticed. You'll be ideal targets. Forget the whole idea.'

This really rubs Pierre up the wrong way. He's come to film some of the country, not to stay in Algiers. As we leave, we reassure him, 'We're not going to give up. But we'll take the bus for the longer trips instead of cycling. That'll give us a break, and we'll be able to travel together and minimize the risks . . .'

Abderrahmane, an Algerian friend of Pierre's father, takes us to visit the Casbah,[1] an old town built on a hill. It's a labyrinth of hundreds of narrow lanes of ochre-coloured earth, bordered with white-walled houses. We could happily lose ourselves here for hours. It's a town within a town. The broad terraces form an irregular stairway leading down to the bay before plunging into the sea. Abderrahmane stops in front of an ancient Moorish house.

'This is a library run by a European. A nun.'

A woman of about 40, in plain clothes, shows us around the property. In the beautiful tiled rooms, several pupils are studying. Then, at Abderrahmane's request, she lets us into a little room off to one side.

'This was Brother Henri Vergès' office.'

'Go on, show them!'

We discover a large, green metal desk, with holes in several places . . . They're bullet holes, from weapons fired in this room, during Algeria's 'Years of Blood'. That was in 1994.

The nun tells us the story. Henri Vergès, a Marist brother, and Paule-Hélène, of the Little Sisters of the Assumption, were 65 and 68 years old. They had lived in Algeria for a long time, and they looked after this library, which was donated by an Algerian businessman. Henri restored it and transformed it into a study room for the young people of the Casbah and Bab El Oued. On 8 May 1994, in the

---

[1] 'Citadel' in Arabic.

early afternoon, two men rang the doorbell. Sister Paule-Hélène led them into Henri's office. As he was getting up to welcome them, one of the two visitors shot him in the face, and the other shot the nun in the back of the neck. The homily given at their funeral several days later by Monsignor Henri Teissier, then the Archbishop of Algiers, began like this: 'Greater love has no one than this: to lay down one's life for one's friends.'[2]

That same evening, as I'm leafing through a French Christian weekly, I come across an article about a new film about the martyr monks of Tibhirine – another terrible episode from those dark years in Algeria. Coincidentally, several weeks later, Xavier Beauvois' film, *Des hommes et des dieux* (*Of Gods and Men*), about this same story, opened in France. It sold over three million tickets.

Later, during dinner, I can't help wondering about the meaning of the monks' sacrifice. Yahya confides that he narrowly escaped being killed. He was then living with another monk, Bruno, in Djebel Bissa, in the Algerian countryside where the Little Brothers of Jesus were based for 40 years.

'It was night-time. I was woken by some unusual noises. I went and hid in some bushes from which I could observe the house. Through the window I saw my companion, Bruno, being tied to the bed. I heard one of the men say, "This lamb here, shall we slit its throat?" My hair stood on end. Another replied, "He's an old man. Leave him." As soon as they'd gone, I untied Bruno. We gathered a few of our belongings, waited for daylight, and fled. When we returned a few days later, the whole monastery had been ransacked, ruined.'

As we talk with people, we learn that Algeria's recent history is marked by extreme violence and bloodshed; the consequences we are aware of are only the tip of the iceberg.

In 1962 Algeria obtained its independence. But disillusionment rapidly set in. The revenue from the increased economic activity only lined the pockets of the corrupt elite, while the general population grew poorer and poorer. According to Houari Boumediene, Algeria's leader from 1965 to 1978, the problems were caused by a failure to modernize, and according to Chadli Bendjedid, who succeeded him, they were

[2] John 15.13 (NIV).

due to the failure to liberalize, which created a fertile breeding ground for religious extremists. In 1988 riots broke out in Algiers and spread to other cities, leaving no alternative but a traditional form of Islam, which presented itself as the solution to all the problems and gave the disaffected an identity. In 1991 the FIS (Islamic Salvation Front) won the first round of the legislative elections and threatened to take the second (January 1992) with a two-thirds majority, which would have allowed it to revise the constitution. The army reacted, prompting a military coup on 11 January 1992. The elections were cancelled and the FIS was dissolved. Out of the chaos, the AIS (Islamic Army of Salvation) and the GIA (Armed Islamic Group) were born. They had no qualms about attacking civilians, both Algerians and foreigners, triggering an uninterrupted cycle of bloody conflicts. Car bombings, bombs in buses, shootings . . . over 200,000 died in the Algerian Years of Terror.

Numerous Catholic communities were repatriated, first to Algiers and then to their home countries. Others made the strange and solemn choice to stay in a country that was, to all appearances, rejecting them. They decided to commit themselves to live with their Algerian neighbours to the very end. In the Diocese of Algiers alone, 18 priests, monks and nuns were assassinated during those years. For the Church, the scar is so deep that even those who have arrived only recently, who didn't live through the events of the 1990s, seem to have been affected. Christians in Algeria know very well what it means to 'give your life', what it means to be the 'Church among the people'. To us the most striking thing is the immense respect for Islam shown by the thousands of believers of the little Catholic community, and their brotherly love for the 35 million Muslims around them.

## Seventh isolated community: Tibhirine

There's one place we desperately want to visit – a place that seems to us to exemplify this 'living among the people' that is the ethos of the local Church. The only one who would be able to drive us there is Jean-Marie. He divides his time between Tibhirine and Algiers. Just as he's retiring for the night I put the question to him, stammering, 'Jean-Marie . . . we would love to come with you . . .'

He looks at me with his penetrating blue eyes and smiles. His hand-shake is strong.

'That's fine. The escort is coming to pick me up at seven o'clock in the morning. Don't be late!'

The next day Pierre and Louis take the car with Jean-Marie while Gabriel and I set off on our bikes. We ride for 60 kilometres as far as the Chiffa Gorge, where the road begins to climb. We take a seat in a plain little restaurant and choose the cheapest thing on the menu. But when we come to pay, they don't charge us.

'Welcome to Algeria!' they say.

The gorge is lush and green. Motorists stop to taste the water that streams down the rock face. Monkeys come down to interact with the humans. On the right, all we can see is rock, on the left, a void. After grinding up an endless series of zigzags we enter the town of Medea. The traffic is lighter. Another climb and we reach the end of the town, through steep little streets bordered by leafy trees and large buildings. It all reminds me of Pagnol's Provence in *Jean de Florette*. Soon we can see the valley, which is surrounded by mountains as far as the eye can see. The monastery stands on one of these hillsides. I wonder how many times the monks took this route to go to market and sell their vegetables. We spontaneously decide to pray the Rosary – a ritual prayer like those recited by Muslims at the call of the muezzin. When we're almost there we ask for some water from the gatekeeper of a big house. We're immediately ushered inside to meet the family. The head of the house is a man of about 30 who works on the metro in Algiers. His wife is welcoming. She shakes our hands, talks with us and serves us tea. She's nothing like the shy, retiring women we met in the Middle East. The children are playing on the floor and watching us out of the corners of their eyes.

'Do you know where Tibhirine is?'

'Yes, very well . . . This is Tibhirine!'

'Do you know Jean-Marie?'

'Of course! I'll drive you to the monastery.'

He takes us 500 metres further on, to a tall iron gate. We knock, and Jean-Marie appears from a little side entrance.

'Oh, it's you! We've just finished bringing in the hay. I'm coming!'

He disappears again and reappears behind the main gate, which he opens enough to let us and our bikes through.

'Come, it's time for coffee.'

He has installed a little kitchen himself for the workers, in one of the sheds. For the three of them, Samir, Youssef and Jean-Marie, morning and afternoon coffee have become a ritual.

We feel deeply moved as we explore the monastery. The ancient buildings are old and imposing, plain but not austere. The monks bought the property in 1938 from an English settler. It has a panoramic view out over the valley to the Mouzaïa mountains. Jean-Marie leads us along the neat little paths, showing us the lodge, the convent, the farm, the apple orchards. Everything is empty and yet very much alive. Jean-Marie is carrying on the work the monks began. He does it differently, in his own way, but the spirit lives on.

In 2001, Bishop André Barbeau, who was at that time Father Abbot of Notre-Dame d'Aiguebelle, head of Tibhirine, asked Jean-Marie to take over the work and look after the land and the monastery. After the monks' assassination in 1996, other Cistercian monks had tried to establish a new community at Tibhirine, without success. Jean-Marie took three days to reflect and then accepted, thus returning to his roots – his training and work as a farmer. In his book[3] he writes: 'Nothing destined me to live at Tibhirine. But everything led me there.' He grew up in a large farming family, studied to be an agricultural engineer and then became a worker-priest with the Mission de France.[4] After his first mission, in Tanzania, he went to Egypt. It was there that he discovered how the Church can be a presence among Muslims. For ten years he consecrated most of his time to Tibhirine, where he lived out his vocation of priest and farmer – the priest working among the people.

'Before they finally left, the monks planted five hectares of apple trees, just young saplings. Today, we market 20 to 30 tons of apples each year! It's a great sign of hope. Life goes on at Tibhirine! Especially

[3] Jean-Marie Lassausse with Christophe Henning, *Le jardinier de Tibhirine*, Montrouge: Bayard, 2010.
[4] The Mission de France was created in 1941 following the realization of the dechristianization of the workplace in France. 'Priest-workers' shared the life of the workers of their times.

through Samir and Youssef, who were working here for the monks at the time of the massacre.'

We realize that work is the key to his presence at Tibhirine. I ask him a stupid question: 'So you alternate the two hats . . . during the day, you're a farmer and, in the evening, you're a priest?'

Jean-Marie winces.

'No, you haven't grasped what I'm saying! I'm a priest even when I'm farming – my feet in the muck, and my hands raised towards the heavens!

'Working with others is an excellent way of living out your faith. There's something very special about it. There are numerous examples that show that the monks' focus changed from their own life within the monastery to their calling to be among the local community. By working the land together with their Muslim brothers, through the activities of the Ribat el Salaam[5] group created by Brother Christian, and the daily acts of service of each community for the other, the monks and the villagers created what he called a "dialogue of life", an ongoing conversation in the context of everyday life.'

We stop in the shade of several large cedars beside the little Tibhirine cemetery. The tombstones stand in a line, side by side. The names of the martyrs are inscribed in stone: Christian, Christophe, Luc, Michel, Paul, Célestin, Bruno. Pierre points the camera at our faces; he wants to get our reactions. But there's nothing to say.

'In spite of the difficulties, we hope this place remains open and welcoming. I'm not allowed to come here for more than two days at a time. I have to go back to Algiers, which means I come up to Tibhirine four times a week, escorted by armed policemen. And the monastery is heavily guarded. Those are the new ground rules and we accept them. The main thing is that Tibhirine continues to be a "sign". When John Paul II spoke to the bishops of the Maghreb [north-west Africa], he said, "You are a sign and a sign is not required to increase in number but to be a sign."'

[5] Ribat el Salaam, or 'Bond of Peace', was founded in 1979 by Charles Rault, a monk who became Bishop of the Sahara, and Christian de Chergé, Prior of the Monastery of Notre-Dame de l'Atlas at Tibhirine. It consisted of Christians and Sufi Muslims. Chosen people used to meet for friendly get-togethers of prayer and sharing around themes drawn from the two religions.

The next day I'm supposed to get up at seven o'clock to pick green peas with Jean-Marie. But I don't hear the alarm. When we emerge, he greets us with a broad smile and points to four little white dots in the distance.

'That's the diocesan pilgrimage on its way here to Tibhirine.'

There are four buses labouring up through the Chiffa Gorge, surrounded by a strong police escort: two plain-clothes policemen on board each bus. It must be a comical spectacle for the villagers, seeing this strange assortment of people getting off the bus. They're a reflection of the Christian community in Algeria: European monks and nuns, expatriate lay people, sub-Saharan Africans and two or three Algerian converts. Led by Jean-Marie and Monsignor Bader, the Bishop of Algiers, they gather around the graves before sharing a picnic, after which they pray and take Communion. The day finishes with Mass in the pretty chapel whose design shows hints of Moorish influence. I think of the words of Father Bernard, at the Mauritanian border: 'In the Eucharist I bring before God all that my Muslim brothers do that is good and beautiful, and that's what I offer.'

As the bishop raises the host, surrounded by the priests who are celebrating with him, I know that Jean-Marie will be thinking of the Tibhirine villagers.

It's a great pleasure to return to home base: the diocesan house in Algiers. Not that it's especially beautiful, or exceptionally welcoming. And its location on the edge of the city is far from ideal. It's the kaleidoscope of strong, endearing personalities we meet here. This is the nerve centre of the little Algerian Christian community, and there are always interesting guests. The residents and visitors form a coherent group because of their link to the Church. This evening, during dinner, I can't help comparing the atmosphere around the long, narrow table to Asterix's banquet. People look out for one another, tease each other, debate passionately – sometimes sincerely, or playing the devil's advocate. And they always come together to eat, many of them several times a week. Their unity is based on the acceptance of their diversity. The house is one, just like the Church is one. And instead of Asterix's banquet, I could liken it to the Lord's Supper, where men who were united only by their relationship with Christ gathered to establish a mission that was far greater than all of them.

I look around the table. First of all there's Yahya, whom I've already described: a young man's heart in the body of an old man, he amazes us with his youthfulness and his faith. One day, when I'm talking to him about the difficulties of being celibate, he confides that he could only have been satisfied with an immense love; that no one woman would ever have been enough. He adds that he needs to be free to serve. So no regrets, even though it has been hard at times. He has a ready laugh, a twinkle in his eye; he loves joking and horsing around. We sense he knows the secret of happiness: living for others, daring to be different, slightly crazy.

And then there's Azzedine, a jack of all trades, who ended up here by accident. About 12 years ago, when he was working in a wealthy part of town as a gardener, he missed the bus and had to walk home. As he was passing the diocesan house he noticed a couple of pretty girls on the doorstep. Preoccupied, at first he didn't hear the head of the house calling out to him, asking what he was looking for. Then, as cool as a cucumber, he answered, 'Er, I'm looking for work, Madam.'

She hired him and he's been here ever since. He and Yahya run the whole place. He buys the bread, mows the lawn, does the gardening, organizes the diocesan fair. And he met his wife here.

And then there's Jean-Paul, 'Papi (Grandpa) Tissot'. Even the most boring things are exciting when you do them with Jean-Paul. I'm deeply touched by this delightful 60-year-old who, having lost his wife several months ago, sold everything and gave his life to serve the poor and needy.

He has a simple heart, tuned in to the beauty of nature, in which he sees the hand of God. Pale blue eyes, pointed nose, bushy beard. He talks a lot. He's filled with wonder at everything around him.

'Look, isn't that amazing?' he exclaims, as he observes a butterfly opening a lime blossom. He confides with us that one day he gave his wife, for her birthday, a magnificent view of a field of cornflowers that he had recently spotted when he was out walking.

At the head of the table is Monsignor Bader, an Arab bishop here among the Europeans. A Jordanian from an influential family, he took over from Monsignor Henri Teissier, a great man who made his mark on Algeria's history through his dedication during the country's darkest years. It is a difficult thing to take on the legacy of another, but that's how the Church functions. No one is irreplaceable. The Church calls, man responds. Monsignor is like a father to us. He kindly listens to us and gives us his advice.

Anne is a dynamic woman in her forties who used to be involved in Jean Vanier's L'Arche[6] community in France. She runs the house, accommodating everyone's feelings and foibles. To her right sits Michael, a young American researcher, with red hair and moustache, a father of two married to an Italian woman who comes to Algiers regularly for her thesis: 'Religiously Friendly Democracy: Framing Political and Religious Identities in Catholic and Muslim Societies'. And then there's Safia, the housekeeper, who is always in and out of the kitchen. She knows better than anyone how things should be run around here; she plans the menus, looks after the logistics. She always has a motherly word for the priests and the guests who pass through. And I mustn't forget Jean-Marie, more talkative when he's amid the trees and fields of Tibhirine than in a large group like this. He sits quietly at the end of the table and is the first to get up to do the dishes.

When the diocesan pilgrimage came to Tibhirine we met Slimane, one of very few Algerian converts. He's a *ritourni* (one who has turned around), a term coined by local Muslims. With his bright eyes, crooked teeth and tall, thin, round-shouldered frame, he's a strange-looking fellow. He looks like a bird that's fallen out of its nest. He came with another convert, a blind man whom he guided around, holding on to his arm. They weren't much to look at, those two, but they were great to talk to. And they invited us to visit them at their home in Tizi Ouzou, in Kabylia.

This time we heed the advice of the French ambassador's security advisor. Leaving our bikes behind, we take the bus to eastern Algeria with Pierre and Louis. After all the threats we've heard about, we have no second thoughts: we relax in the back seats, enjoying the wonders of motorized transport. In a few hours we reach Tizi Ouzou, capital of

---

[6] An organization for the disabled.

Kabylia, the town where four members of the Missionaries of Africa, or White Fathers,[7] were assassinated in 1996.

As soon as we step off the bus, several men sitting outside a café warn us of the risk of abduction, something we've become totally paranoid about. Slimane comes to pick us up from the bus station and we follow him for 500 metres during which I'm continually turning to look behind me. Slimane leaves us at the entrance of the White Fathers' presbytery, where we find a young African priest who has come to lead the sub-Saharan students. There are two other White Fathers here, one Dutch and one French.

Pierre asks if he can film the Mass. Father Jones, a young man, refuses, and when he asks the Kabyle Christians, they also refuse. Not even from behind, or with their faces hidden. Some come to Mass without their families knowing. Others have 'come out' and faced the consequences: they've lost their jobs, suffered rejection by their families, received death threats. Some have even been physically assaulted or become complete social outcasts. Slimane has even had stones thrown at him.

Mass is wonderful. It's an 'anticipated' Sunday Mass since, in Algeria, Sunday isn't a holiday. As well as Kabyle Christians there are sub-Saharan students, who lead the liturgical songs. As we leave I notice a guard posted at the entrance to the compound. They explain that he's there as much to prevent another attack as to keep an eye on the people who come to Mass.

Converts pose a problem in a country where Islam is the state religion. According to Mustapha Krim, President of the EPA (Protestant Church of Algeria), there are 50,000–100,000 converts in Algeria – a figure that is contested by the authorities, who put it at 11,000. The Church has never 'organized activities aimed at taking people away from their community', to use the words of a senior official of the Catholic Church. Those who show a deep desire to be baptized must follow the path of catechism, which may take several years. And baptisms are generally done on the quiet, to avoid all suspicion of proselytizing.

We stay in Tizi Ouzou for three days without seeing Slimane again. As in Rosso, in Mauritania, the White Fathers run a library

[7] The Missionaries of Africa, or White Fathers (Pères blancs), is an international Catholic missionary organization founded in Algeria in 1886.

for local students to use, irrespective of their religion. Many young Muslims come to study for their exams. The Dutch priest looks after them. He is, by turns, a school librarian, a teacher and a maintenance man. When we meet him he's absorbed in a language primer; at over 60 years old, he's learning the Kabyle language.

'There's no choice. How can you live among a people if you don't speak their language, and communicate if you don't understand their culture?'

After Tizi Ouzou we come back 'home' to the diocesan house in Algiers, where we watch a show put on by local theatre school students. The teachers and students are all Muslims. A group of Catholic nuns enjoy the performance and applaud heartily. Monsignor Bader says a word of welcome. One of the teachers congratulates himself on the initiative, tapping me on the back.

'You see! That is what you call dialogue! It's tangible, very real!'

Pierre has shut himself away in his room to edit the film so that it's ready for submission to French television channels on his return. Ours was the first footage to be taken inside the monastery at Tibhirine in ten years. While Pierre is busy, we wander the streets of Algiers with Louis. Slowly but surely we unwind, both mentally and physically. Perhaps it's because we're cycling less, or maybe it's all the ice creams and pastries Louis treats us to. Or else it's because we know there are only a few weeks to go before we return to France. Anyway, we feel as if we're on holiday.

In the evening we go out to celebrate Pierre and Louis' departure; they're leaving the next day. In a wide, deserted avenue in the centre of Algiers, we're attracted by shouts erupting from a little door; inside men are drinking beer, wine or pastis and smoking like chimneys.

Pierre and Louis have returned to France. In less than a month it'll be our turn. The closer our return comes, the less I like the idea. I like this custom-made life of ours. I take my seat in the back of a shabby bus at the Algiers bus station. We're heading for le Grand Sud – southern Algeria. A way of distancing ourselves temporarily from the reality of our final border crossing.

Sitting in the back row, above the engine, we almost die from the heat. After six hours on the bus, we reach the oasis of Ghardaïa. The bus station reminds me of a modern-day caravanserai – touts everywhere, cars and buses parked at random, and passengers running in all directions. We have to race to catch another bus heading for Tamanrasset. Twenty hours on the road, through the middle of the desert. In the dead of night the bus stops in the tiny central square of a small town. We all get off and pile on to another bus. The precise rendezvous is impressive. Later we stop again and two policemen board the bus for identity checks. They wake Gabriel and order him off the bus. A blond guy with a ginger beard doesn't go unnoticed. But with my dark hair, I melt into the background. I sink down into my seat, furtively watching my friend getting picked up by the cops. I pretend to be fast asleep when one of the officers climbs back on the bus and taps me on the shoulder. I've been spotted.

After about 30 hours on the road we reach Tamanrasset.

Passers-by point us to Charles de Foucauld's house. We knock on the door and a European nun opens up for us. She's one of the Little Sisters of Jesus, followers of de Foucauld. She tells us to follow her. In the overwhelming heat we walk along sandy roads lined with miserable little shops. The few animals we see are mangy and thin. The nun leaves us at the entrance of another house with mud walls. Here we find Béatrice, a French volunteer who has been in Tam for two years. She's been expecting us. She appears in the open doorway, wearing a Tuareg tunic, her blonde hair drawn back into a plait. She welcomes us graciously and shows us to our rooms.

'Be careful not to waste water. Use a facecloth and only one basin of water to wash yourself.'

Later in the afternoon she takes us to visit the little fort where Charles de Foucauld lived, a square block, four to five metres high, ochre coloured walls. We enter through a tiny gap in the wall that opens on to a courtyard. A well, four walls, three dark corridors: one for storing weapons and food, one for prayer, one for work. Perhaps? We try to imagine how the hermit lived. A little external staircase leads up to the ramparts. In 1916 Charles de Jesus moved into this little fortress. He was assassinated here on 1 December of the same year.

In the evening, Mass is celebrated by a clone of George Clooney: the handsome Father Daniel, who has completed two years of *Fidei Donum*[8] service in Tam. There are nine of us: George Clooney, a Little Brother of Jesus, the nuns, Béatrice, from Chad, and us. The altar is made of stone. Here too the Church is small and inconspicuous. We quietly pray for the people in the community around here.

The next day we hop on a 4x4 heading for Assekrem, Charles de Foucauld's summer hermitage. When the heat in Tam became unbearable, he used to escape to the mountains of the Hoggar Desert.

*One has to pass through the desert and sojourn there to receive the grace of God; it is there that one empties oneself, that one drives away from oneself all that is not of God, and that one completely empties the little house of our soul, to leave space for God alone.*       *Charles de Foucauld*[9]

In 1864, at the age of six, Charles was orphaned. He and his sister Marie were brought up by their grandfather. Charles was smart but rebellious. As an adolescent he fell right away from his faith and led a life of debauchery. He joined the army but left it in order to undertake a dangerous mission to Morocco (1883–4) disguised as a Jew. Witnessing the Muslims' faith caused him to wonder about the existence of God. He called out: 'God, if you exist, let me know you.'

The road is deserted; a deserted desert road in a barren, rocky landscape. It's like a Western film set, with the jagged silhouettes of craggy outcrops in the distance. Everything is parched and lifeless, sharp and severe. And yet so beautiful – a raw, harsh beauty. Our driver leaves us at a guard post with enough pasta to last us three days, and we climb the last few hundred metres on foot. We come out on a wide, rocky plateau where we see several little huts made of flat stones piled one on top of the other. They're reserved for those on retreat and are spaced well apart to preserve the hermits' solitude.

But today there's no one here but us. Charles de Foucauld's former hermitage has been converted into a chapel. On one wall are the words 'I want all the people here, Christians, Muslims, Jews, non-believers,

---

[8]  Gift of Faith priests come from dioceses in European countries to work in a diocese in the developing world, especially in Africa.

[9]  'Lettre au Père Jérôme, Trappiste de Staouëli', 19 May 1898, in Denise and Robert Barrat, *Charles de Foucauld et la fraternité*, Paris: Éditions du Seuil, 1958; 2002, p. 103.

to look on me as their brother, a universal brother'. The Church among the people. Again.

'Hey, this is paradise.'

We spend three days here, time out of time. We see not a single soul. The first two days, we talk very little, only during meals. We each go off on our own for long walks. Not a sound disturbs the silence, save the whistling of the wind around the rocky peaks.

How often must de Foucauld have contemplated these mountains as he talked to the All-Powerful One? This entrancing plateau is surely a favoured place where Creator and creature meet. The isolation, the calm, the height of the mountains. We've never been so close.

On his return to France, Charles de Foucauld came across a priest named Abbot Huvelin, who had a profound influence on him. With lightning speed, in October 1886 he was converted and returned to the God of his childhood. He was then 28 years old. 'As soon as I believed there was a God, I understood that I could do no other than live only for Him.' He went on pilgrimage to the Holy Land and while there he heard a call: to follow Jesus in his life in Nazareth, before he began his public ministry, and to imitate him in the simplest years of his existence. Charles became a monk and spent seven years with the Trappists, first at Our Lady of the Snows in the Ardèche, and then at Akbès, in Syria, before returning to Nazareth to live near a convent of Poor Clare nuns.

In the evening, as I'm peeling the vegetables for dinner, Gabriel interrogates me in front of the camera.

'So, how does it feel to be here, chez Charles de Foucauld?'

'It's great . . . and small at the same time. In here it's very small – it must be only three metres by two. But outside, it's huge. It all depends on how you see it.'

I had better watch out . . . I'm becoming a mystic!

The next day is 10 June. Today we manage to get up before the sun. Thousands of tourists come here every year to feast their eyes on this view at dawn. And it seems that less than ten per cent come because of Charles de Foucauld. So it must be because it's so very beautiful. In spite of the mist, the sun lights up the mountains, one by one, like candles. And at dawn on this day, 10 June, I've planned the most beautiful present imaginable for Gabriel's 25th birthday. Just as Jean-Paul gave

**Celebrating the dawn**

his wife a field of cornflowers, I'm giving Gabriel – who is certainly not my wife – a sunrise. It's an instant Kodak. The advantage of a present like this is that it's sure to please, it doesn't break the bank, it shows undeniably good taste, it's original and it's totally unbeatable. When you give an instant and the infinite at the same time, you stand on the podium as one of the world's best present givers.

'Happy birthday, old chap.'

He had lost track of the date. He doesn't say much, but I know he's happy.

Most of the morning we spend reading and talking. After 11 months, we've still got something to say to each other. *Hamdoulilah!* Thank you God! We use our time here to look back at the highlights of the past months. It's an isolation chamber in which we have uninterrupted time to digest what we've experienced. We try to synthesize the untellable into a two-sentence response to the question, 'So how was your tour of the world?'

We make a grand tour of the east side of the plateau. From the top of a nearby hill we shout at the top of our lungs, causing an echo that reverberates around the peaks and rock faces, gradually becoming distorted before it finally dies away. The wail of a distant wind grows louder and more high pitched as it crosses our mountains. Far below a stray donkey replies to our shouts, braying with all its might.

That evening I write out a part of T. S. Eliot's long poem 'Ash-Wednesday', where he prays that he might forget matters that he discusses too much with himself.[10]

Back in Tamanrasset we visit the Little Brothers of Jesus. We have not met any of them so far, but if they're of the same calibre as Yahya, we must meet them at all costs. These successors of Charles de Foucauld are keeping the flame alive. Béatrice takes us to visit them.

Charles de Foucauld was ordained as a priest when he was 43 (in 1910). He went off into the Sahara, to Beni Abbès, to be among the Tuareg people of the Hoggar mountains. He wanted those around him to see him as their brother. He wanted to 'cry out the gospel with his whole life', with great respect for the culture and faith of those among whom he lived. When he was killed in 1916, he was the only member of his religious community. But since then several communities have been created with the desire to embrace, as he did, the life of Jesus of Nazareth.

In the fraternity's tiny courtyard we stand in the shade beside a planter box overflowing with little orange flowers. Behind us some dry laundry is hanging on a line. Gabriel interviews; I film.

'Who is Brother Charles de Foucauld? What does he mean to you?'

Jean-Marie (a different Jean-Marie) replies first. Little moustache, grey hair, ageless.

'Foucauld was converted by an obvious work of grace. His life changed from one day to the next. But what I find most moving is that he orientated his whole life to the life of Jesus of Nazareth. He thought that since Jesus, who had a message for the whole world, spent his first 30 years living in anonymity, leading an ordinary life, then this must be significant for us. He thought that if we realize the significance, it could lead us to consecrate our lives more deeply. That's why I'm here. Ultimately, daily life is a path towards God. I live very simply here – working, sharing, connecting with others – in a cultural environment

[10] From T. S. Eliot, 'Ash-Wednesday', *I*, in *Collected Poems 1909–1962*, London: Faber & Faber, 1974, p. 96.

that's very different from my own. Accepting the other, loving him as he is. In this situation we can apply the imperatives of the Gospel, to truly live as Christians.'

Taher is bald headed with a thin moustache and metal glasses. He came to Algeria when he was 22; he's now over 60 and has Algerian nationality.

'The Gospels say almost nothing about the first 30 years of Jesus' life. There's a profound mystery in the fact that God could become a man. Our lives are at once ordinary and, at the same time, inhabited by a mystery that we'll spend a whole lifetime seeking to understand.'

We've met several members of the Algerian Church before, and once again we're touched by their humility. They witness to a Church that is self-effacing, making itself insignificant.

'You're not here to evangelize?'

'It all depends on what you call "evangelizing". If evangelizing means helping others to open up, then yes, we're here to evangelize. If it's proselytizing to try to get conversions, then no. We want to help people to be more true to themselves and towards God. In this context, it means helping them to be true Muslims and to interiorize their faith. I like to think that we're here in the same way Jesus was in Nazareth – to manifest the presence of the mystery of the love of God among men.'

Jean-Marie is the gardener at Tamanrasset. Taher spent 40 years in a Tuareg village in the Hoggar. He used to be a truck driver in the desert. As the interview goes on, they grow more relaxed in front of the camera.

'You know, living here allows us to confront the difference in a very tangible way. Accepting the difference is not so simple because it involves not wanting the other to become like oneself! Creation is full of diversity. There are Muslims, Jews, Christians . . . it's very beautiful! Charles de Foucauld used to say that we must give first place to the other and take for oneself the last, the smallest. It's a whole different way of thinking.'

'Living in community is a first step towards accepting others. We brothers obviously share the same faith and the same calling, but we have different ideas and different temperaments. We must first learn to live together with all our differences before we can live with Muslims.'

To Jean-Marie, the way of Christ is marvellous because it leads those who take it to put to death their ego, their natural automatic reactions, the prejudices they've inherited from their culture; this enables them to accept the other. I feel all fired up. I don't think anyone has ever explained all that so clearly. Jean-Marie, though, remains impassive, looking straight ahead, his face inscrutable. The legacy of years in the desert.

'Spiritually, I become fully alive when I fully leave a place for the other. In this is the whole mystery of God. When we say that God died, it's because he's so discreet that we no longer see him! Jesus, in taking the lowest place, first in Nazareth, then all through his life, shows us the way of humility. This is the mystery of God's love.'

We went away to discover the forgotten Church. That Church has served us a double portion. It seems that the Church here does everything possible to be forgotten. On the founding of the monastery at Tibhirine, Father Christian de Chergé chose a text from El Madhi Ben Barka to address a group of young French Franciscans in 1965. It's still relevant today:

> In order to one day establish a dialogue in an atmosphere of trust, we must follow as closely and as best we can what your brothers have done in Morocco, that's to say, to live among us providing for your needs and that for several centuries, accepting suffering and death, perhaps a violent death, until the day when we, who are also believers, will ask you, 'Brothers, in whose name do you live like this among us?'[11]

On the bus back to Algiers it's hard to sleep. I'm impressed and troubled at the same time. I'm confused. I understand, with Jean-Marie and Taher, that evangelism too often makes the other a target, refusing to accept him in his difference. But if you consider the faith as a source of joy, isn't it natural to want to share it? To enable those who have never heard it before to discover it?

In the end it seems that if we understand the situation and context, we will get a clearer idea of how to relate to our Muslim neighbours. There's probably a happy medium to be found between the direct proclamation of the gospel and the example of our lives. Christ did both. Not always at the same time. The presence of these men and

---

[11] Lassausse with Henning, *Le jardinier de Tibhirine*, pp. 24–5.

women who freely give their lives is awe-inspiring. Their way of life here in Algeria speaks to us about the calling of the Church as a whole, the Church universal: giving ourselves to the world unreservedly, full of love and hope, regardless of whether we feel we're compatible or effective. The gospel tells us that Christ's disciples are the 'salt of the earth'. Here in Algeria, Christians are in such a minority that they're no more than a few grains in a bowlful of maize. But they give flavour to the world around them by the witness of their lives, by creating a dialogue, by their prayers for their neighbours. And I wonder if I enhance the lives of those around me in France. I think I'm the type of salt that is low in iodine.

We're now on the home stretch before our Mediterranean crossing. I make the most of every moment I have to spend with Yahya, following him around all day like a puppy. This old man really fascinates me. Just looking at him brings tears to my eyes. He seems at once fragile and solid as a rock, full of life. He's crazy but also full of a crazy love for the person of Christ. I join him in the garden, where he's trying to position a hose on an umbrella stand.

'Ah! You see! It's like automatic gun fire, don't you think? There, I don't even have to touch it. It's watering the garden all by itself!'

He's wearing an oversized, threadbare, green polo shirt tucked into his jeans, and a baseball cap that sits on his head sideways. Yahya style. In the shade of the trees sitting on the low wall around the well, while the hose sprays water over the garden, he tells me of his years in seminary. His superiors used to be at their wits' end with his lack of obedience. He tells me the story of his first job as a labourer, which allowed him to save up and go into business on his own, with three francs and six centimes. He tells me how one day he set out to find some land to develop. He bought a property that day and started working it the next. He moved into the ramshackle old house with a thatched roof that leaked in the rain. He fixed it up, planted potatoes, then bought some cows. And then one day he threw it all in to follow the example of Charles de Foucauld. These were his 'nomadic' years, as he calls them. He talks about the time he spent in the Sahara, behind the steering wheel of a truck. I ask if he was happy.

'Yes . . . I think I've been happy all my life. I've had my struggles, at times. That's normal. It makes no difference. I may not want to be in this situation; but it doesn't matter because the Lord gives us what we can bear and no more. His grace helps us keep going . . .'

We've been talking for over an hour. Yahya has forgotten about the watering and the presence of the camera.

'Do you know, my only regret is that I haven't loved enough. But I don't think I'm the only one.'

His eyes glaze over slightly and he gives me a big smile.

'Ah, you've finished filming, have you? Do you often interrogate people like this?'

That evening we attend Mass at Notre Dame d'Afrique, Our Lady of Africa, the church we found by accident when we first arrived. We've come full circle. After giving the homily, the Vicar General presents us with a cross that used to belong to Henri Vergès, the monk who was assassinated in the Casbah, the ancient quarter of Algiers. We hand over the matchstick cross from the Senegalese Christians. We pray for Pandiénou and also for our parish in Paris, where the final gift will be given. It's the end of a chain that has linked seven villages that had no idea of each other's existence.

Brother Henri's cross is nothing to look at. It's made of unattractive, raw metal, very plain and simple. The kind of cross you don't really notice; it melts into the background. But it really is there.

# 16

## Epilogue

## In which the hosts become the visitors

26 JUNE, 11 MONTHS AND 21 DAYS AFTER DEPARTURE
The stern begins to open and a shaft of light penetrates the hold. In the haze of exhaust fumes, the cars, which have been sleeping during the passage from Algiers, stretch and purr. The Algerian operating the ramp glances at us, amused. He examines Gabriel's cycling jersey.

'Are you going to do the Tour de France?'

'Not exactly.'

'Do you take drugs?'

'Some . . .'

We cruise along the quay – the French quay. Yachts are tacking back and forth out in the bay. Marseilles welcomes us with a big blue sky.

'Here we are, old boy. Back home!'

'Yeah.'

### Fourteen months later, 17 August 2011, Madrid

Pierre's little film production company has moved. Within a few months he's lost his job, lost his business and rebuilt it all again. Like us he's a firm believer in Providence – and in his lucky star. Sometimes a series of random events aren't random at all. He has started a new venture in new premises with a new name: Tprod.

All three of us are in Madrid. We are three among one and a half million people. The city streets are packed with young people, singing for the sheer delight of being there, in the holiday heat. Gabriel and I have been home for just over a year now. I remember the last few days of our world tour as if it were yesterday. In the half-light of the Madrid cinema, as the rows begin to fill, I sink back into my seat, a slight knot in my stomach, and I think back to our arrival. I love dipping into my pool of memories. They're all good, even those that weren't at the time. Even canoeing down the Amazon. As they say, time is a great healer.

At the end of this year spent meeting the forgotten Church, we wanted to make use of the final stretch, between Marseilles and Paris, to meet people who are easily overlooked by typical Parisians like us who, though we don't admit it, think that life begins and ends in the capital. In Paris, parishes offer a wide variety of activities; there's something to please all tastes. Every priest has something different to offer. But what about those outside Paris? Bernanos[1] wrote about a country priest of his times, but who are the country priests of today?

We decided to take the back roads on our way back to Paris, hoping to come across some remote parishes. If it worked for 2,000 kilometres in India, why not in France, the Church's older sister? But in Arles we found the church was firmly locked and the priests were off on a jaunt somewhere. A parishioner and her family invited us to stay. The next day, in Vigan, the priest answered the door, but with his 18 bell towers he was very busy and didn't have time to chat. We spent the night with Marie-Hélène, who invited us to stay in her family campervan. At Figeac, we stubbornly insisted and the three priests at the parish house agreed to show us the church, but couldn't put us up for the night. We spent the night in a gîte on the Way of St James, the ancient pilgrimage route to Santiago de Compostela in Spain, and met a motley band of joyful pilgrims. Some were walking the trail in order to pray, others wanted to find themselves or were accompanying their spouse. Some were walking a long way, others not so far. Some were young, others old.

The French countryside seemed to us to possess a rare and overwhelming beauty. Strong silent oaks, laughing hazels, expansive limes, parasol chestnuts. In the Cévennes, every bend revealed a new vista. The vegetation was fresh and green, not yet scorched by hot summer

---

[1] Georges Bernanos (1888–1948), French author who wrote *The Diary of a French Country Priest.*

sun. The air was clean; no vicious dust, no smell of diesel. We tasted it again and again, never tiring of it. We sniffed the air like a drug; too pure, it burned our nostrils and lungs.

'It's good stuff!'

A Spanish voice fills the cinema. '¡*Por favor señoras y señores, siéntese! Vamos a empezar!*'[2] A young girl wearing the green volunteers' polo shirt passes down the aisle and smiles at us. I glance at Gabriel sitting next to me. On our return, he spent the summer with his family and then joined the Year of Discernment programme at Sainte-Anne-d'Auray in Brittany, to consider his life calling. He has just finished. He told me he's going to seminary, to become a missionary in Asia.

On the fourth day we reached Rocamadour. We stayed there for three days, honouring a promise made a year before: we said we would come to the sanctuary to thank the Virgin for her protection throughout the journey. We arrived right in the middle of a celebration dinner. The young Father Ronan, priest of Rocamadour, welcomed us like royalty. Five young men had just been ordained as deacons and were celebrating with their families. And we were invited to the banquet. Seated at a long, rustic wooden table laden with dishes of roast mutton with gravy, oven-roasted potatoes, duck rillettes, game terrine and all kinds of salads, we reacquainted ourselves with *la gastronomie française* and toasted the happy reunion with a wine that, to us, seemed quite exquisite.

Clinging to the rock, perched above a cliff that towers over the Alzou Gorge, the sanctuary of the Black Virgin of Rocamadour has attracted pilgrims for almost a thousand years. They say that St Louis[3] himself came here to venerate the Virgin, and that it's the second most visited site in France today, after the Mont Saint-Michel.

'*Attention les amis!* You're under surveillance. Be careful what you ask for because your prayers might be answered!'

---

[2] 'Ladies and gentlemen, please be seated. The film will commence shortly.'
[3] Louis IX (1224–70), the only King of France to be canonized.

Father Ronan was smiling at us – a toothy smile on his mischievous face. For some years he has been working on the resurrection of the sanctuary.

He told us some of the stories from the book about the miracles of the rock sanctuary. There's one about a mother who found her two kidnapped children, after 18 years of searching; and a young couple, non-believers, who were saved from a violent storm at sea; they were convinced that they owed their lives to the Black Virgin. One of his stories made us smile. A woman once said: 'Virgin Mary, I came to you three times in this chapel to ask that I might have a baby. I had triplets. Thank you.'

After a while we came back down to earth. We noticed how crowded it was in the sanctuary. Thousands of tourists visit during the summer months, 20 per cent of whom are pilgrims. Outside the chapel, visitors from all over the world struggle up the steps to get a good photo of the cave sanctuary. Inside, pilgrims come to kneel and adore the Blessed Sacrament. Stone dominates here in Rocamadour; there's a powerful blend of the spiritual and the mineral. It's a magical place. We treated ourselves to a three-day retreat before the end of our journey. Although the context is different, we continued what we began in Assekrem. Sitting in the darkness of a little chapel, with eyes closed, we prayed.

About 300 kilometres from Paris the terrain finally flattened. From then on the going was easy. Jacques and Virginie invited us to stay in Saint-Benoît in the Loire Valley, in comfortable beds, which helped us endure the last few kilometres. During these blessed evenings, with the miracle welcome extended to us night after night, hesitantly we tried to tell our story. But the words came out wrong; our thoughts were muddled. It was too soon.

Just for the heck of it, we cycled 200 kilometres in one go. We gorged ourselves on asphalt. So what? There was no more risk of indigestion. We spent our last night on the lawn of a housing estate, behind a hedge. This time we wanted to be alone. Gabriel opened a bottle of cheap Cahors[4] while I cooked up a last, giant bowl of pasta. It was 4 July. The next day we'd be home, exactly a year after we left.

---

[4] Cahors is a wine-making region in south-west France, known for its red wines.

Why do they say coming home is difficult? Only a few kilometres left. No need even to think. And our legs were still functioning. We dutifully obeyed the red traffic lights in the Paris suburbs, but inside I was far away. I thought about my friendship with Gabriel; not a new friendship, but a transformed one. The little things we had to do to make it work, and the pride in returning still friends. I thought about our faith in the Providence of God, and the little tell-tale signs that we had consistently seen. In the welcome we received wherever we went, in the Good Samaritans we found on our way to help us just when we needed them, in the problems we managed to avoid in the Amazon, in Iraq, in Tibet, I had the radical experience of a God who never fails us, and with whom there is never a dull moment.

A car tooted and the driver overtook us, shaking his fist in the rear-view mirror. I thought again about how we're always running after time. We passed the Porte d'Orléans as if we were racing to cross the finish line, and whizzed past the Church of Saint-Pierre-de-Montrouge. Some demonstrators made us stop to take their leaflets. They were inviting us to take part in the general strike. I had no idea what they were talking about.

The little cinema is now full to bursting. There must be about 200 people seated and about 50 more sitting on the floor. In the darkness I can make out several of my friends' faces. Pierre, Gabriel and I go forward to introduce the film. Pierre takes the microphone. He says he's feeling quite overcome, that the film is the fruit of a whole year's work. His voice is quavering. People are clapping.

'It's called *Face to Faith*.[5] I hope you enjoy it!'

I'm feeling great. This is awesome. We present our documentary about the world's forgotten Christians to young people who have come to what is actually the largest assembly of people in the world, World Youth Day. Started by John Paul II at the beginning of the 1980s, these gatherings have been held every two or three years since then. This time there are one and a half million young pilgrims from all corners of the earth who have come together, with Pope Benedict XVI.

---

[5] *Il était une foi.*

In the cinema the majority are French, with a few Spaniards, which justifies the subtitling of the film in the local language, Castilian.

And then, best of all, among the spectators there are 17 special young pilgrims. They're from the countries we visited, so they're witnesses of our journey, directly or indirectly. At Rocamadour I prayed to the Black Virgin that we would be able to communicate something of what we'd seen. Father Ronan was right when he said that we ran the risk of our prayers being answered. We're happy that the film has been made, but the thing that has given me the most joy is being able to invite these friends who were our hosts several months ago. Now they're our guests, and this time it's their turn to discover the incredible diversity of Christians in the world – and many of them have never before even travelled out of their own country, or even out of their own little area.

First there are four Lepchas, who've come down from the lofty heights of Darjeeling; they had to battle hard to get exit visas. Among them is young Marcus, the most saintly man in the world, who took us from family to family to pray with his friend Gilbert.

Five young Syrians have also joined us. Sadly, since we left their country, the situation has developed into open conflict. It's a joy to meet up with the smiling Jamil, Monsignor Audo's student in Aleppo. With him are two of his fellow seminary students, Slimane and Pierre, and two other young people, Alex and Albert, nephew of the prelate. As in Tal Arboush, with them we rediscover how good it is to 'take our time'.

There are three Romanians from Beclean village, Tania, Alex and Ovidiu, whom we met at an exchange evening organized months ago in Romania by Father Alin. They've visited Spain once before on a tour that he organized, faithful to his objective of opening the minds of his young people to the world and bringing an end to the fratricidal struggles of their parents.

From Senegal there's only Karl, who is the son of Georges and Leonarda, a couple we met in Dakar. His brother intended to come but wasn't granted a visa. Karl is cheerfulness and politeness personified.

And then there are four Iraqis. We didn't meet them in Iraq but much later, in France. They're refugees from an attack in Baghdad in which they narrowly escaped death but lost their whole family. On

31 October 2010, the Catholic Cathedral of Our Lady of Salvation was attacked during Mass by terrorists wearing explosive belts. Fifty-eight people were taken hostage for five hours and then killed. Our friends each have in their wallets a portrait of their priest, killed that day. Melad has metal rods in his leg until the broken bones heal. Ghassan, the tubby one of the group, bears a scar on his stomach from machine-gun fire. Salam is still alive only because his aggressors thought he was dead; they walked all over what they thought was his corpse. Their grief is unspeakable.

Just as the film is starting, someone passes us a message: 'I'm out-side with my group. Help! Aliocha.' Aliocha, our friend and guide on our Himalayan treks. A few moments later, in he comes, followed by 10 or 12 others. Among them there are two Tibetan Catholics. He too has invited friends!

Something becomes quite clear to me in the middle of this diverse crowd who are all looking in the same direction. *I love this Church*. We hardly dare say it. I hardly dare say it. We whisper it reluctantly for fear of being thought 'trad' or passed off as naive, a bit simple. As if buying into the whole package isn't an option for someone of normal intelligence. And yet this realization is the greatest good that has come out of our year away, which was transformed into a year of pilgrimage: I learned to *love the Church* and to feel comfortable, at home, in her many different forms. No matter where. She's made up of imperfect people, ordinary people, but still I find her beautiful. It's quite mys-terious. But now, to me, she's no longer ethereal and cold. The faces of our friends – the Karen, Tibetans, Amazonian, Iraqis, French – as they cross the screen, put flesh on her and bring her to life.

# Afterword

The account of Charles and Gabriel's travels from July 2009 to July 2010 is a series of snapshots of the places they visited during that year. Some areas have changed greatly since then. This is certainly the case for Syria and Iraq, which have been torn apart by war. In fact, even as the pair cycled through Syria and the north of Iraq in late 2009, terrorism was spreading its tentacles across the landscape. In spite of the gentle rhythm of life that Charles and Gabriel experienced in the Christian villages of Tal Arboush in Syria and Qaraqosh in Iraq, the inhabitants were well aware of how precarious their situation was, and had begun to express their concerns about the rise of Islamic terrorism. They had all already endured violence and forced displacement to some degree.

In Iraq, the American-led invasion in 2003 and the fall of Saddam Hussein reawakened sectarian tensions. Violence spread across the country. The city of Mosul was plagued by insurgents of the group 'Al-Qaeda in Iraq', and the Iraqi army lost control of some parts of the city. This situation became extremely difficult for the Christians still living there. In Baghdad and Kirkuk, the number of kidnappings increased. Between 2003 and 2014, about 1,000 Christians were killed in Iraq, including a number of priests and a bishop. In contrast, the Christian village of Qaraqosh, on the plain of Nineveh, about 30 kilometres from Mosul, seemed a haven of peace. Many Christians from the cities took refuge there, but, in 2014, the group Islamic State (Isis) undertook an offensive that shattered the apparent tranquillity. On 10 June 2014, they took control of Mosul without meeting any resistance. Thousands of Christians fled the city. Some 500,000 people were displaced. Within a few days, Isis began marking the houses of Christians with the dreaded letter *N* for *Nassarah*, the term used for Christians in the Qur'an. They then issued an ultimatum to those who remained: convert to Islam, pay a 'religious tax' or flee, leaving behind all their possessions. *'After this date, there is nothing between us and them but the sword'*, the statement said. And so the last Christians left

Mosul. Then, on the night of 6 August, the jihadists unleashed a wave of destruction as they took the entire plain of Nineveh. A few hours before Isis moved into the region, the 120,000 Christians who populated this plain fled to nearby Iraqi Kurdistan. Today, exactly two years after this exodus, many more Iraqi Christians have left the country, hoping for a better life elsewhere. Some have been welcomed by Western countries; others have joined the millions of displaced persons in surrounding countries (Turkey, Jordan and Lebanon), waiting for the situation in Iraq to improve. Living conditions in the camps are so difficult that some families choose to return to Iraq.

The displaced Christians who remain in Iraq today live mainly in Erbil, the capital of Iraqi Kurdistan, where they are struggling to rebuild their lives, little by little. Others have found refuge in the Christian communities of Dohuk, in the north of Iraq, Kirkuk, Baghdad and even Basra, in the far south. A combined offensive by the Kurdish Peshmerga, the Iraqi army and the international coalition to take back the city of Mosul has been carried out since the summer of 2016. They are making slow progress. At the time of writing, the people of Qaraqosh have expressed fresh hope that their town will be liberated, but many uncertainties remain. In what state will they find their houses? Will there be landmines in the towns? And, above all, will it be possible to live again in peace in this region where the ideology of Isis has become deeply rooted in certain sections of the population? Despite their exodus, Christians continue to look to the future. Hundreds of marriages and baptisms have been celebrated over the last two years. Two churches have been built in Erbil and three Syrian Catholic priests have been ordained for the diocese of Mosul.

In Syria, not far from the border with Iraq, lies the village of Tal Arboush, which Charles and Gabriel visited towards the end of 2009. It is one of a string of 30 Christian villages nestled along the Khabour River, which crosses the north-east of Syria before flowing into the Euphrates. The inhabitants are Catholic Chaldeans and Assyrians, who are the descendants of the escapees of the genocide of 1915 in Turkey and massacres in Iraq in 1933. On 23 February, at five in the morning, Isis launched an attack on these Assyrian villages, especially the village of Tall 'Amar, which is a strategic point on the route between Raqqa, Islamic State's base in Syria, and Kobanê, a town near the Turkish border that serves as an entry point for weapons and jihadists wanting to join Isis in Syria. The villages were defended by Kurdish fighters and the Assyrian militia Sutoro. Thousands of Christians fled. About 2,000 sought refuge in Al-Qamishli, a town situated about 100 kilometres east, near the Turkish border, while thousands more found refuge in Hassaké, only a few kilometres away. They have been taken in by various Christian churches there. Over 250 Christians were kidnapped during this attack. Most have now been freed. In May 2015 the jihadists were expelled by the Kurds from the Khabour villages, including Tal Arboush. About 500 families have now returned.

More generally, Syria is highly fragmented. The government of Bashar al-Assad controls the so-called 'useful Syria' – Damascus, the coastal towns of Tartus and Latakia, Western Aleppo and Homs – while insurgent militias divide up the rest of the country into dozens of little potentates. Isis holds the region of Raqqa and the banks of the Euphrates, while the Al-Nusra Front, which recently renamed itself Fateh al-Sham, controls the city of Idlib. In the north and west, the Kurds have retaken the strategic towns of Kobanê and Manbij and declared them autonomous regions.

*Laurence Desjoyaux, journalist for* La Vie, *specialist in Christians of the East*

## Useful websites

For French NGOs (with pages in English) that help Christians in Iraq and Syria, please see the following websites:
<fraternité-en-irak.org.en>
<filles-de-la-charite.org>

# Acknowledgements

To all our hosts, only some of whom have been mentioned: we thank you with all our hearts for making life so easy for us!

To Laetitia Buffet, for her patience and kindness, and her pertinent suggestions throughout the writing of this book.

To our families, particularly our parents, who accepted a year that gave them more than a few grey hairs.

To those who opened their doors so I could work in the peace and quiet of their homes. In particular, the priests of the Missions Étrangères de Paris, the monks of Sept-Fons Abbey, the Monastic Fraternity of Jerusalem in Strasbourg, the priests of le Mont Saint-Michel and the monks of Kergonan Abbey.

To all those who helped us, a little or a lot, before we left and when we returned, particularly Inès Azais, Vianney Auzou, Henri Barbé, Pierre Barnerias, Domitille Blavot, Simon and Charlotte de Beauregard, the parish of Beauvais Nord, Laurent Bibard, Mrs Billaudel, Hélène Bodenez, Hubert and Marianne de Boisredon, Christian de Boisredon, the Bone family, Jean-Baptiste Bonhoure, Nicolas and Thérèse Bonhoure, Véronique Bréchot, Monsignor Philippe Brizard, Jean-Claude Breuil, Monsignor Nicolas Brouwet, Brunor, Agnès Buchet, Marie-Hélène de Chérisey, the group of kind, anonymous donors, Father Georges Colomb, Father Yves Combeau, Agnès de Couesnongole, Alain Courau, Sébastien de Courtois, Véronique de Thuy-Croisé Pourcelet, Marc Delacroix, Baptiste Deleplace, the Dezobry family, Mrs Dufresne, Anne-Céline Durrande, Guillaume Fauchère, the Foulon family, Marc Fromager, the Gadenne family, Arnaud Gehenne, Philippe Groleau, Claire de Guillebon, Jacques de Guillebon, Amaury Guillem, Jean-Paul Guilhamon, Romain Guinier, Vincent Hervouet, Father Denis Jachiet, Monsignor Jean-Paul James, Arnaud Jehenne, the Lacroix family, Ambroise Landier, Anne Landier, the Lassagne family, Hadrien Lecoeur, Thomas Lerudu, Sophie Lelasseux, Brother Majid, Laure Martin, Christophe Meherenc, Michel and Augustin, Francois Moog, Emmanuel Naves, Hughes

Noirot Nerin, the Paillusseau, Benoît Perier, Philippe Person, the du Plessis family, Alexandre Poussin, Father Marc de Raimond, Gratien Regnault, Monsignor Jean-Yves Riocreux, Riton, Vincent Roux, Stéphanie de Sansal, Olivier Schweitzer, Constantin de Slizewicz, Jeremie Siccoli, Hugues de Tailly, Aurélie Testinière, Geoffroy et Loïc de la Tullaye, Falk van Gaver, the Villeroy de Galhau family, Monsignor André Vingt-Trois, the Zarrouati family.

To the great team at Corpus 2008–2012: Henri Barbé, Claire Bastier, Marc Blanchet, Laetitia Buffet, Angélique de Chabot, Soizic de Clock, Father Yves Combeau, Laetitia Croizé-Pourcelet, Hélène Croizé-Pourcelet, Laurence Desjoyaux, Marie Desrieux, Aymeric Dezobry, Rodolphe Duffour, Guillaume Dupuy, Anne-Coco Elluin, Anne-Charlotte Georges, Florence Guyon, Émilie Humann, Paul Jacquelin, Maxime Laot, Jean de Lépinau, Louis de Lépinau, Anne-Marie L'Huillier, Agnès Lot, Antoine Meffre, Sophie Milcent, Anne Myon, Aurélie Nys, Laetitia de Saint-Louvent, Anaïs Thomas, Sixtine Wallaert, Charlotte Weber.

To the equally great team at Tprod, each one devoted, inspired and enthusiastic. To Jérémie and dear Pierre, whose faith is like a beacon.

To the wonderful people who agreed to proofread some or all of the book: Laetitia Buffet, Father Alain Bourdery, Father Georges Colomb, Laetitia Croizé-Pourcelet, Laurence Desjoyaux, Father Jean-Marie Dubois, Tanneguy Gaullier, Emilie Guibaud, the Guilhamon family, Marie-José Guilhamon, Jacqueline Juglar, Father Jean-Marie Lausausse, Laure Noyelle, Damien Oursel, Christophe Sanche.

To those future travellers who will share their adventures with others. From now on they can apply to the Bourse de l'aventure chrétienne created after our journey: <www.labach.fr>.

To Jeannine Balland for being willing to trust me. To Cécile Rivière and Vincent Brochard.

To those I've forgotten here. (Forgive me!)

To you and me!

# Translator's note

In creating this translation I have sought to remain faithful to Guilhamon's style in *Sur les traces des chrétiens oubliés* to convey his sincerity, energy and wonderfully understated sense of humour to an English-speaking readership. I am indebted to Claire Stirrat, June McArthur and Alison Morton for their help and support, Associate Professor Deborah Walker-Morrison of the University of Auckland School of European Languages and Literatures for sharing her wealth of experience and skill in French translation, and my husband Colin, without whose constant support and advice this translation would never have been brought to fruition.

23657419R00186

Printed in Poland
by Amazon Fulfillment
Poland Sp. z o.o., Wrocław